I WAS THERE!

JOE BUCK, BOB COSTAS, JIM NANTZ
AND OTHERS RELIVE THE MOST EXCITING SPORTING EVENTS OF THEIR LIVES

By Eric Mirlis

FOREWORD BY
MARV ALBERT

SPORTS
PUBLISHING

Sports Publishing books may be purchased in bulk at special discounts for sales promotion, corporate gifts, fund-raising, or educational purposes. Special editions can also be created to specifications. For details, contact the Special Sales Department, Sports Publishing, 307 West 36th Street, 11th Floor, New York, NY 10018 or sportspubbooks@skyhorsepublishing.com.

Sports Publishing® is a registered trademark of Skyhorse Publishing, Inc.®, a Delaware corporation.

Visit our website at www.sportspubbooks.com.

10 9 8 7 6 5 4 3 2 1

Library of Congress Cataloging-in-Publication Data is available on file.

Cover design by Tom Lau

Cover photos: AP Images

ISBN: 978-1-61321-936-2

Ebook ISBN: 978-1-61321-941-6

Printed in the United States of America

To Keri and David
You make it all worth it

CONTENTS

ACKNOWLEDGMENTS

Aproject like this warrants many thank-yous, but none of them are more important than the ones I must say to all of the people who are featured in the following pages. In some cases, it started with a blind email, in others it was a connection through a friend or coworker. In all cases, it ended with me being a royal pain in the behind, so my deepest and most sincere thank-you to each and every one of you.

This book was a labor of love for me, and, frankly, wouldn't have happened without the continued support and encouragement from my friend Kenny Albert, who has been bugging me to do this for the last few years. Not only did he push me to get rolling on this, but his assistance throughout the process, from enlisting people to participate to listening to all of my hairbrained ideas along the way, was invaluable.

They say the hardest thing in the world when writing is proofreading your own work. I can attest to that and owe Todd Behrendt a huge debt of gratitude for all of his hard work handling the fact-checking, proofreading, and mistake-saving.

Of course, it goes without saying that there were a lot of people involved in helping me line up all of the participants. Many favors were called in, and for those, I say thank you to Rich Ackerman, Chris Antonacci, Kent Camera, Stosh Cienki, Jennifer Cingari, Steve Craddock, Andrew Crawford, Bill Dallman, Jennifer Davis, Mark Feinsand, Lorraine Fisher, David Fried, Dave Goren and the National Sports Media Association, Matt Gould, Dan Higgins, Tom Hoffarth, Mike Hughes, Rick Jaffe, Dan Kaufman, Matt Ketaineck, Rick Leonard, Melissa Miller, David Neal, Lou Oppenheim, Jeff Pearlman, Dan Quinn, Alex Riethmiller, Alex Rozis, Dan Sabreen, Alan Sanders, Matt Schnider, David Scott, Eric Spitz, Jacob Ullman, Brad Zager, and Adam Zucker.

When I set out on this project, there were going to be 100 people in the book. I would be remiss if I didn't acknowledge those people whom I interviewed but whom I needed to place to the side for book length considerations: Greg Amsinger, John Anderson, Hal Bodley, Cindy Brunson, Jim Caple, Heather Cox, Howard David, Colleen Dominguez, Amin Elhassan, Neil Everett, Travis Haney, Benjamin Hochman, Tom Hoffarth, Kostya Kennedy, Michael Kim, David Lloyd, Alex Marvez, Tony Massarotti, Ryan McGee, Scott Miller, Beth Mowins, Rob Neyer, Dave Pasch, Steve Physioc, Bill Pidto, Pete Prisco, Bill Reiter, Dave Revsine, Peter Schrager, Dave Sims, Susan Slusser, Lyle Spencer, Bob Wischusen, Van Earl Wright, and Adam Zucker. I wish I had the room to run them all. Thank you all for your time and understanding.

Most important, a thank-you filled with love to my wife, Keri, and son, David. There were quite a few ups and downs while I was writing this book, and some spots along the way where I lost my focus. If it weren't for their love and understanding, though, I'm not sure I would have gotten it back on the rails. They are the ultimate definition of "I couldn't have done it without you."

FOREWORD

By Marv Albert

Sports broadcasters and writers see so many events that it is easy for us to take it all for granted. We know we are the conduit between the games and the fans, so it is our responsibility to relay the importance of the big events or moments when we see them. At the same time, we often forget why we are all in this business to begin with. We are all fans, too, and we are all fans because of those great moments.

Whenever we get a chance to step back and reflect on the moments that stand out the most to us, the memories come flooding back, and the stories start rolling off our tongues. At heart, we are all storytellers . . . we just usually tell those stories as they are unfolding, not as recollections. That is what makes it so much fun to put together a list for this book. It gives all of us a chance to look back at everything we have seen and done and tell stories about the moments in our careers that have meant the most to us. Maybe they had personal meaning, maybe it was something historic. Regardless of why it stands out, though, each story resonates in some way.

As you read each of the stories in the book, try and remember where you were for those moments you saw that are being shared by myself and my peers. Compare your memories to ours. In most cases, you'll realize that they don't differ very much, with the exception that some of us were lucky enough to be there to provide the soundtrack for you to hear or postgame story for you to read. And that is all it is . . . we were simply lucky enough to be there to see all of these wonderful moments.

Marv Albert, a recipient of the Basketball Hall of Fame's Curt Gowdy Award, is currently a broadcaster for Turner Sports.

INTRODUCTION

How do you define the top sports moments you have ever seen? Basically, it can be summed up in two words: You can't.

"What were the top five sports moments you have seen in person?" was the question posed to the people interviewed in the following pages. All of them answered in different ways. Each story is presented in that person's own words, and each list is in chronological order, so that no one had to rank one event over another. The cutoff for all lists was Super Bowl XLIX in 2015, when Malcolm Butler of the New England Patriots provided a moment that more than one person mentioned on their list, and all of the interviews were completed before the end of that calendar year.

Of course, there are a number of common threads throughout the answers.

The most obvious theme, and the one that immediately comes to mind when thinking about "Top Sports Moments," is exactly what you would think . . . the seminal moments in sports. The events mentioned the most won't surprise anyone. Vince Young's touchdown to win the 2006 Rose Bowl. The ball going through Bill Buckner's legs in Game Six of the 1986 World Series. David Tyree's catch against his helmet in Super Bowl XLII. Michael Jordan's final shot with the Chicago Bulls in the 1998 NBA Finals. The entirety of the 2001 World Series. These are the games and moments where you know where you were when you saw them. You felt the excitement through your television. You'll never forget exactly what happened and how it happened. They are the moments you wish you were there to see in person.

What is cool about many of these moments, which provides a neat theme throughout the following pages, is how different people describe the same event. Everyone has a slightly different (or, in some cases, very different) perspective on what happened. It might have been because of where they were sitting or standing. It might have been because they were there as a fan, rather than a working member of the media. It might have been who they were with.

But each individual story is different, and that is something to keep in mind as you compare the stories.

There is more, though, to how people define the top moments they have seen. Just because an event wasn't expected to be a "big event" doesn't mean it can't be memorable. That happens every time someone pitches a no-hitter, for example. No one buys a ticket expecting to see one, which makes the idea of being in attendance for one even more special. The same goes for a game-winning shot or unforgettable ending. Sure, these are magnified in playoff games, but the unexpected nature of them doesn't cause their memorability to be lessened during the regular season. The Olympics are especially conducive to stories like this, and you are going to read many stories that are truly resonant throughout the lists for exactly that reason.

There are other events that might not strike most people as memorable but hold a special place in the hearts of others. Every sports fan can relate to these, be it the first baseball game someone has attended or a professional accomplishment that one of the participants never expected to experience. There is a common thread through all of these that everyone can understand, whether you work in the media or not.

The last theme you'll see is family. In many ways, these stories are probably the most important. They remind everyone that even the most accomplished broadcaster or journalist is, first a foremost, a sports fan. It is those memories, the ones that drove people to work in their chosen profession, that are most important. They changed the soundtrack of sports for all of us, because they provided the basis for the people we listen to or read to do what they do.

As you read everyone's lists, think back to all of the great moments you have seen, and remember, they don't have to be the most famous moments to qualify. You'll read about little league baseball games, ticker-tape parades, exhibition baseball games, and even bowling You'll read stories from people's childhoods. You are even going to read about the conception of someone's child. Every one of these stories qualified as a Top 5 Sports Moment for someone in the book.

And at the end of the day, these are stories anyone can tell, whether you are a sports broadcaster, sportswriter, or sports fan.

Kenny Albert

Broadcaster, FOX Sports/MSG Network

1992 Summer Olympics, Men's Basketball, Palau Municipal d'Esports de Badalona, Badalona, Spain, July 26–August 8, 1992

Four years after the stunning upset by the Soviet Union of the U.S. Olympic basketball team in Seoul, South Korea, in 1988, the United States sent a "Dream Team" of NBA stars to the Summer Olympics for the first time. Michael Jordan, Magic Johnson, Larry Bird, and Charles Barkley aligned together as teammates to try to avenge the loss suffered by the collegians. I had a front-row seat in Barcelona, Spain (handling statistics for NBC), as Team USA rolled through the Olympics with a perfect 8–0 record, from the opening 116–48 victory over Angola through the gold-medal-winning game against Croatia. I have had the privilege of working at six Olympics. I also handled research for NBC at the boxing venue in Seoul in 1988 and called men's and women's ice hockey play-by-play for NBC at the Winter Games in Salt Lake City (2002), Torino (2006), Vancouver (2010), and Sochi (2014).

1994 Stanley Cup Finals, Game Seven, Vancouver Canucks at New York Rangers, Madison Square Garden, New York, New York, June 14, 1994

I had the fortune of calling the series for NHL Radio. The Rangers' Cup hopes almost ended in the conference finals, as they trailed the New Jersey Devils, three games to two. Captain Mark Messier "guaranteed" a Game Six victory and delivered. Then in Game Seven, the Devils forced overtime with a goal in the final 10 seconds, again putting the Rangers' season in peril. Stephane Matteau sent the Rangers to the Finals with a goal in double overtime; Howie Rose's "Matteau, Matteau, Matteau" call on WFAN Radio will be remembered by New Yorkers for decades.

On to the Finals, and the Rangers took a commanding three-games-to-one lead over the Vancouver Canucks. New York City was ready to celebrate on June 9; however, the Rangers lost Game Five at home. The Canucks forced a decisive Game Seven by winning Game Six at home, and the Rangers won the clincher in a 3–2 nail-biter. A sign held up at the final buzzer by one Ranger fanatic said it all: Now I Can Die In Peace. I will never forget the emotions of the series, especially during the final frantic moments. Madison Square Garden erupted with chants of "We Want The Cup" and "No More 1940," while the Rangers celebrated on the ice. When NHL Commissioner Gary Bettman handed the Stanley Cup to Messier, fifty-four years of frustration were erased.

California Angels at Baltimore Orioles, Camden Yards, Baltimore, Maryland, September 6, 1995

Cal Ripken plays in his 2,131st consecutive game, breaking the record set by the Iron Horse, Lou Gehrig, fifty-six years earlier. Having grown up in Aberdeen, Maryland, Ripken was one of Baltimore's own. The city of Baltimore has a small-town feel, especially at sporting venues. The city celebrated as it never had before, as a native son reached a mark most sports experts thought would never be attainable. Eighty-year-old Joe DiMaggio, Gehrig's former teammate, gave a poignant speech during the ceremony.

Cal Ripken Jr. during ceremonies to celebrate his breaking of Lou Gehrig's record of 2,130 consecutive games played. (AP Photo/Denis Paquin)]

2003 American League Championship Series, Game Seven, Boston Red Sox at New York Yankees, Yankee Stadium, Bronx, New York, October 16, 2003, and 2004 American League Championship Series, Game Seven, Boston Red Sox at New York Yankees, Yankee Stadium, Bronx, New York, October 20, 2004

I could feel the tension in the ballpark throughout my entire body. I will always cherish the opportunity I was given to handle the post-series interviews for FOX on the podium in the winning clubhouse both years (Joe Torre and Mariano Rivera in '03 following Aaron Boone's walk-off home run, Terry Francona and Tim Wakefield in '04) as Jackie Autry handed the hardware to the winners.

While I watched the first eight innings of both games from the photographers' box directly to the right of the Yankees' dugout, I did not see Boone's homer in 2003 in person. I was watching on a 12-inch monitor in the hallway just outside the Yankees' clubhouse, because I had to enter the winning clubhouse immediately to set up for interviews at the conclusion of the game. Seconds after Boone ended the series, I sprinted toward the clubhouse and was nearly knocked over by clubhouse attendants and other team personnel as they ran the other way toward the tunnel leading to the dugout so they could join in the celebration.

After I concluded my postgame interviews in the Yankees' clubhouse, I noticed Mayor Michael Bloomberg standing to the left of the podium. One of his aides climbed toward me and asked in a hushed tone if I would mind interviewing the mayor. I explained that due to the extra innings, we had already signed off and transitioned to the late local news. The mayor's aide whispered to me, "Can you fake it?" Sensing that his future employment may be in jeopardy if I did not interview the mayor, I asked the cameraman to act as if he were recording the interview. I then spent the next three-to-five minutes interviewing one of the richest and most powerful men in the world, knowing that nobody outside the TV truck would ever hear or see our chat.

2010 Winter Olympics, Men's Hockey Final, United States vs. Canada, Canada Hockey Place, Vancouver, Canada, February 28, 2010

During the 2010 Winter Olympic Games in Vancouver, I called play-by-play for twenty men's and women's hockey games in the span of fifteen days. After calling the men's bronze-medal game between Finland and Slovakia on February 27, I returned to Canada Hockey Place the next afternoon as a spectator for the gold-medal game between the United States and Canada. The United States had not won a hockey gold medal since 1980 in Lake Placid, while Canada beat the U.S. to win gold in Salt Lake City in 2002. Once the U.S. and Canada had won their semifinal games two days earlier, the gold medal matchup became one of the most highly anticipated hockey games of all time. Two North American teams filled with National Hockey League stars playing in a North American venue. Canada took a 2–0 lead in the second period before a raucous crowd. Ryan Kesler of the Vancouver Canucks (booed in his home arena throughout the game) scored for the U.S. later in the period to cut the Canada lead to 2–1. Eighteen thousand hearts palpitated inside the arena throughout the third period. Over 50 million tuned in on television throughout the U.S. and Canada. When Zach Parise tied the game with 25 seconds remaining in regulation, you could hear a pin drop. And when Sidney Crosby scored the "Golden Goal" in overtime, it set off a wild celebration inside the arena, which spilled out onto the streets of Vancouver.

Marv Albert

Broadcaster, Turner Sports/CBS Sports

Recipient of Basketball Hall of Fame's Curt Gowdy Award, 1997
Elected to National Sports Media Association Hall of Fame, 2014

1970 NBA Finals, Game Seven, Los Angeles Lakers at New York Knicks, Madison Square Garden, New York, New York, May 8, 1970

This game is considered the largest audience for a sports event in New York radio history; the game was on tape delay on television, so unless you had a ticket, this was the only way to follow it live. I taped the pregame show, and at that point, most people did not think Knicks center Willis Reed was going to play after he injured his leg in Game Five and missed Game Six. I interviewed Willis for the show just before he was about to get a cortisone shot and asked whether he was going to play, and he told me there was no way he would not be out there. During warm-ups, Willis was not on the floor, and everyone in the building was more concerned with where he was than anything else. The Lakers were looking around for him, as were his Knicks teammates. The game was getting close to starting, but there was still no sign of him. Then, at 7:27, he dramatically came out of the tunnel to the court, and I said on the air, "Here comes Willis," followed by a deafening roar from the 19,500 in attendance. Everything in the building stopped, and the crowd was going berserk. Wilt Chamberlain of the Lakers couldn't believe what was happening and just stood there with his mouth wide open—apparently, his mindset was that he wasn't going to have to play against Willis. Both teams abruptly stopped warming up as Willis trotted onto the floor and hit a couple of practice jumpers, causing the crowd to go even crazier, all just moments before the game was about to start. Once the game actually got underway, he hit his first two jump shots, and I've never heard an NBA crowd that loud. Normally, a couple of early baskets wouldn't be that meaningful in the first quarter of an NBA game, but this seemed to provide a great deal of inspiration. As it turned out, Walt Frazier had one of the greatest games in Finals history, and undoubtedly one of the most forgotten great games ever, but Willis's mere presence in uniform gave everyone the feeling that there was no way the Knicks were going to lose. The Knicks won in a romp, 113–99, to take their first NBA championship.

1988 World Series, Game One, Oakland Athletics at Los Angeles Dodgers, Dodger Stadium, Los Angeles, California, October 15, 1988

Bob Costas and I cohosted the World Series pre- and postgame shows for NBC. We would each do a postgame interview, and, this night, I was in Oakland's dugout as the game was coming to an end. The Athletics held a 4–3 lead in the ninth and were starting to celebrate, since it appeared that they were going to win the game. Hall of Fame closer Dennis Eckersley, who had 45 saves that season, was on the mound to shut the door, and I was standing right near then-Oakland manager Tony LaRussa when the injured Kirk Gibson came hobbling out of the dugout following a Mike Davis walk with two outs. The entire Oakland dugout was astonished that he was about to pinch-hit; he could barely walk due to a painful knee injury, so no one thought he could actually step up to the plate and produce. I was all set to interview Oakland's Jose Canseco once the final out was made, since he was the star of the game to that point, when Gibson remarkably homered into the right-field pavilion to give the Dodgers a 5–4 win. The moment he made contact, Canseco knew the ball was gone, just from the crack of the bat. Of course, the crowd went wild at that point. As Bob interviewed Gibson after the game, Eckersley, who looked crushed after giving up the homer, agreed to talk with me without any hesitation. He looked at it as just one of those things that happens and you have to talk whether things went well or not. Gibson didn't make another plate appearance in the Series, but that home run will go down as one of the most extraordinary moments in the game's history, and it spurred the Dodgers to the Series win.

1992 Summer Olympics, Men's Basketball, Palau Municipal d'Esports de Badalona, Badalona, Spain, July 26–August 8, 1992

It was chilling for me just to watch the original Dream Team take the court for the first time in the Olympics. This was clearly the most incredible group of players ever assembled in a team sport, from Jordan to Bird to Magic to Stockton and Malone. Obviously, the games were blowouts, but to see this group performing together was daunting. When they took the floor, the crowd, which was comprised mostly of fans from overseas, went crazy. Once the tournament started, though, the games weren't even close, and the U.S. won every one by at least thirty-two points. It meant a lot to the team to win the gold medal, but the games themselves were actually difficult to broadcast since they were all so one-sided. Most of the excitement surrounding the team was off the court, usually centered around Charles Barkley, who was all over the city, soaking up the Olympic experience and the adulation, with throngs following him everywhere. Throughout the two weeks in Barcelona, it felt as if we were covering the exploits of the Beatles, not a basketball team.

Members of the USA basketball "Dream Team" pose with their gold medals at the 1992 Summer Olympics. (AP Photo)

1994 Stanley Cup Finals, Game Seven, Vancouver Canucks at New York Rangers, Madison Square Garden, New York, New York, June 14, 1994

As I was broadcasting the game, I remember gazing at the seats surrounding the radio booth in Madison Square Garden, which was located in the middle of the lower stands. As the clock wound down and the Rangers won their first Stanley Cup since 1940, I remember seeing people all around me in tears, reminding me how emotionally Rangers fans reacted to the team. While this was all going on, I thought back to my earlier days as a broadcaster for the team, when they were often contenders, with guys like Rod Gilbert, Jean Ratelle, Vic Hadfield, Eddie Giacomin, and others, but it was the era of the Montreal Canadiens, and Bobby Orr's Bruins, then the Philadelphia Flyers, and the Rangers were never quite good enough. It was fifty-four years between Rangers Stanley Cup wins, and chants of "1940" were prevalent for a long time. So, this night was more about the fans as the final seconds ticked off. Growing up as a Rangers fan, with firsthand knowledge of the frustrations from all of the disappointing conclusions to seasons, it felt like this day would never happen. When the buzzer sounded, I said on the air, "The New York Rangers have won the Stanley Cup, something most people thought they would never hear in their lifetime." I can recall looking to my left, where I saw a fan holding up the sign that read: "Now I CAN DIE IN PEACE." That said it best of all, and I can only imagine how many people in the building that night shared in those sentiments.

1997 NBA Finals, Game Five, Chicago Bulls at Utah Jazz, Delta Center, Salt Lake City, Utah, June 11, 1997

To me, this was one of the most remarkable individual performances I have ever seen. Michael Jordan reportedly had eaten some bad pizza and was weakened by food poisoning or a stomach virus. He could barely stand up before the pivotal Game Five in Salt Lake City, with the series tied at two. He was dizzy and dehydrated to the point where I remember newspaper reports the next day describing him as being "deathly ill." I did a five-minute interview with him a few hours before the game, as we always did, but he didn't give us any indication that he wasn't feeling right, so we didn't even know about that until after the game started. Of course, we discussed it on the air for the television audience, but those in attendance had no idea of the extent of his physical condition—what they were watching really was amazing. As the game went on, Michael became weaker and weaker, but somehow he just kept going, and I remember we showed him, at times, being helped to the bench or being propped up by Scottie Pippen during timeouts. Despite his debilitating illness, he scored 38 points in the game, 15 of them in the fourth quarter, to lead the Bulls to a 90–88 win. It was incredible just to watch him preserve his energy and will himself to lead his team to its most important win of the season. Afterwards, Pippen said he had never seen Michael that sick and that he didn't think he'd even be able to put his uniform on. I have been fortunate to call a host of memorable Jordan games, but I've never seen anything quite like this one. The series would end two nights later in Chicago.

Harvey Araton

Columnist, *New York Times*

1970 NBA Finals, Game Five, Los Angeles Lakers at New York Knicks, Madison Square Garden, New York, New York, May 4, 1970

Most people remember this championship series for the Willis Reed game, which was Game Seven, so Game Five of the series is often overlooked, and the impact of it was lessened by the events two games later. The series was tied, 2–2, and I was a seventeen-year-old high school student living in Staten Island. I grew up in a New York City housing project and our whole lives were centered around the concrete court in the middle of the housing project, so it was impossible not to love that Knicks team. They were clearly the dominant pro basketball team in New York. A friend of mine had relatives in Manhattan who had season tickets but couldn't use them that night, so we took the ferry into the city and rode the subway up to the Garden. That day happened to be the day of the Kent State shootings, so there was a pall over the city that night, and you felt a bit guilty about attending a sports event.

The Knicks came out and fell behind early, when Willis Reed was driving on Wilt Chamberlain. He stumbled forward and went down with a thud, and as the play went to the other end, he was still down on the court, stretched out in agony. The immediate thought was that this incredible season was going to go up in smoke. They played without him and had Dave DeBusschere, who was 6-foot-6, guarding Wilt. After a huge rally, the Knicks won the game, and it was only when that happened that everyone put the day's proceedings aside and got involved in the spirit of the comeback and the underdog. Forty years after the game, I was writing a book on the Knicks of that era and sat with Willis to watch this game, since he told me he had seen Game Seven numerous times but had never watched Game Five. After we were done, he said this was their greatest victory. Combining that experience with being at the actual game gives this one great meaning to me.

1992 Summer Olympics, Men's Basketball Final, Palau Municipal d'Esports de Badalona, Badalona, Spain, August 8, 1992

As I got deeper into my career, one of the things I always appreciated about working for the *New York Times* was that I got to go to a lot of international events. When I was young and a clerk at the *New York Post*, I used to go in on Friday nights and work the desk and often would listen to columnists like Vic Ziegel and Lester Bromberg reminisce about things like the Ali days, when the guys that covered Ali went on international journeys to places like Kinshasa or Manila to cover his fights. They talked about it with reverence, referring to them as the stories that defined their careers. I would always wonder if I would have that one defining story. Looking back now, if I have to pick one story I covered like that, it would be the globalization of professional basketball, because it was the kind of story that was bigger than the NBA or one particular series. It was all crystallized with the 1992 Dream Team at the Barcelona Olympics. I covered the team from the early practices in San Diego to the qualifying tournament in Portland and then to Monte Carlo for the pre-Olympics training camp and then finally in Barcelona. Aside from the wonderful travel and hotels, it was incredible to see the responses in Europe to players like Michael Jordan, Larry Bird, and Magic Johnson. Those three in particular were the most identifiable faces around the world, and Michael, in particular, was becoming arguably the most popular athlete in the world. Being around them for that long and watching the world converge on a sport that I love was a wonderful thing to participate in.

What made the event even more spectacular was that the world was changing at the time, with the fall of the Soviet Union and all of these small countries breaking away. During those Olympics, besides the Dream Team, who were the basketball Beatles, you had other storylines about the small countries playing for nationalistic pride. Countries like Lithuania were able to qualify on their own, while other former Soviet players played for the Unified Team, which also included players from former Soviet countries that didn't qualify for the Games. There was also the breakup of Yugoslavia and the Croatian team, featuring Drazen Petrovic and Toni Kukoc, that qualified, as well. So, the teams from Lithuania and Croatia were playing with a real fervor and passion. The bronze-medal game actually came down to the Unified Team against Lithuania, with Lithuania winning a real impassioned, tense game. The Croatian team ended up playing in the gold-medal game against the Americans, who won in a blowout. That made the medal presentation an amazing sight, with the Americans and all of these icons of the game representing wealth and power, and standing right next to them on one side were the Lithuanians, who were so poor that their warmup jerseys were tie-dyed and supplied by the Grateful Dead, and the Croatians on the other side, who were hugging and crying and proud just to hold up their flag after what their country had just gone through. It was an amazing contrast in that event. With all of the talk about the Dream Team, everything else that was going on represented the true Olympic story.

1994 Winter Olympics, Men's 1000 Meter Speed Skating Final, Vikingskipet Olympic Arena, Hamar, Norway, February 18, 1994

This is another story about what the Olympics are supposed to be. My first Olympics were in 1988, when I was working for the *New York Daily News*, and I was the only reporter there for the paper. One of the stories in Calgary that year was American speed skater Dan Jansen, who had a sister who was dying of leukemia. Jansen was the favorite in two events—the 500 and the 1,000. He had spoken to his sister the morning of the 500, but she was too weak to converse with him and would die later that day. With this on his mind, he ended up falling and losing the race. He would end up skating poorly in the 1,000 after that. We then move on to 1992 in Albertville, France, where he was also a favorite to win the 500 and contend in the 1,000, and again he failed to medal, finishing 26th in the 1,000. Now it looks like he is going to become one of these Olympic-failure athletes over the course of multiple Olympics. After 1992, the Winter Olympics shifted their schedule to alternate every two years with the Summer Olympics, giving Jansen one more serious chance in 1994 in Lillehammer, Norway to finally win a medal.

He was a strong candidate to win the 500 but was not expected to do as well in the 1,000. By this point, I was covering the event for the *New York Times*, and in the 500, he slipped again and finished out of the medals. That meant the 1,000 was his last chance to medal. The sport is very popular in Norway, and as the skaters are making their way around the oval, their times are flashing up on the big board. For Americans, the times happen too fast to register, but Norwegians follow the sport so closely, they are quick to pick up on what the times mean, and it immediately becomes obvious to them that something is happening. And what was happening was that Dan Jansen, in an event he wasn't supposed to win, was in the process of setting a world record and winning a gold medal. When he finishes and the final time registers, the crowd erupts. What came next was the most amazing thing. All of the competitors from the other countries, including the other contenders and rivals, were cheering him as he did his victory lap. Between the 1992 and 1994 Olympics, Jansen and his wife had a baby girl named Jane, after his sister. His wife handed Jane to him and he carried Jane in one arm and a small American flag in the other hand, and a spotlight came down on him as he was skating. I don't think there was a single person in the building, including journalists, who wasn't in tears. It was the most beautiful sports event and in stark contrast to the other big event from those Games, the women's figure skating circus featuring Nancy Kerrigan and Tonya Harding.

1998 NBA Finals, Game Six, Chicago Bulls at Utah Jazz, Delta Center, Salt Lake City, Utah, June 14, 1998

My older son loved basketball from a very early age, especially Michael Jordan, and he followed the Bulls religiously. Whenever they came to town to play the Knicks, I would buy one ticket and my wife would go with him, and he would sit on her lap. That takes us to the final act in Jordan's career (at least in Chicago). The Bulls were up, 3–1, and going for the clincher in Chicago. I wrote a column for the *Times* where I stood by the Jordan statue outside the United Center and asked the fans what it meant to them, as they worshipped in front of the altar to him. The Bulls lost the game, though, so we all had to go back out to Utah, where there was a chance the Jazz would win both of the games to win the title. The Bulls came back late, and Jordan hit the game-winning shot over Bryon Russell. He probably pushed off but got the superstar call, and the Bulls stopped the Jazz at the other end to seal the win. On the court, it was pandemonium, and I'm on a ridiculously tight deadline. I had two versions of my column written and just needed to fill in the details, but just couldn't resist calling home, because I knew my nine-year-old son was watching this. He was so excited that the Bulls had won, and I just felt like I needed to share it with him for a couple of minutes. One of the things that we lose as sportswriters, because we are away a lot, is moments like that with your family. I decided that if I was five minutes late with my column, so be it. I was going to spend this moment, which was going to be the last one of the Bulls' run, with my son, because I knew how important this was to him.

The 2009 Wimbledon Championships, Gentlemen's Final, Andy Roddick vs. Roger Federer, The All England Lawn Tennis Club, London, England, July 5, 2009

I was never into tennis until my late twenties and covered the sport for the first time during the New York newspaper strike in the late '70s, when I did some work for one of the strike papers everyone went to work for. It was a great time for American tennis, with Connors and McEnroe, plus Bjorn Borg from Sweden. After that, I started covering and enjoying the sport more and more, especially Wimbledon, which is like the Fenway Park of tennis stadiums. In May of 2009, the *Times* moved me into feature writing for all of their weekly sections in the Sunday paper. With both the economy and the newspaper industry in free fall at the time, I took this as a real threat to my job, since they were moving me off the sports section, where I had an identity. I had already been scheduled to go to Wimbledon, though, so they let me go and I would start my new role after I got back, with the mindset that my last sports assignment would be this tournament that I really love. At this point, Roger Federer is well into his run as the world's top player and has fourteen Grand Slam titles, to tie him with Pete Sampras. On the final Sunday, Federer faced American Andy Roddick. Roddick won the first set, then they played a tiebreaker in the second set, which Roddick led, 6–2. Somehow, Federer got back to 6–5, and Roddick missed a fairly easy backhand volley that would have ended the set. Federer eked out the tiebreaker to even the match at one set. It eventually went to a fifth set, which seemingly went on forever, ending at 16–14 for Federer. As that set progressed, I went back and forth on thinking about who I wanted to see win, since both would be great stories. It also hit me that this could be the last sporting event that I would ever cover, so there was great personal meaning for me, as well. I decided that if I was going out, I wanted to see a record broken, so I started hoping Federer would win, which he did. When I got to the airport the next day, I was waiting in the airline lounge while waiting to board, and former New York mayor David Dinkins walks in. He was always a big tennis fan, so I went over to introduce myself, and we spent the next half hour talking tennis. As he got up to leave, he told me that he was a reader of mine for many years, going back to when I was at the *Daily News*. I told him this was probably my last tennis column, and he said he would miss my work and wished me luck. I remember getting on the plane thinking about how wonderful that was—it was just a really nice, serendipitous moment and emboldened me to go home and embrace whatever came next and do the best I could. I did leave sports but went back a year later in a slightly different role, but if my sports career had ended on that note, it would have been a good way to go out.

Roger Federer of Switzerland leaps into the air after defeating Andy Roddick to win at Wimbledon in 2009. (AP Photo/Alastair Grant)

Michelle Beadle

Broadcaster, ESPN

Waco Wizards at Austin Ice Bats, Luedecke Arena, Austin, Texas, October 19, 1996

The only historic significance that night was that the team made its debut. I was an intern for the team, though, and basically we were a bunch of kids and newbies that started a hockey team. I was in school at the University of Texas, when they decided to start a hockey team in Austin in the new Western Professional Hockey League. So, a bunch of us show up and are all interns, and it turns into one giant family. All of these Canadian players had moved down to Texas to bring hockey to the masses. We literally started working in a barn with the head coach, former NHLer Blaine Stoughton, and a team full of misfits that couldn't get picked up anywhere else. You don't get to be part of something from the bottom level very often in life, but here we were on a Friday night, and we would bring in some six-packs and put the rink together. I had never even been ice skating, but I now knew how to put the Plexiglas up around the ice. It was the most fun you could ever have doing an internship. When we debuted in the barn, we would run into weather problems. There were bats, there was fog, it was too hot . . . the typical hockey arena problems. It is sad, because the team doesn't exist anymore, but to have been a part of something like that every night was awesome.

Chicago Bulls Home Game, United Center, Chicago, Illinois, 1997–98 season

A friend of mine that I worked with at the Ice Bats was from Chicago and is one of the biggest sports fans I've ever known. I'm not sure what really sparked it, and neither one of us had any money, but we knew Michael Jordan might be retiring after the '98 season and decided to go to Chicago specifically to be able to watch him play in Chicago just once. Our seats were way up at the top of the building, but it didn't matter, because it was amazing to be there and see him play in person. We did the whole thing—we took our pictures in front of the statue, we went to the ESPN Zone, and I took my picture at the *SportsCenter* desk (who knew!!!). But to be in that building and see the greatest basketball player of all-time, and have the chance to be surrounded by all of these superfans, it was worth it. I can't even tell you who they played that night. But when that intro music started, I was so happy we made the trip. And now I can always say that I saw Michael Jordan play in that building.

2006 Rose Bowl, Texas vs. USC, Rose Bowl, Pasadena, California, January 4, 2006

CSTV was still very new, and going to this game was a very big thing for us. We took a bunch of people to Pasadena to do shows and cover the game. I was assigned to run onto the field after the game ended to do interviews. Of course, I also went to Texas, so there was some conflict for me because I had to be "unbiased," but I was also wearing this topaz Longhorn necklace tucked under my shirt, so that was my way of rebelling against the system. Late in the game, everyone thought USC was going to win the game, so all of the media was piling onto the Trojans' sideline. I remember how chaotic it was and had never actually done this before, so all I really knew was just to hold onto my cameraman's backpack and just go. But all of a sudden, Vince Young became a superhero, everything went nuts, and UT figures out a way to win the game. We were still on the USC sideline and watched the mood there change very quickly, from this very happy place to depressing. As we ran onto the field, I remember screaming and cheering, then reminding myself that I wasn't supposed to be doing that. We finally got out to do the interviews, but it was such an adrenaline rush that I wasn't totally sure what to say, and I probably looked like an idiot because of the way I was jumping up and down in excitement. That game, though, is why we all love sports. We all thought it was over, and we all got ready to do our jobs, but then the ending changed and made it even more fun. Of course, everyone around me was probably asking who the unprofessional ass jumping up and down was.

Vince Young rushes for the game-winning touchdown in the 2006 Rose Bowl. (AP Photo/Paul Sakuma)

WWE Survivor Series, Madison Square Garden, New York, New York, November 20, 2011

Survivor Series is one of those events where a big name will usually come back, and this night, it was The Rock. I had become friendly with Jim Ross through Twitter. I hate to ask people for tickets, so I asked him how I could buy some. He was nice enough, though, to get me ringside tickets, and I felt like I was twelve all over again. We made a sign with Jim's cowboy hat on it to hold up and were sitting basically at one of the corners at the bottom of the entrance ramp, where they turn to go up into the ring. Some of them saw me sitting there and had some fun with it, like CM Punk coming over to mess up my hair. When the DVD of the night came in, I saw us losing our mind as The Rock came out and did his promo. Any event at the Garden is pretty cool (except for a Knicks game), but it is fun to be there for a big WWE event. It gets so loud, and everyone gets amped up to be there. The nerdiest part of it for me was when the DVD came out and you can see me yelling like a kid, chanting, "You still got it!" at The Rock. I'm sure there is a part of me that is supposed to be embarrassed, but that was just the greatest night ever. It was so much fun, and it makes you feel like a kid again.

2014 NBA Finals, Game Five, Miami Heat at San Antonio Spurs, AT&T Center, San Antonio, Texas, June 15, 2014

I've been a Spurs fan since I was a kid, and the rise of the Miami Heat with LeBron James made for a very interesting chapter for Spurs fans, especially after the loss in 2013 on Ray Allen's buzzer-beater. My dad is a season ticket holder, and his seats just happen to be right next to the visitors' bench. The only game I was able to get home for in that series was Game Five, so I went with my brother and my boyfriend. We basically had three butts in the two seats for the entire game, but since nobody was sitting the whole game, it didn't even matter. We had so much fun sitting there and yelling all game. It got to the point where Chris "Birdman" Andersen wanted to get my brother and my boyfriend kicked out because of all of the trash we were talking. I know some of the guys that were on the Heat, and LeBron was looking at me with this sad face, since he knew who I was. I kept trash-talking, though, but wouldn't make eye contact with any of them. At one point, I was staring at the scoreboard and yelling at Andersen, who knew it was me yelling because he was standing around two feet away from me, but I wouldn't look in his direction. I have never been so sweaty and so happy at a game. There are screen shots of this idiot blonde person (that would be me) with her mouth open, screaming and yelling, arms in the air. After the Finals the previous year, and the bad taste that it left in our mouths, this night was the most perfect ending for me. It is, hands down, my most favorite sports moment of my life.

Mike Breen

Broadcaster, ESPN/MSG Network

1986 World Series, Game Six, Boston Red Sox at New York Mets, Shea Stadium, Flushing, New York, October 25, 1986

The press box was so crowded that the Mets were just putting people wherever they could find seats. I was working for NBC Radio at the time, and they happened to seat me in the Red Sox radio booth, where there was enough room for the broadcasters to sit in the front, while others sat in the back. I was really young and had just started working in the business, so I hadn't really learned the proper etiquette yet. Being a Mets fan my whole life, I was dejected because it appeared that they were going to lose the World Series. So when the ball went through Bill Buckner's legs, I lost all journalistic perspective and started jumping up and down like everyone in the stands. I can't remember if it was the producer or one of the Red Sox radio guys, but one of them turned around and shot me the dirtiest look. I should not have been acting that way, and I quickly quieted myself down. But it was such an unexpected great moment for a Mets fan that I believe even the most hardened journalist would have had a difficult time not reacting.

1994 NBA Finals, Game Five, Houston Rockets at New York Knicks, Madison Square Garden, New York, New York, June 17, 1994

NBC was broadcasting the NBA at the time, and during the game, the O.J. Simpson chase was going on. On our TV monitor, NBC put up a split screen of the game and the O.J. chase; then, at some point, it just became O.J. I found it too distracting while broadcasting the game, so I asked our statistician, Harry Robinson, to shut the monitor off. When he went to turn the TV off, all the fans sitting around the booth objected and asked if I would leave it on. The radio booth at Madison Square Garden is right in the middle of the stands, and you become friendly with the people sitting around you all the time, so we turned it back on for them. I remember thinking, here was the biggest game I had ever broadcast, and people are more interested in watching O.J. Simpson and a white Ford Bronco. It was a very bizarre experience.

1996 Summer Olympics, Women's Basketball Finals, Georgia Dome, Atlanta, Georgia, August 3, 1996

The American women had lost in the 1994 World Championships to Brazil and were no longer considered the best team in the world, so they completely changed how they prepared for the Olympics. They hired Trish VanDerveer from Stanford, who took a leave of absence to coach the team. All the women on the team toured around the country and the world for a year and a half to become a cohesive unit and make sure they won the gold. They didn't lose a game the entire time they were together while preparing for the Games in Atlanta, so the pressure on them to win the gold was enormous; any loss would have been a huge disappointment.

They won the Olympics going away, destroying Brazil in the finals. After the game in the Georgia Dome, they gave the medals out immediately, since this was the final event of the Games. When the national anthem played, it felt like every one of the 40,000 fans in the building sang the anthem. I've never been in a building where so many people sang the national anthem. You could see that the players became very affected by the outpouring of patriotism and began crying. I still get chills thinking about it.

2002 FIBA World Championships Finals, Yugoslavia vs. Argentina, Conseco Fieldhouse, Indianapolis, Indiana, September 8, 2002

NBC was scheduled to broadcast the semifinals and finals, with the expectation that the United States would be in one of the two semifinals. Well, that didn't happen, as the Americans were knocked out in the quarterfinals, leaving us to broadcast the rest of the tournament without Team USA on American television. Argentina and Yugoslavia won the two semifinal games to make it to the championship and were clearly the two best teams in the world at this point. The finals were in Conseco Fieldhouse in Indianapolis, thousands and thousands of miles from either country, yet there was a huge core of fans from both Yugoslavia and Argentina.

One of the great things about international basketball is how emotional and passionate the fans are. They chant and sing all game long as they cheer their country on. Yugoslavia won the game, and at the final buzzer, the players on the Yugoslavian team, along with their fans, were all crying with tears of joy. The players and fans from Argentina were all crying, but with tears of disappointment. It was one of the best-played games and certainly the most emotional game I've ever seen, from both a player's and a fan's standpoint.

2013 NBA Finals, Game Six, San Antonio Spurs at Miami Heat, AmericanAirlines Arena, Miami, Florida, June 18, 2013

This game will always affectionately be known as the "Ray Allen Game." His has to go down as one of the great clutch shots in the history of the NBA, especially when you consider the stakes and the situation. It didn't win the Heat a championship, but it prevented them from losing it. If anyone was ever prepared to take a shot like that, it was Ray Allen. He had practiced that particular shot thousands, if not tens of thousands of times. Every single game that I've covered that Ray Allen played in, I would never beat him to the arena, and I would usually get there at least two and a half hours before the game. He was always at the arena on the floor shooting, every single game with zero exceptions. He wasn't just a good shooter. He was a guy that put years and years into being ready for that moment.

A few things stand out from that night. The NBA had set up the rope that they put up around the court when a championship is decided and they are going to award the trophy, and the Heat players noticed it. Even LeBron James admitted that he noticed it and thought it was over and they weren't going to win. The Spurs had gone up five with 28.2 seconds remaining before everything started to change. When it looked like it was over, people started to leave the arena in droves, but after the three-pointer and the game headed into overtime, we had a shot of people trying to get back inside. They were pounding on the glass to get back in but weren't allowed back in. So all of these people who left early missed not only one of the greatest shots in the history of basketball, but a thrilling overtime, as well.

If there was ever evidence of the fine line between winning and losing, this game was it. The championship was decided by one rebound, one missed free throw, or one made three-pointer. In the last 20 seconds of that game, there must have been seven or eight things that, if one of them had happened differently, San Antonio would have won the title that night. It is pretty incredible that a whole season would come down to that and how one play completely changes the narrative of a season and of players. People get crazy about someone's legacy, but a legacy can be altered by one missed free throw or just missing a rebound. If Allen's shot doesn't fall, it changes everything. But that is the beauty of sports and why we love them so much.

Ray Allen ties the game with a three-pointer at the end of regulation of Game Six of the 2013 NBA Finals. (AP Photo/Lynne Sladky)

Thom Brennaman

Broadcaster, FOX Sports

Chicago Cubs at Cincinnati Reds, Riverfront Stadium, Cincinnati, Ohio, July 16, 1994

I was doing Cubs games at the time. Major League Baseball did not have a national TV contract, so they formed what was called The Baseball Network, which televised regional games across the country one night each week. They asked if I would be interested in doing a game with my dad, Marty, who is a Hall of Fame broadcaster with the Reds. My first inclination was to say of course, but when I thought about it, I realized I had never done a game on national TV, which was a big deal. I was still so inexperienced at the time. Additionally, neither one of us is an analyst, but I realized it was something that I just had to do. I recall the night of the game, and standing there to do the open for the telecast next to my dad, holding microphones that had "ABC" on them. It was, without question, one of the most surreal moments that I think a young man could ever experience. I was really nervous, but I remember how calm my dad was, although I knew he was nervous, as well, but nervous for me, not for him. All of these moments were flashing through my head. I remembered being in spring training when I was ten and my dad got the job with the Reds, going into the clubhouse for the first time, and the first four people I met were Johnny Bench, Pete Rose, Joe Morgan, and Tony Perez. Then I thought about being a batboy for the team during spring training, and working as a fourteen-year-old cleaning up the suites at Riverfront Stadium. All of these memories came rushing back to me, and I just thanked God for the opportunity to do what I was doing that night.

2001 World Series, New York Yankees vs. Arizona Diamondbacks, Yankee Stadium, Bronx, New York, and Bank One Ballpark, Phoenix, Arizona, October 27-November 4, 2001

I was hired to be the play-by-play announcer for the Arizona Diamondbacks two years before they even started playing, so having been with the organization since its inception made this a really exciting time. I remember all of the New York press writing that it would be a short series with the Yankees winning but chalked that up to them being on the East Coast and not seeing the Diamondbacks play very much. The team had Randy Johnson and Curt Schilling, so nothing was going to be over too fast. Schilling was dominant in the Game One win. Johnson was even better in Game Two, getting the complete-game shutout to put Arizona up, 2–0.

Now we go back to New York, and all of this, far more important, was happening on the heels of 9/11. To walk into Game Three that night, on that hallowed ground of baseball, with the crowd, the anticipation, the emotion, and the excitement, and see President Bush walk out to the mound so proud and strong and fire a fastball, then see a bald eagle soar into the stadium and land right behind home plate, I will never again in my lifetime see anything like that. For those of us who love this country, it was a moment where you just said, "Wow!" I'm not sure there were many dry eyes in the stadium that night; even the most hardened of New Yorkers felt that emotion that night. For the next three nights, all of that emotion is packed into the World Series, and we witnessed the next two nights, in Games Four and Five, something that had never happened in the history of the World Series—a team blowing a ninth-inning lead and losing in extra innings in back-to-back games. That put the Yankees ahead, 3–2, but the energy in that city and that stadium for those three games was beyond description.

We know what happened after that, when the series shifted back to Arizona. Game Six was a blowout with Johnson pitching again to tie the series, bringing us to Game Seven. I will always maintain that the best big-game pitcher that I've ever seen in my career is Curt Schilling. It was Schilling against Roger Clemens in Game Seven, and it just doesn't get any better than that. The Diamondbacks jumped out in front, the Yankees came back to take the lead, and now the clock is ticking. The Yankees are bringing in Mariano Rivera, and we find out the Yankees are setting up their locker room for the postgame celebration. When Rivera came out of the bullpen for the ninth inning, it was just electric, even though it was a Yankee road game. It never rains in Arizona that time of year, and the roof was open at the stadium, but all of a sudden, a light rain started to fall. It felt impossible and made you wonder whether we were going to see something else impossible happen on the field, which would have been Mariano Rivera blowing a save in a World Series game. It was so eerie. And that is exactly what happened, culminating with the Luis Gonzalez single to center that scored Jay Bell to give the Diamondbacks the first championship by a professional sports team in the state of Arizona.

2003 National League Championship Series, Game Six, Florida Marlins at Chicago Cubs, Wrigley Field, Chicago, Illinois, October 14, 2003

I had the chance to call Cubs games for six years, and I think anyone who has had the opportunity to have any sort of affiliation with the Cubs comes to understand the pain and suffering of the team's fans. After Josh Beckett threw a shutout in Game Five to keep the Marlins alive and shift the series back to Chicago, the scene at Wrigley Field was something I had never witnessed in my life. There were probably five times as many people outside the stadium as there were inside for the game, in anticipation of the Cubs' winning and going to the World Series for the first time since 1945. All of the streets in the neighborhood were closed off for multiple blocks in every direction, and people were completely jamming the streets but really kept themselves under control.

The Cubs took the lead into the eighth inning and were five outs away from clinching the series. As everyone knows, the Marlins scored eight runs in that fateful eighth inning. The play that is unquestionably the most remembered was the foul ball down the left-field line that was touched by Steve Bartman as Moises Alou attempted to catch it. At that moment, we had no idea the Marlins were going to go on to score eight runs. I still maintain to this day that Alou wasn't going to catch the ball, but we'll never really know for sure; all I know is that from where I was sitting, he wasn't going to catch it. Alou's reaction, and he has apologized for it since, had a lot to do with the subsequent reaction of those in the stands, because there were multiple people that went for that foul ball. After it happened and the game resumed, we had an in-house camera in the broadcast booth that was able to show us that the situation in the stands was starting to get a little ugly. Security finally came down to get Bartman out, and while they were walking him out, people were yelling at him and throwing things at him, and we knew it had a chance to get really, really bad.

The game eventually ends, and with the streets mobbed with people, our production team decided to meet at the corner of Clark and Addison and walk

Chicago Cubs fan Steve Bartman attempts to catch a foul ball that could possibly have been caught by outfielder Moises Alou during Game Six of the National League Championship Series at Wrigley Field. (AP Photo/Amy Sancetta)

seven blocks to get in the car and go back to the hotel. To leave the stadium, we cut through the team's offices and went out a singular door, so there weren't many people around that exit. As I opened the door, there stands, by himself behind an eight-foot cement wall, Michael Jordan. I don't know him at all, but my natural reaction was to ask what he was doing there. He says to me, "You haven't been out there yet. There are one hundred thousand zombies walking around out there. It is scary." We invited him to walk with us to help protect him, but he told us there was no chance and that he would spend the night there if he had to.

2007 Fiesta Bowl, Boise State vs. Oklahoma, University of Phoenix Stadium, Glendale, Arizona, January 1, 2007

I think this game, perhaps more than any other, ignited the flame that became the College Football Playoff, because it proved that there are teams out there that could compete with the BCS Conference schools, if given the opportunity. Not many people really gave Boise State a chance against an Oklahoma team that featured Adrian Peterson, had lost only once that season, and might have been playing for a national championship if it hadn't lost that one game. Because our broadcast crew for FOX was doing not only this game, but the national championship game seven days later, as well, we split our group to visit different campuses. I happened to go to Boise, and unlike most people, I knew more about them than their blue field, because I had watched a number of their games during the season. When I got there, I realized that team really believed that they could win the game. I'm not sure anyone else believed it, but when we left Idaho, we knew they believed.

The Broncos dominated the first three quarters and were ahead, 28–10, until Oklahoma ripped off the next 25 points, with the go-ahead touchdown coming on an interception return with 1:02 remaining, and everyone started thinking that was it. Boise gets the ball back and are faced with a fourth-and-18. They pull off the hook-and-lateral play to get not just the first down, but also the tying touchdown to send the game into overtime. On the first play of OT, Adrian Peterson runs 25 yards to give the Sooners the lead. Boise State gets the ball and eventually ends up with a fourth-and-2 at the Oklahoma 6 and decides to run their second trick play; wide receiver Vinny Perretta threw the touchdown pass. The crowd was going crazy, knowing Boise could now tie the game or go for the win with a two-point conversion. We just let the natural sound of the crowd tell the story and stopped talking. I looked over at Barry Alvarez, who was one of my partners, and took my headset off to ask him what he would have done if his offensive coordinator had called that play. He said, "I would have fired his ass right on the spot." The Broncos decided to go for the win and pulled off the Statue of Liberty play; Ian Johnson ran the ball into the end zone untouched for the win.

Chris Myers, who was our sideline reporter, was on the field and went to interview Johnson, who promptly dropped down to one knee and proposed to his girlfriend, one of the Boise State cheerleaders. I can't remember exactly what I said, but it was along the lines of "No Hollywood producer would ever buy this story if you tried to sell it to him." It was just an incredible final quarter and the most exciting quarter of any sport (at least among those sports that have quarters) that I've ever been blessed to witness. It is amazing how many people through the years come up to me and tell me they can't believe I had a chance to see that game.

Appalachian State at Michigan, Michigan Stadium, Ann Arbor, Michigan, September 1, 2007

I had moved back to Cincinnati from Arizona as FOX Sports launched the Big Ten Network, so since I was now living in the Midwest, FOX asked me if I would be interested in working some football games for the new network with Charles Davis. This was the very first game on the network. Appalachian State was the defending FCS national champion but had lost a number of players from that team and was starting a freshman quarterback named Armanti Edwards. Michigan was ranked No. 5 and was loaded with stars, including Chad Henne at quarterback and Jake Long, who went first overall in the NFL draft. When we met with the Wolverines and head coach Lloyd Carr as we were getting ready for the broadcast, they had a palpable aura about them. Then we met with Appalachian State and were at Michigan Stadium when they arrived. It was a beautiful Friday afternoon, and as they walked in, you could see the awestruck look in the kids' eyes as they saw the huge stadium for the first time. I think it is pretty safe to say that there weren't many kids on that team who were recruited by Michigan. You couldn't help but be happy for the kids that they were going to get a chance to play on a stage like that. We talked to their coach on the field for around ten minutes, and when we were done, Charles looked at me and said, "I don't know about you, but that guy thinks they can win this game." It was the same feeling I had after meeting with Boise State while preparing for the Fiesta Bowl a few months earlier. But that was Boise State. This was Appalachian State.

Michigan got the ball to start the game and just rammed the ball right down the Moutaineers' throats for an easy touchdown. Right away, you felt like it had a chance to get really ugly. And it did . . . for Michigan. As soon as you saw Armanti Edwards play, you couldn't figure out how Michigan was going to stop him. They couldn't, and Appalachian State was handling the Wolverines. Michigan had one last shot and got close enough to kick a game-winning field goal and just survive. It was a long attempt, but they had a good kicker so they went for the kick, and it gets blocked. I'm not sure there has ever been a quieter gathering of 105,000 people than that day in Michigan Stadium. You could hear the Appalachian State players celebrating in the press box all the way at the top of Michigan Stadium. There are a lot of people who know more about college football than I'll ever know who say this was the greatest upset in the history of college football.

Ric Bucher

Columnist, Bleacher Report

1993 NBA Finals, Game Three, Phoenix Suns at Chicago Bulls, Chicago Stadium, Chicago, Illinois, June 13, 1993

The image is Charles Barkley beating Michael Jordan in triple overtime in Chicago Stadium, but it is underscored by the great quote by Charles afterwards, when he said that "God wanted us to win." There was a lot of talk at the time about Michael Jordan and his gambling, so he wasn't talking to the media. Charles was laughing it up all series and was like Joe Namath at the Super Bowl. He was regaling everyone to the point that, before that game, Hannah Storm walked into the locker room to show Charles her engagement ring. Without missing a beat, Charles said, "Damn, girl. That is the biggest piece of zirconium I've ever seen." The fact that he would take a shot at Hannah in front of all of the newspaper reporters only endeared him to the ink-stained wretches. It was one of those games where you had the sense that Charles refused to lose in the same way that Michael always refused to lose. This was a time where you saw somebody get the better of Michael. There was a moment late in the game where Charles took a mid-range, fadeaway jumper. You could see the smokiness of Chicago Stadium, which I really miss. This was also the first NBA Finals that I ever covered, and to this day, I think it was one of the best. I was looking at it with fresh eyes, and it was Charles vs. Michael. This game is one of the all-time Finals games. In some ways, it embodied both of their careers. Michael ended up winning at the end, but Charles had moments where he could put a team on his back but could never get a team over the top.

Phoenix Suns at Golden State Warriors, Oakland-Alameda County Coliseum Arena, Oakland, California, November 16, 1993

It was the first time that Chris Webber and Charles Barkley faced off in a game. I'm not sure *apocryphal* is the right word to describe it, but there was a play where Webber blocked a shot at one end, then, at the other end, went behind the back to dunk on Barkley and, after the dunk, whispered something to him before running down the court. Later, he told everyone that he told Barkley,

"I want to be just like you." It is meaningful in a number of ways. It was the first time that I covered a team of any significance. The Warriors had basically mortgaged their future to get Webber but weren't prepared for a guy who was already coming in as a superstar, with a bigger identity than the normal college player has. The template was set for him and who he wanted to be, especially looking at how they now work together on TNT. Webber developed into a great player, although he never made it to the Finals, but there was always that little something that seemed to be missing. Barkley was never afraid to take the big shot with the game on the line, while there was always that question around Webber and whether he really wanted to be that guy.

Personally, as a brand new guy covering the league, having the opportunity to see up close the politics and everything else that happened with Webber and the team was a tremendous initial learning experience. And then you have this one play that proved to be the highlight of Webber's career with the Warriors. It was the first time that I saw a single play, along with the exchange on the court after it, be more of the story than the outcome of the game. Strange as it may sound to a sports purist, it taught me that who won or lost wasn't always the most important thing. Who said what, and did what, to whom, could prove to be most memorable. It certainly was in this case.

1998 NBA Finals, Game Six, Chicago Bulls at Utah Jazz, Delta Center, Salt Lake City, Utah, June 14, 1998

I was covering this series for the *Washington Post*, and the whole question around it was whether this was finally Karl Malone and John Stockton's year, and how Michael Jordan was going to get it done against them. Scottie Pippen was having back issues during the series, and, at this point in Jordan's career, he was really relying on Scottie to do more of the dirty work so that he could conserve his energy to close out the games. Utah was leading for most of the game and had a bunch of opportunities to build a big lead, but they looked like they were comfortable just leading by a handful of points. In the back of my head, I kept thinking that it wasn't enough, and that you need to create a gap that Jordan can't come back on.

The start of the final comeback was set up by a steal at the other end, where they ran a basic post play for Malone; (Jeff) Hornacek throws it to him on the left block and then runs by him to the far corner. Sometimes guys run plays so often that they just go through the motions, and Jordan recognized that Hornacek was not looking to get the ball back, so he didn't have to worry about guarding him. You could also tell Malone didn't know where Jordan was and was trying to decide what move he wanted to make. Jordan saw that little opportunity to double back and tipped the ball away from Malone for the steal. To me, that was the beginning of the end. Even after Jordan scored to put the Bulls ahead, Utah still had that confidence that they were OK, but no one else in that building thought that. This was Michael Jordan, and you if give him a small window, he is going to cause problems. By the time it got to the final play, long before Jordan took the shot, it felt like that game was over and the damage had already been done. From where I was sitting near the top of the lower bowl, I saw all of the fans behind the basket standing up, and all of them had that open-mouthed "Oh, no" look on their face. It felt like the entire state of Utah was having their fate decided right in front of their eyes, and, of course, it was Michael Jordan doing it. In all my time covering the game, I don't know if I've ever had that vantage point to watch one man break that many hearts at one time. It had less to do with the Utah Jazz, and Stockton and Malone, than it did the entire state that Jordan was subduing with this one shot. After that ending, in no way did I want Jordan to come back, and I wrote that and got killed for writing it. There was no way to top that moment as a way to go out. This was the storybook ending of all storybook endings.

Yao Ming's Final Home Game with Shanghai Sharks, Pudong Yuanshen Gymnasium, Shanghai, China, March, 2002

The first time I got to see Yao Ming play was in his final game in the Chinese Basketball Association. It was interesting then, particularly anticipating that he was going to be the first pick in the NBA draft. I initially went there because I was approached about doing a book with him, and my first response was that I needed to know whether the guy could play or not. I didn't want to write a book about a guy who turned out to be the great bust from China, so I wanted to see if he could play. It was an unheated gym, and he clearly wasn't in great shape. The competition was probably Division III college level, but there was a play where there was a loose ball on the floor and he went down to get it. He flipped it behind his head to find a teammate for an easy basket. He had a decent jumper and the size was legit, but you could also see he had a nice touch and feel for the game. After that little instinctual play, though, I wasn't sure how great he was going to be and didn't expect him to be an All-Star every year he was going to be in the league, but he had that little deft touch that nobody else on the floor had. He was able to make a play out of nothing, and in the NBA, there is a lot of that. That is what separates guys, and I think that translates to any level. If you have a feel for where the ball is going to go, or where to go with the ball when everything breaks down, then you have a gift that you need to have to survive in the NBA. All these years later, I've never forgotten that moment. It made me believe that he could play in the NBA. When I look at what he meant as far as bridging cultures, with all of the weight he had on him after being the first pick and representing his country, he never had a misstep.

2004 NBA Western Conference Semifinals, Game Five, Los Angeles Lakers at San Antonio Spurs, SBC Center, San Antonio, Texas, May 13, 2004

Everyone remembers Derek Fisher's shot with 0.4 seconds left, but few remember that play was preceded by Tim Duncan hitting an unbelievable shot from long range. You really felt like the balance of that playoff series and whoever was going to win it all that season was in that game, and with 0.4 seconds remaining, there seemed like there was just no way the Lakers would win. That shot symbolized Derek Fisher's role with the team. Kobe entrusted him to take shots like that. As much as anything, it was about being there live and experiencing the incredible sway of emotions in San Antonio. You could tell from Duncan's reaction that even he was surprised he made this circus shot, so the Spurs and their fans had that feeling that they had the game won at that point. I can still see Derek Fisher's body and Manu Ginobili's outstretched arm, and how pure that shot was. I was sitting courtside at an angle looking down the court, so I had everything framed in front of me, with Fisher to the left and Ginobili coming over to contest the shot. Fisher had to catch, turn, and shoot in one motion, and for the direction that he was going, it only added to the difficulty of the shot. That shot has its own name now, just like many other famous plays in sports history. Say "point four" to sports fans, and they'll know exactly what you are talking about.

Derek Fisher celebrates after his basket with 0.4 seconds left won Game Five of the 2004 NBA Western Conference Semifinals. (AP Photo/David J. Phillip)

Joe Buck

Broadcaster, FOX Sports

1982 World Series, Game Seven, Milwaukee Brewers at St. Louis Cardinals, Busch Stadium, St. Louis, Missouri, October 20, 1982

Watching the Cardinals celebrate at home was something I had never seen in my lifetime, so it was the first time I was really exposed to a celebration like that. I was thirteen years old and was sitting with my mom in the broadcast booth while my dad and Mike Shannon were doing the game on the radio. The radio booth was relocated for the Series by the national TV broadcast, and for some reason Tug McGraw was sitting in the booth with us. People assume the Cardinals were always good, but in the '70s, they were terrible, and those were the years I was going as a little kid, so seeing this team overcome all of that to beat the Brewers in seven games, it was the first time I remember witnessing the sheer joy of fans as their team won a championship. Fans were running onto the field and ripping up pieces of the turf, while mounted police were trying to keep them off the field. It was just mayhem and was the first time I understood what these events and sports can mean to people, especially when they get to celebrate in their hometown.

2001 World Series, Game Three, Arizona Diamondbacks at New York Yankees, Yankee Stadium, Bronx, New York, October 30, 2001

After the events of September 11, you couldn't help but feel vulnerable sitting inside a stadium, and if there was ever an opportunity for a terrorist group to make a statement, making one at Yankee Stadium in New York was its chance. What's more representative of America than the New York Yankees? I remember I had Cipro in my backpack, in case there was some sort of nerve gas attack. Tom Ridge, the director of the newly created Office of Homeland Security, was giving updates every five minutes, with the terror level raised and new colors being added to the terror scale almost daily.

Of all the moments I've seen, maybe the single most powerful moment was President Bush throwing out the first pitch before Game Three. I say that because there was a lot on the line. He was showing power and strength. It wasn't political at all. It was a rousing ovation because he was a symbol that we weren't scared and our President was going to walk out to the middle of the field and not just wave, but throw the first pitch to the catcher. If that didn't give you chills, nothing will. Baseball that autumn was our national pastime, and it really served a role for everybody.

2004 American League Championship Series, New York Yankees vs. Boston Red Sox, Yankee Stadium, Bronx, New York, and Fenway Park, Boston, Massachusetts, October 12-20, 2004

Every game in this series with the exception of Game Three could stand alone. The Yankees won that game, 19–8, to go up three games to none in the series. After the series, all of the revisionist historians were coming out and saying that the Red Sox knew they still had a chance and just had to win one and keep the series going, but in reality, everyone was basically congratulating the Yankees on the field before Game Four.

It wasn't just that the Red Sox came back in the series, but the way they did it. There was Curt Schilling and the bloody sock, David Ortiz hitting the home run to send the series back to New York for Games Six and Seven, plus Pedro Martinez and Johnny Damon and a whole group that were a lot of fun to cover. That was the best series I've ever been a part of, and only because of the way it ended. It was like an avalanche and ended completely flipped.

Super Bowl XLII, New York Giants vs. New England Patriots, University of Phoenix Stadium, Glendale, Arizona, February 3, 2008

Eli Manning became a completely different quarterback in the playoff run leading up to the Super Bowl. He went from an all-potential, erratic quarterback to someone who just refused to turn the ball over. The Giants won in Dallas against the top-seeded Cowboys, and Eli was just a different guy. Beating New England—a team that not only looked unbeatable, but that was going for 19–0—the way they did, and the fourth quarter being back and forth the way it was, this was another game that when you are calling it, your heart feels like it is about to jump out of your chest. Not only are you aware of the size of the audience that is watching, but this was a great game on top of it.

David Tyree catches Eli Manning's pass against his helmet during the winning drive in the fourth quarter of Super Bowl XLII. (AP Photo/Gene Puskar)

2011 World Series, Game Six, Texas Rangers at St. Louis Cardinals, Busch Stadium, St. Louis, Missouri, October 27, 2011

This one might be at the top of memories from my career. I say that because I've watched the replay a couple of times, and even having been there to broadcast the game to a national audience, you can't believe the game ends with the Cardinals winning. Not only were they down to their final strike twice, but they had to come back in extra innings, which was just stunning. To snatch a win away from not just the jaws, but the throat of defeat is something that took your breath away. It was one of those games where you don't have to be a Cardinals fan or a baseball fan. You don't even have to be a sports fan. A game like that just triggers something in your inner sense of drama. I go back to one of my dad's calls: "I don't believe what I just saw." You just didn't see it coming. You walk away from the game shaking your head.

It was fun to call the end of the game the way I did, almost twenty years to the day from when my dad did it after Kirby Puckett's home run. That wasn't really why I did it, it just hit me at that moment to do it. And if nobody else liked it, at least my mom did.

Kevin Burkhardt

Broadcaster, FOX Sports

Philadelphia Eagles at New York Jets, Giants Stadium, East Rutherford, New Jersey, October 3, 1993

I was an Eagles fan my whole life and had season tickets since I was old enough to drive. On this day, I was eighteen years old and went to the game with my younger brother. The Eagles looked like they were going to get buried that day. This was one of the first I had ever gone to, even though it was in enemy territory. The Jets ran out to a 21–0 lead, and Boomer Esiason was on fire. Randall Cunningham, who was one of my favorite athletes growing up, got hurt in the game, and left the field on a cart. Nothing was going right that day. But Bubby Brister comes into the game, and the Eagles start moving the ball. But while they eventually tied the game, you still had that feeling that the only way they were going to stop the Jets was by getting a turnover. After a safety gave the Jets the lead, New York took the free kick and moved right down the field again, and it felt like the game was over. Then Eric Allen picks off an Esiason pass on the 6. We were sitting on the opposite end and side of the field from where he intercepted the pass, so from where we were, we could see Allen pick off the pass, but then he disappeared behind all of the bodies on the field. Finally, he emerges from behind the crowd and is racing toward the end zone. We couldn't believe that he was still running and missed all of his zig-zagging on the field, but there he is to score the winning touchdown. My mouth was agape, and I kept asking myself what had just happened. My brother and I were wearing some Eagles gear, and we had to cover our heads while leaving to make sure no one saw.

2001 NCAA Division III Men's Basketball First Round, Hampden-Sydney at William Paterson, William Paterson Recreation Center, Wayne, New Jersey, March 3, 2001

I went to William Paterson, and after I graduated, I did public address for the basketball games for a few years. A couple of years earlier, over Christmas break, a kid showed up to play basketball. His name was Horace Jenkins, and

41

he was a little older than the other students. He was a 6-foot-1 guard, and I had never seen a player at the Division III level this good. He had a vertical jump that was out of this world and won the college slam dunk contest in 2001. William Paterson had some good teams, but Jenkins completely turned that program around. Jenkins was actually a bit of an urban legend in the area. Jose Rebimbas was the team's coach and was in a park in Newark trying to recruit a player, and all of a sudden sees Horace playing. It turned out he had dropped out of school and became an electrician to support his family.

This was the last home game he would play, and if William Paterson won, they would move on to a game elsewhere. And he was unbelievable that night. There was one sequence where he blocked a three-pointer, came down and hit a three-pointer, then blocked another shot and came down and had a tomahawk dunk. He was so much better than the other players that it was stupid. The team ended up losing in the Division III championship game, but Jenkins had a chance to play in the NBA after that. It was so cool to see his story unfold and watch him play at this tiny school in New Jersey, where you just don't get players like that.

2003 NFC Divisional Playoffs, Green Bay Packers at Philadelphia Eagles, Lincoln Financial Field, Philadelphia, Pennsylvania, January 11, 2004

The Eagles were the top seed in the NFC but were down 14–0 in this divisional playoff game before you could blink. Philadelphia fought back to tie it, but Brett Favre hit Javon Walker with a long pass to help the Packers retake the lead on a field goal in the fourth quarter. Of course, that led to the usual Eagles fan reaction: the team was going to blow being the top seed and choke in the playoffs again. There were less than two minutes left, but after a penalty and a long sack of Donovan McNabb by the Packers, it was fourth-and-26 for the Eagles. My tickets were midway up the upper deck around the 5-yard line where they were headed, and at this point, the obvious thought is that the game is over. I remember looking at where the ball was, then looking at the scoreboard and seeing the fourth-and-26, looking to see where the Eagles needed to get on the field to get the first down, looking at the scoreboard again and trying to figure out how the Eagles were going to possibly get a first down to keep the game going. The ball was snapped, McNabb dropped back and threw a line drive pass over the middle to Freddie Mitchell, who caught it and was hit immediately. As soon as he got hit, I looked to the sideline marker and couldn't believe that it looked like he got it. The whole section couldn't believe it, but we had to wait for the measurement on the field first. Even after the referee said it was a first down, we still couldn't believe they actually got the 26 yards on fourth down. It was jubilation, but also a little confusion; we just couldn't figure out how the Packers' secondary even allowed it to happen. The Eagles still had to go a little farther to get into field goal range, but they did it and tied the game. Going into overtime, you just felt like the momentum had totally changed. On the Packers' first possession, Brett Favre threw a bad pass that Brian Dawkins picked off, leading to the eventual game-winning field goal. The range of emotions from not believing that the Eagles were going to lose the game to seeing them convert on the long fourth down was wild. You don't see plays like that too often, especially in the playoffs.

St. Louis Cardinals at New York Mets, Citi Field, Flushing, New York, June 1, 2012

Pretty much every Mets fan knew that no Mets pitcher had ever thrown a no-hitter before this night. Every time I ever had to miss a game, I was always worried that I was going to miss the game where they finally threw that first no-hitter. It was always on your mind at every game. There were so many close calls, whether it was Tom Seaver or John Maine, that it just seemed like it was never going to happen. Before the game, Terry Collins was talking about pitch counts with Johan Santana, because he was making his way back from shoulder capsule surgery and was looking good, but they still were being cautious. Someone asked him what he thought would be his limit for pitches that night, and he said it would be maybe 110, 115 at the absolute most.

The game itself never really felt like a no-hitter game. A lot of the time, it feels like there is going to be something special, but this wasn't one. Santana didn't have great control and walked five guys in the game, he wasn't crisp, and, to be honest, I didn't even realize he had a no-hitter until the fifth inning. I was walking around the ballpark and was doing some stories for SNY, but watching the game at the same time, it just didn't feel like he was locked in. Normally, I kept score at every game while doing the sideline reporting but had bounced around a little more than usual that night. I remember being in the restaurant in left field, looking at the scoreboard after the fifth inning and realizing Santana hadn't allowed a hit, but couldn't believe it. I hustled down to the field and was next to the Mets' dugout, and, at that point, you started to feel the excitement. Santana knew what was going on and knew the history, as well—that it had never been done by a Mets pitcher. He got better as the game went on but still struggled to throw strikes, and by the seventh inning, he was already at that pregame pitch count. I tried to put myself in Terry Collins's shoes and figure out what you do in that spot. Everyone knows the history, and everyone knew what Santana was coming back from and that Johan really wanted to do this. It was a very tough spot; how do you take him out of the game in that situation, while also knowing that you could risk his career by leaving him in? It was so intense looking into the dugout and seeing how Collins and pitching coach Dan Warthen were struggling with it. Johan made the decision, though, that he wasn't coming out of the game. Maybe deep down inside he didn't know how long his shoulder was going to last anyway and felt that this was his chance at baseball immortality. I think that had something to do with it.

There was so much drama when Santana came out for the ninth, and the pitch count keeps going up. When he threw that 134th and final pitch, a changeup to strike out David Freese, it was the coolest thing ever. To be there and know you just saw something that an entire fan base had been dreaming of and watch Santana come off the field as emotional as he was, with tears on his face . . . he came into the dugout and actually gave me a hug! You felt all of the emotion with him. I was the guy who got to do the first interview with him, and I pulled him out onto the field to do the interview. I hate not asking questions in an interview, but there was so much emotion that rather than ask a question, I just said, "You've just thrown the first no-hitter in Mets history." I thought it was appropriate, and he just went with it. It was so neat to be there for that and for him. The Mets have had so many great pitchers over the years, but I think he was the perfect guy to do it, especially after coming back from the type of surgery he had.

2014 World Series, Game Seven, San Francisco Giants at Kansas City Royals, Kauffman Stadium, Kansas City, Missouri, October 29, 2014

You don't see things like what Madison Bumgarner did in this game. Guys like Gibson and Koufax did them, but it just doesn't happen anymore. The whole story on our pregame show on FOX that night was about when was Bumgarner going to come into the game. As soon as the game started, I was sitting with Frank

Thomas, Gabe Kapler, and Nick Swisher, and all we were wondering was when he was coming in. I don't ever remember a game where that was the overriding story. It started with the first pitch, and then, when he started warming up, we couldn't believe he was coming in as early as he did. Then, the thinking was that he could only go a couple innings, but he keeps going. It is one thing for me not to believe what is going on, but to be sitting with someone like Frank Thomas, and watch him shake his head in disbelief, was enlightening. To see Bumgarner do what he did, in a day where managers routinely take guys out after 100 pitches, it was uncanny. The most incredible thing to see up close, though, was that the Royals looked like they were defeated the moment he came in. That is something you don't see often. I really am lucky to have seen this performance, and to be on the field when he wrapped it up is something I'll never forget. I'm not sure we'll ever see something like this again.

Madison Bumgarner runs out to the mound to pitch during the fifth inning of Game Seven of the 2014 World Series. (AP Photo/Charlie Neibergall)

Jeffri Chadiha

Broadcaster, NFL Network

1993 NCAA Men's Basketball Tournament Finals, North Carolina vs. Michigan, Louisiana Superdome, New Orleans, Louisiana, April 5, 1993

It was my senior year at Michigan, and I made the trip to New Orleans with some friends, because there was a sense that Chris Webber wasn't going to be around after that season and the Fab Five was going to break up. We had tickets for the championship game way up in the Superdome, but Kentucky fans were giving their seats away after losing in the semifinals, so we ended up sitting in what would have been their band's seats right near the court instead. It was a fantastic game, with the Fab Five going up against a very experienced North Carolina team led by guys like Eric Montross. Michigan had won a lot of close games during the season and the tournament, but the Tar Heels were up by one late and were shooting free throws. Pat Sullivan made the first but missed the second, and Webber grabbed the rebound. He started to pass, then dragged his plant foot and walked, but it wasn't called. At that point, it felt like it was Michigan's game; the Wolverines had just caught a break, and here comes the winning basket. He came up the right sideline with the ball, stopped right in front of his bench, turned around, clutched the ball, and called timeout. No one in the arena realized Michigan had no timeouts left, so we thought they would get a better play off than before, but one of the referees signaled for a technical foul and we couldn't figure out why. Then it dawned on me to look up at the scoreboard, where I saw that they didn't have any timeouts left. I could see Webber cursing at the bench, and it was later found out that backup guard Michael Talley, who had lost his job to one of the Fab Five members, might have told him to call the timeout. North Carolina hit the ensuing free throws, and the game was over. I'll never forget Webber walking off after it was over and putting his jersey over the front of his face. It was such a long walk to the locker room, and even though he is a huge man, he became so small as he walked off. My heart just went out to him. There aren't many moments in my life where I looked at someone and felt so horrible for him.

Colorado at Michigan, Michigan Stadium, Ann Arbor, Michigan, September 24, 1994

I had just started to work at the *Ann Arbor News* but was in the stands for this game. There was a lot of buzz around the game, because Colorado head coach Bill McCartney had started his career at Michigan and his kid went to school there. It was a great back-and-forth game, with the Wolverines ahead late, 26–21. I was sitting there with my buddy talking about how good Colorado's quarterback Kordell Stewart and receiver Michael Westbrook were and wondering what they were going to do on the last shot at winning. Michigan had a habit of losing these kinds of games, usually because of a big play by someone on the other

Colorado quarterback Kordell Stewart throws a 64-yard game-winning "Hail Mary" touchdown to teammate Michael Westbrook to defeat Michigan. (AP Photo/Jon Freilich)

team, but the Buffaloes needed the craziest thing in the world to happen to score and win the game. They ran a couple of plays and moved the ball to their own 36 with six seconds left. My friend asked me if I thought Stewart could throw the ball that far in the air, but I thought it was too far. Stewart dropped back, and it seemed like it took minutes for the play to unfold. I was sitting behind Stewart and have never seen a ball thrown that far, that high and with that much velocity by a human being. It was such a heave, and I can still see Westbrook running across the field to the post, and Ty Law backpedaling. As the ball was coming down, I heard someone say it had a chance to get there, and all of a sudden, a hand popped up out of the middle of the pack. The ball popped in the air, and Westbrook came from the back of the pack in the end zone, dove, and cradled the ball for the win. Over 100,000 people went silent almost immediately, and I thought it was the most athletic feat I had ever seen in person. From where Stewart released the ball, it went 73 yards, and I don't think I'll ever see someone throw a ball that far and that accurately again.

Super Bowl XXXVI, New England Patriots vs. St. Louis Rams, Louisiana Superdome, New Orleans, Louisiana, February 3, 2002

This was the beginning of the Patriots dynasty. I had gone to the University of Michigan and earlier that year had pitched a story to my bosses at *Sports Illustrated* about Tom Brady, who had just become the Patriots, starting quarterback following an injury to Drew Bledsoe. Brady was a nobody at that point, but he had a coolness to him that you picked up on immediately, and that always stuck with me. Going into the Super Bowl, there was a debate about who should start at QB, since Bledsoe was healthy again and had actually come in to replace an injured Brady in the AFC championship game. I'll never forget Bill Belichick telling me during the interview for that story I wrote that the team had kept him around after drafting him in the sixth round because of his intangibles, and I think those intangibles are why Belichick started Brady. He saw something there that he felt Bledsoe didn't have. The Rams were the previous version of the Patriots, with Kurt Warner leading the "Greatest Show on Turf" and this was their second Super Bowl in three seasons, but Ty Law returned an interception 47 yards for a touchdown in the second quarter, which set the tone for the game, then Brady threw a touchdown pass to David

Patten to put New England up, 14–3. Eventually, the game came down to a game-winning field goal by Adam Vinatieri, but I'll always remember Brady spiking the ball on the play before the field goal. When he spiked it, it popped right back up and to his hands and he caught it, and I couldn't help but think that this was the coolest football player I had ever seen.

I was assigned to talk to Brady after the game and get quotes from him for Michael Silver's main story, and we walked out of the stadium together toward the team buses. We were talking about the game while walking, and he invited me onto the bus to go to the hotel. I eventually ended up in his hotel room talking with him, while his girlfriend and buddies were there watching the highlights, when his agent came in and told him that he was invited to Disneyland the next day because he was the MVP. He said he needed to ask Belichick first, so he went to the coach and came back a short time later. I asked him what Belichick said, and he told me, "He said I just won the Super Bowl and could do whatever the fuck I wanted." That moment sticks with me, because I think that was the last time Tom Brady was Tom Brady, regular guy.

Super Bowl XLII, New York Giants vs. New England Patriots, University of Phoenix Stadium, Glendale, Arizona, February 3, 2008

I always seemed to have a knack for covering teams that went on improbable playoff runs, and being around the Giants late that season for ESPN, I started to get that weird feeling again that this team had something special about it that could help them go deep into the postseason unexpectedly. After they beat Dallas to get to the NFC championship game, you started to hear stories about head coach Tom Coughlin, and how he had changed during the season and wasn't as tough on his players as he had been in the past, and how the players appreciated that. Eli Manning was playing better, and the team was starting to come together at the right time. Then they won in Green Bay in frigid temperatures to get to the Super Bowl against the unbeaten Patriots.

As the game got closer, I was one of the few people in America saying on record that they thought the Giants could win, since everyone was expecting a blowout. There was a quiet confidence about them that week, and they knew they could play with the Patriots. When the game started and the Patriots didn't immediately blow the Giants out, people started to realize they did have a chance. The game was pretty even and the lead went back and forth, but when Randy Moss scored with less than three minutes to go, you could see the Patriots' sideline celebrating. At no point in his career did I ever think Eli Manning was capable of doing what he ended up doing on the next drive. There were some little things early in the drive, but the big moment was the play everybody remembers. Eli was under a lot of pressure but escaped. I was sitting behind the Giants as they moved down the field away from us, and when he planted his feet and threw the ball downfield, I couldn't figure out where he was throwing the ball. You couldn't even see a receiver, just open field, and it was almost like he just picked a spot on the field and hoped a receiver would end up getting there. When David Tyree got there and jumped, even from where I was sitting, you could see the ball cling to his helmet as he went to the ground, and the refs weren't waving it off. After seeing the replays, it was the most amazing catch, and maybe the most amazing play, I've ever seen in a football game, given the magnitude of it and everything that was on the line. When that play happened, I immediately thought the Giants were going to score to win the game, and as one of the only guys who thought they could win, my instincts were proven right.

2014 World Series, Game Seven, San Francisco Giants at Kansas City Royals, Kauffman Stadium, Kansas City, Missouri, October 29, 2014

I moved to Kansas City in 2005 and love the environment at the football games, but I had never really gone to many baseball games. I knew there was a great baseball tradition in the city and was intrigued by the excitement of Opening Day every season, even though the team was always coming off a losing season. It left me wondering what the atmosphere would be like if the team was winning, and that happened in 2014, as the Royals made it to Game Seven of the World Series. I've never been in a city that was so captivated by a sports team. This town was so hungry for a contender and, more specifically, a certain kind of team. They found a team that understood what that franchise meant to the city. So when Game Seven rolled around, there was so much buzz.

It had built up for a month through the playoffs, and this was the culmination for a team that hadn't won in twenty-nine years.

It is hard even to describe the level of energy and anticipation in the stadium that night. People were on pins and needles throughout the entire game. When Madison Bumgarner came out of the bullpen for the Giants, the big question was how much he had in him—how many innings or pitches was he going to throw? There was a sense of dread, because you knew it was going to be bullpen versus bullpen, but also the feeling that there was no way the Royals were going to lose Game Seven at home. Bumgarner dominated the game the rest of the way, until Alex Gordon hit what should have been an easy play in center field. Gregor Blanco missed it, though, and the entire crowd rose in unison. It was like we were levitating as the ball was misplayed, and what first looked like a single ended with Gordon on third base. I was sitting behind third base and remember watching him out of the box and thinking that he looked like he was trying to figure out how he could get to second on the play. Just that little hesitation in his mind might have been what kept him from being able to score, and by the time he reached third base, I could see the ball being relayed back to the infield. I know it was debated for weeks afterwards, but that was the smart play. The stadium was shaking at that point, the emotion was palpable and the anticipation was real. It wasn't just that night, but it was twenty-nine years of emotion coming out. When Salvador Perez popped out to Pablo Sandoval, and Sandoval fell to the turf, it was like they were playing in someone's living room. It got so quiet as everyone went from exhilaration to heartbreak. As we started to leave, the building erupted in a "Let's Go Royals!" chant, which then morphed into a "Thank You Royals!" chant. I grew up a Tigers fan in Michigan, but for a month, I couldn't help but be a Royals fan, and that chant epitomized how easy it was to fall in love with that team.

Freddie Coleman

Broadcaster, ESPN

Grambling vs. Morgan State, Yankee Stadium, Bronx, New York, September 20, 1969

This was the first sporting event my parents ever took me to. Grambling means so much to black college football, so going to my first college football game and seeing them play at the old Yankee Stadium, with the pageantry of the bands and Eddie Robinson on the sideline, really left an impression on me. It is one of the main reasons I still talk a lot about black college football. I was only three years old at the time, so the memories of the game aren't as important as the memories of the actual experience.

Grambling was a national program. Everyone talked about USC and Penn State and schools like that, but for African-Americans, Grambling was on the same level as those schools. Eddie Robinson created something special there, and that program carried the banner for schools like Southern and Florida A&M for black college football. Having the chance to see them play as part of the first sporting event I ever saw in person was unforgettable.

1973 National League Championship Series, Game Five, Cincinnati Reds at New York Mets, Shea Stadium, Flushing, New York, October 10, 1973

When my dad told me he got tickets to the game that morning, I told him I had to go to school. "Not today, you don't," was his reply. And we were off on the train ride to Shea Stadium. There was a lot of bad blood between the teams after Pete Rose and Bud Harrelson fought earlier in the series, so the Mets fans were ready to go for the game to decide who went to the World Series. No one thought the Mets had a chance in the Series, but it was the famous "You Gotta Believe" Mets team. The Reds had the better record, in fact, but the Mets had home-field advantage because they alternated each year between the divisions at that time. That proved to be enough, as New York won 7—2 to claim just its second pennant ever. To see that game, with a championship on the line, was pretty cool.

1983 Big East Conference Championship Game, Boston College vs. St. John's, Madison Square Garden, New York, New York, March 12, 1983

St. John's had Chris Mullin and David Russell, and those guys led the Redmen to their first Big East title. It was the first year where the Big East Tournament was held at Madison Square Garden. It was only a three-year contract, but the tournament still hasn't left after all these years.

When St. John's made the final, a bunch of friends and I drove from school in Pennsylvania all night on Friday so that we could be at the championship game on Saturday afternoon. St. John's just destroyed the Boston College press time and time again, and Russell had a bunch of transition slams as a result. I honestly believe that game really put the Big East on the map and made it bigger than ever before. People had always looked at the league as one where they played good basketball but still wondered if the teams were really that good. With St. John's at the Garden, though, it was like a Broadway play. It had a very special vibe about it, and this game is the one that showed the rest of the country that the league was for real. Of course, three Big East teams went to the Final Four two seasons later, proving that.

1984 Summer Olympics, Los Angeles, California, July 28-August 12, 1984

Seeing the Olympics in person is so much different than it is on TV. They call it the Olympic Experience for a reason, with people from different countries and a sense of camaraderie and competition. Getting to see the Opening Ceremonies was really cool, with all of the athletes parading in behind their flags. When you are eighteen and you grew up watching this on TV, it takes your breath away to see it in person.

People talk about the "Dream Team" in basketball from 1992, but the 1984 Olympic team had guys like Patrick Ewing, Michael Jordan, the late Wayman Tisdale, Steve Alford, Sam Perkins, and Chris Mullin, plus Bob Knight as their head coach. They had assembled a bomb squad, with so many players that became top NBA picks after their college careers. We went to so many events while we were there, including Joan Benoit becoming the first American woman to win the marathon. I still get chills thinking about her running into the stadium and waving to the crowd.

The Olympic flame is flanked by a scoreboard signifying the formal opening of the 1984 Olympics in Los Angeles. (AP Photo/Eric Risberg)

Army vs. Navy, Veterans Stadium, Philadelphia, Pennsylvania, December 5, 1992

My uncle Douglas played for West Point, but I never got the chance to go to an Army-Navy game until I was working for the Army Radio Network. I knew all about the game and how special it was from watching on TV, but getting to see it in person for the first time was amazing. All of the pomp and pageantry associated with the game is something that has to be seen to be appreciated. I also got the chance that day to meet my football hero, Roger Staubach. Even though he was there for Navy and I was on the Army side, when I saw him across the field, I couldn't help but think that there was the original Captain America. I walked over and introduced myself and called him "Mr. Staubach." He immediately corrected me and said, "No, Roger." I still couldn't bring myself to call him anything but "Mr. Staubach." I must have sounded like a five-year-old kid just babbling about how much of a hero he was to me!

The game itself was even better than meeting my hero, though. Army was down 24–7 and came all the way back to win on a field goal in the final seconds. That game means everything to those schools, so to see all of the emotion and watch the game won the way it was, you really can't beat that as your first experience at an Army-Navy game.

Bob Costas

Broadcaster, NBC Sports

Recipient of Basketball Hall of Fame's Curt Gowdy Award, 1999
Elected to National Sports Media Association Hall of Fame, 2012

1986 World Series, Game Six, Boston Red Sox at New York Mets, Shea Stadium, Flushing, New York, October 25, 1986

It was my job to interview the winners of the World Series, so entering Game Six, the only team that could win was the Red Sox. I perched myself in the corner of their dugout and was sitting next to Tom Seaver, who wasn't on the team's active roster (but who, ironically, is the best player in Mets history), and Don Baylor, who was Boston's DH but wasn't in the lineup since it was a game in a National League park. When Dave Henderson homered to put the Red Sox ahead in the 10th, I went down to their clubhouse, and they were already preparing for the celebration. They set up a podium for me to do the interviews and had covered the lockers to protect them from the champagne that was about to be sprayed. The Red Sox added an insurance run to make it 5–3, and, as the Mets came up in the bottom of the inning, MLB commissioner Peter Ueberroth entered along with some other league executives as the championship trophy was wheeled in. Also with him was the very frail Jean Yawkey, widow of Red Sox owner Tom Yawkey. The first two outs were recorded, but then Gary Carter singled, and Kevin Mitchell singled. I was still standing there thinking about the Red Sox interviews. Not just about this game, or this series, but about the curse and all of the near misses along the way. Not only was I mindful of it being a Red Sox championship, I was also mindful of it being the first Boston title-clincher ever broadcast, since they didn't even have games on the radio in 1918. But then Ray Knight comes up and fists one over Marty Barrett's head to make it 5–4, and I remember asking my producer, Mike Weisman, who was in my ear, what I should do if the Mets tied the game. His response? "Get your ass out of there as fast as you can." Mookie Wilson comes up, and there is a wild pitch, allowing Mitchell to score the tying run and moving Knight to second. They ushered Mrs. Yawkey out, and I'm not sure what state of shock she was in. The commissioner left with the trophy, and they started breaking down all of the preparations they had made in the room, including the platform. By the time Wilson rolled the ball through Bill Buckner's legs to score Knight, all traces of any celebration were gone. It got done, but just barely. I slipped out a side door and was standing against the wall as the players came trudging down the hallway ashen-faced. Not a word was spoken, except somebody crashed a bat against the cement wall along the corridor, and I heard one word: "Fuck!" I don't think anyone even noticed me standing there. The combination of the unlikely series of events and the delirium of Shea Stadium, plus the real pathos of this Red Sox team, is what I remember the most. I think it was Jimmy Breslin who said the best stories are always in the loser's locker room. In my mind, even though that band of Mets was a great team that was colorful and unforgettable, this was more about the Red Sox losing than the Mets winning.

1988 World Series, Game One, Oakland Athletics at Los Angeles Dodgers, Dodger Stadium, Los Angeles, California, October 15, 1988

I was in the corner of the Dodgers dugout when Kirk Gibson homered. Technically, at that time, no one is supposed to be there other than team personnel. I've always had a great relationship with Tommy Lasorda, but he was pacing up and down the dugout before the homer and sees me, and says, "Look at that. NBC thinks the fucking game is over!" So I tried to make myself as inconspicuous as possible and moved to the end of the corridor from the dugout. That spot allowed me to hear Gibson hitting balls off a tee. I wandered down to take a peek, and there is a batboy putting balls on a tee and Gibson is hitting each of the balls, but with each swing, you hear the "thwack" of the contact, followed by an audible grunt of pain. Everyone assumed Gibson wasn't going to play in the game, and, in fact, I opened the broadcast by saying, "First order of business. Kirk Gibson will not play tonight and is not available for so much as pinch-hitting duty." Everyone assumed that was the case, but he was on the trainer's table and heard Vin

Scully reiterate that late in the game, and it lit some sort of competitive fire in him. Hitting coach Ben Hines went to check on him, and came walking back past me, and tells Lasorda (and it was just like a line in a B-baseball movie), "He says he has one good swing in him," and Lasorda just kind of nods. When Mike Davis came up for the Dodgers, they put someone not named Kirk Gibson in the on-deck circle—it was the light-hitting utility infielder Dave Anderson. As I look back on this, A's pitcher Dennis Eckersley, who was basically untouchable and walked next to nobody, was a teammate of Davis when he hit 22 homers the previous season. The 1988 Mike Davis, however, hit .196 with two homers. Even so, if you're looking at Dave Anderson in the on-deck circle, maybe you are pitching carefully to Davis, because he was the only guy who could hurt you with one swing. Maybe that accounts for why he ended up walking Davis.

It wasn't until after the walk that Gibson got up off of the bench in the dugout and headed to the plate, and we all know what unfolded next. To this day, when you watch the at-bat, it is almost impossible, when you see all of the weak swings that preceded it, to figure out how he hit the ball as far as he did. He hit it flat-footed; it was all arms. It was so stunning that it not only turned the game around, but it turned the entire series around. The Dodgers had Orel Hershiser pitching at home in Game Two, and Hershiser was on one of the great rolls in the history of baseball. He beat the A's that next night, and the Dodgers were on their way. The Gibson home run was so theatrical that people stayed for a half hour after the game, belying the few that had left early and whose tail lights you can see in the parking lot when you watch a replay of the homer. Two of the greatest calls in the history of baseball came on this play—Jack Buck's on the radio and Vin Scully's on TV. They were distinctly different but are two of the best ever. After Gibson made it around the bases, it was my job to get him for the postgame interview. My questions weren't anything special, but it was a genuinely exhilarating moment. It was so improbable, exciting, and dramatic that you knew instantly that it would be part of baseball lore forever.

Kirk Gibson celebrates his home run in the bottom of the ninth inning to defeat the Oakland Athletics in Game One of the 1988 World Series. (AP Photo/Rusty Kennedy)

1996 Summer Olympics, Opening Ceremonies, Centennial Olympic Stadium, Atlanta, Georgia, July 19, 1996

I've done a lot of Olympics and Opening Ceremonies, and most of the time you are given a little bit of a tip-off as to the combination of people who are going to be the final torch bearers and who is going to light the cauldron. In this case, it was such a well-guarded secret that maybe a half dozen people knew, and Dick Ebersol, who ran NBC Sports, was one of them. All he said at the production meeting to me and Dick Enberg, whom I was working with, was "I want you and Dick to respond as spontaneously as possible. Just trust me. You'll recognize the person or persons, so you won't need any notes, but I'm not going to tell you who it is." I started trying to figure out who it was, and who was connected to Atlanta. Was it Evander Holyfield or Hank Aaron? Who was it? Holyfield was one of the torch bearers, and Janet Evans was the second-to-last one. She climbed up the steps, and we found out later that they rehearsed this at three in the morning with no one in the stadium.

How they got Ali into the stadium without anyone knowing, I still don't know. But he was in the shadows, and when she got to the top of the steps, she handed the torch to him. He was already in bad shape at that point, and he stood there, holding the torch while trembling as he got ready to light the cauldron. When you are in a stadium, it is usually a symphony of sounds. One thing you rarely hear in a stadium, though, is a gasp. This time, however, there was an audible gasp, and it took a second or two before it sank in and an uproar of cheers and applause began. It wasn't just a dramatic moment, but, in a sense, a moment of reconciliation. Here was a guy who had been a polarizing figure. You can be as cynical as you want about the Olympics and the commercialization of them, or the politics that are always involved, but then you have moments like this one, which symbolized what the Olympics are supposed to be about. Every time I think about it, I still get goose bumps. I don't remember what Dick and I said, but it didn't have to be much. It was a stunning and dramatic moment that, to me, was *the* moment of the 1996 Olympics.

1998 NBA Finals, Game Six, Chicago Bulls at Utah Jazz, Delta Center, Salt Lake City, Utah, June 14, 1998

I was doing the play-by-play for Michael Jordan's game-winning shot. For me, a good sports broadcast of a live event, if it is an important event, ought to hold up as if it were the first draft of what a well-written story about the game would be. It isn't just play after play after play followed by the final score; it should be about the narrative of the game. When Jordan came across the midcourt line with the ball, I said something like, "Here comes Chicago, 17 seconds left. 17 seconds to Game Seven or to championship number six." Then he makes the basket. He hadn't announced his intentions yet, and after Doug Collins and Isiah Thomas analyze what occurred, the teams went to the bench for a timeout, and I said, "Five point two seconds left and Michael Jordan running on fumes with forty-five points." We couldn't be sure, but I knew that might have been the last shot of his career, and that is the bigger story. One of the epic careers in the history of American sports might be ending, and if this is the end, it might have been the best ending ever for an important athlete. It gave them the lead, plus the way he held the pose and the perfect swish as it went through the basket were classic. Utah could still score, though, since there were 5.2 seconds to go, and they could force a Game Seven, or Jordan *might* not retire. So I say, "Who knows what will unfold in the next few days or months, but that may have been the final shot that Michael Jordan will ever take in the NBA. And if that is the last image of Michel Jordan, how magnificent is it. If this is the final chapter, what a way to close the book." John Stockton barely missed a shot after the timeout, and that is basically the end of Jordan's career; the rest is just footnote stuff.

Super Bowl XLIX, Seattle Seahawks vs. New England Patriots, University of Phoenix Stadium, Glendale, Arizona, February 1, 2015

Seattle's defense was arguably the best in the league, and Tom Brady has to score twice in the fourth quarter, which he does to give the Patriots a four-point lead. Seattle comes right back, though, and Jermaine Kearse makes this ridiculous catch with the ball bouncing around and ending up in his lap. Now the Patriots are looking at another situation where a one-in-a-thousand catch, just like David Tyree's in Super Bowl XLII, was going to lead to a Super Bowl slipping away. Malcolm Butler made a great play to jump the route and come up with the interception on the goal line to seal the win, though. A great sports event not only has what actually occurred, but almost always has a moment of "what if." There is always some debate attached to it, and in this case, the question was whether they should have given the ball to Marshawn Lynch instead of passing. Or if you are going to throw, why don't you throw on third down if Lynch doesn't score on second down, since Seattle still had a time out left? You can also question Bill Belichick not using timeouts after Kearse's catch, because a touchdown would have put them down only three and they had Brady at quarterback and a very good kicker. There was all that stuff at the end that made it so memorable.

Colin Cowherd

Broadcaster, FOX Sports

1991 NCAA Men's Basketball Tournament Semifinals, UNLV vs. Duke, Hoosier Dome, Indianapolis, Indiana, March 30, 1991

I was in Denver when UNLV won the national championship against Duke, but the next season, the Runnin' Rebels were even more dominant. Then they met Duke again, this time in the national semifinals. Duke was a year older and had added Grant Hill, who was becoming a star. The Blue Devils were playing with a chip on their shoulder after getting the crap beaten out of them the year before and because UNLV was supposed to win. I remember watching Hill score an easy layup on the opening play and thinking that things felt different than the year before. This wasn't the same. I had covered that team all year and watched them practice without Greg Anthony, who had hurt his jaw during the season. So when he fouled out late in the game, I knew they were a different team. I turned to the person next to me on press row and said that they were in big trouble without Anthony, and they were a mess at the end of that game. After it ended, I went to interview UNLV coach Jerry Tarkanian and was walking with him. I had never seen a sadder coach than at that moment. He thought he was going to be mocked by people for losing that game because he had such a great team. He was so vulnerable and so sad, not pissed off. Tark always had this incredible vulnerability. He lived for basketball and had no hobbies. I felt so bad for him, and he wasn't always the easiest guy to root for. He was like a little boy while walking down that hallway. It wasn't just a loss, it was a blow to his self-esteem and not measuring up to his idols like Bob Knight. When he talked, there was no filter, and as we were watching, we could feel just how awful it all was for him.

Riddick Bowe vs. Evander Holyfield, Caesars Palace, Las Vegas, Nevada, November 6, 1993

I was working in Vegas when I went to this fight. Louis Farrakhan was a very polarizing figure in the country at the time and was at the fight. He had this huge entourage with him and lots of security, because he was always receiving death threats. The fight was outside and we were sitting on the other side of the ring from him when, all of a sudden in the middle of the seventh round, I look up, and a guy comes flying in from over the stands with a parachute and a huge fan. It looked like one of those hovercrafts, and the guy, who would come to be known as "Fan Man," crashes into the ropes and lands in the stands right near Farrakhan. I looked at my friend who I was sitting with at the fight and said to him, "Someone is trying to kill Farrakhan!" His guys started jumping on him and pummeling him. I told my buddy that if one guy shot a gun, we were going to be in the middle of a riot. You couldn't explain what was going on, and the fighters couldn't figure anything out. My friend started laughing so hard at the whole thing, saying this was the greatest thing ever, but I was scared to death. People talk about a buzz in the crowd, but after this, that is exactly what it was for the next hour.

1996 Fiesta Bowl, Nebraska vs. Florida, Sun Devil Stadium, Tempe, Arizona, January 2, 1996

This was the funniest game I've ever been at. Nebraska was college football royalty and had been in so many of these big games previously that it brought a certain class and dignity to their fan base. They had been there before. Florida was a shitstorm for a very long time, and then got really good, really fast with Steve Spurrier. I was in the press box, where it was open air, covering the game for WTVT in Florida, and these Florida fans were so obnoxious and had a few beers in them. They were just vulgar, loud, and cocky and were taunting the Nebraska fans, who were classy and older. It was new money versus old money, Jets fans versus Giants fans. That game was over before halftime, thanks to twenty-nine unanswered points in the second quarter by the Cornhuskers, and was one of the few games I've ever been at where I actively rooted against the team I covered. The Florida fans were that obnoxious, and I witnessed it. The Nebraska fans had such class and dignity, and this game got ugly. It was one of the worst bowl games ever and perhaps the biggest ass-kicking I've ever seen in a big game. It wasn't even physically competitive. At some point during the fourth quarter, I actually yelled out from the press box to the Florida fans asking them why they got so quiet.

2000 NBA Western Conference Finals, Game Seven, Portland Trail Blazers at Los Angeles Lakers, Staples Center, Los Angeles, California, June 4, 2000

I was covering the Portland Trail Blazers for KGW in Portland, and it was the seventh game of an unbelievable Western Conference Finals. That was the deepest Blazer team I've ever seen or covered, with Scottie Pippen, Steve Smith, Bonzi Wells, Damon Stoudamire, Arvydas Sabonis, Rasheed Wallace . . . it was a virtual All-Star team. Kobe and Shaq were just coming into their prime, but the Blazers were a much deeper team. You might have taken Kobe and Shaq, but after that, you were taking Portland players three through nine. It didn't matter who won this game, you just knew they were going to destroy the Pacers in the Finals. The Lakers couldn't stop Wallace. At one point, I asked Phil Jackson how they were going to stop him, and he said, "You don't. You just hope he stops shooting." In the fourth quarter, Staples Center was so tense. The Lakers had trailed for much of the game, and while Portland had the better roster, the NBA has always been a league about closers. Portland couldn't get a break in that fourth quarter. Everybody was getting their shots, and they were all great shots, but none of them fell. Mike Dunleavy took the blame, but it was a really well-coached quarter. Then there was the play where Kobe alley-ooped to Shaq, which is now iconic. I was behind the Laker basket, so I saw it happen right in front of me. I turned to my left and made eye contact with Blazers GM Bob Whitsitt, and he just looked at me and knew it was over. You could feel the air come out of the city of Portland and the Trail Blazer franchise. This was their last shot, because everyone knew that Lakers team was only getting better. I don't think I had bigger goose bumps as a reporter than during that game.

2006 Rose Bowl, Texas vs. USC, Rose Bowl, Pasadena, California, January 4, 2006

I went to this game as a fan and wanted to do that because it was the biggest college football game of my life. The weather was perfect, and the sun was coming over the San Gabriel Mountains. I was sitting next to a guy named Chad Scott, and we were right on the line dividing the two fan bases. When the Stealth Bomber went over the stadium during the pregame flyover, I turned to Chad and said, "I think this is the coolest thing I've ever seen live." What I remember more than anything is that it might have been the only college game I've ever been to that felt like an NFL game. There were so many pros on the field: Leinart, Reggie, LenDale, Vince Young, Bo Scaife. Everything was big. The pregame was huge, Reggie Bush's lateral was huge, Roger Clemens was on the Texas sideline. It was just a series of big moments. I've never been to a college football game where everything felt big the whole game.

Frank Deford

Writer, *Sports Illustrated* **/ Correspondent,** *Real Sports with Bryant Gumbel*

Elected to National Sports Media Association Hall of Fame, 1998

Chicago Bears at Baltimore Colts, Memorial Stadium, Baltimore, Maryland, September 27, 1953

I grew up in Baltimore, and the closest we had to a major-league team was the Colts, who were in the All-America Football Conference. Then, in 1952, the Dallas Texans of the NFL folded, and the franchise was granted to Baltimore, on the provision that they could sell 15,000 season tickets within six weeks. The price was around $30 or $40, which of course sounds ridiculous by today's standards. My father bought two tickets, and the city of Baltimore reached the ticket number to get the team. My mother and I actually went to the first game, something the two of us never did again by ourselves. With the Orioles coming a year later, this was the first major-league game of any kind in Baltimore since 1902, the last season before the Orioles moved to New York, where they eventually became the Yankees. The Colts beat the Bears that day. The amazing thing from that day was right before halftime, when a guy named Bert Rechichar made a 56-yard field goal. Today, nobody blinks at kicks that long, but at that time, the kick was the longest in NFL history. There were no specialists at that time; Rechichar also played defensive back and linebacker in addition to handling the team's placekicking. He also kicked straight ahead, not soccer-style. I was fourteen years old, and for Baltimore, which was a big city but had no teams, including college, the whole thing was really special.

Princeton vs. Michigan, Madison Square Garden, New York, New York, December 30, 1964

In those days, holiday tournaments were really big in college basketball. Teams didn't fly around the country very much, and the only time there was a lot of travel was right before and after Christmas. Michigan was one of the best teams in the country and featured Cazzie Russell. I'm a Princeton alumnus, and this was Bill Bradley's senior year. Bradley wasn't an unknown quantity —he was the captain of the United States Olympic team earlier that year and was eventually named Player of the Year. The Princeton team, however, wasn't considered in the same league as Michigan, although they ended up making it to the Final Four that season (where they lost to Michigan). Bradley didn't have much help from his teammates and, on this night, put on a show that was unbelievable. All of the fans at Madison Square Garden began rooting for Princeton, which was unusual, because everyone looked at Princeton as an Ivy League school filled with rich kids. The place just fell in love with Bill Bradley, though. He fouled out of the game with less than five minutes to go after scoring 41 points and with the Tigers up twelve. After he fouled out, though, Michigan came back to win by two, 80–78. Princeton couldn't even get the ball over halfcourt. I know I was an alumnus, but it was the most despairing loss I'd ever seen. They may have lost to Michigan again that season in the Final Four, but this was that game that tore out your heart.

1973 South African Open, Ellis Park Tennis Stadium, Johannesburg, South Africa, November 14-27, 1973

I went with Arthur Ashe to South Africa, where he played in the South African Open. It was the breaking of the color line in that country, not only in sports, but I believe in entertainment, as well. It was a major story, well beyond anything having to do with sports. In the first match, he played Sherwood Stewart and eventually went all the way to the finals, where Jimmy Connors clobbered him. The tennis wasn't the point, though. This was the only time in my career as a sportswriter where I was a part of history. The match against Stewart was the first time you had whites and blacks sitting together, which was one of the qualifications the Ashe camp had made—it couldn't be segregated seating. It was a traumatic and extraordinary experience and really was the first dent in apartheid. Nelson Mandela was still in prison, and the idea that apartheid would end wasn't even on the horizon. Sportswriters don't usually cover events of significance like this one. I might have seen thirty-five Super Bowls, but so what? I was very close to Arthur, so seeing history made like this was unforgettable.

The 1980 Wimbledon Championships, Gentlemen's Final, Bjorn Borg vs. John McEnroe, The All England Lawn Tennis Club, London, England, July 5, 1980

This was the best game or match I've ever seen. Some people have said the match between Federer and Nadal in 2008 was better, but you can argue that forever. To me, this was extraordinary. It wasn't just the best two players in the world playing against each other in the cathedral of the sport. The amazing thing was the tiebreaker in the fourth set, which ended 18–16. After it got to 5–5, every other point was either a match point or a set point. Borg and McEnroe were entirely different characters, so you really had everything in this match. It was for the championship of the world, with both players at the top of their games. If either one of them had a bad day, it would have been straight sets the other way. They were both over the moon that day, though.

1992 Summer Olympics, Men's 4x100 Meter Relay Final, Estadi Olimpic de Montjuic, Barcelona, Spain, August 8, 1992

I was friends with Carl Lewis, and he was nearing the end of his career. In track and field in the United States, you have to win a place on the team, regardless of who you are or your past success. When they had the trials, Lewis was sick, so he didn't make the U.S. team in either 100 or the 200. He got well enough to make the team in the long jump, however, and barely qualified for consideration for the 4x100 relay. But when Mark Witherspoon was injured in the semis for the 100, they not only put Lewis on the relay team, they acknowledged what everyone already knew, which was that he was the best sprinter on the team, so they made him the anchor on the relay team. Who finished second or third isn't even significant, because the U.S. team was so much better than everyone else. Rather than staying in the press box, I went down and stood by the track for the race. When Carl got the baton, the race was already over. He roared by in front of me and it was the most beautiful, graceful, athletic vision I ever had. It made no difference how much he was ahead or how much the team won by. It was the epitome of everything that is beautiful about sports.

Gregg Doyel

Columnist, *Indianapolis Star*

Florida at Auburn, Jordan-Hare Stadium, Auburn, Alabama, November 4, 1989

This was the first college football game I ever covered as a sportswriter. I was 19 at the time and was on the road covering the Gators, and it just boggled my mind that I was actually making the drive to Auburn, sleeping in a hotel room, having all of my expenses covered . . . it just blew my mind. I couldn't believe that my job was to watch football.

The game itself was interesting, too. Bill King was the writer for the *Gainesville Sun* at the time and is a super-talented writer. Auburn won with around 20 seconds left, on a TD pass that was caught right in front of me. I think I was actually closer to the receiver than any of the Florida defensive backs. Well, Bill's lede that night has become infamous. It read, "Shayne Wasden was open. That is all you need to know." I'm not sure it was really a bad lede, but because he was so talented and people were envious of that talent—and also ticked off that the Gators lost—people mocked that lede in Gainesville for years.

Dinner at Steve Spurrier's House, Gainesville, Florida, March 28, 1992

I was writing for the school newspaper at the University of Florida, and Steve Spurrier was the football coach at the time. He tried to do something to foster some goodwill with the media in the spring—which is ironic, since he later tried to get a columnist fired while at South Carolina—and invited everyone, including the writers from the student paper, to his house for an evening for dinner and to watch some basketball. His previous job before Florida was at Duke, and he has always had a soft spot in his heart for them. The night we had dinner at his house ended up being the night of the Christian Laettner shot against Kentucky. The funny part about the evening was that all of the writers were rooting for Kentucky, and it wasn't until around halftime that we all realized our mistake and that Spurrier was rooting for Duke. So that attempt at camaraderie backfired on him, with all of the writers on one side of the room, while Spurrier and some of his coaches, who all either went to and played at Duke or coached there, were on the other side.

1997 World Series, Game Seven, Cleveland Indians at Florida Marlins, Pro Player Stadium, Miami Gardens, Florida, October 26, 1997

I was covering the Marlins for the *Miami Herald*. This was pre-Internet, so the daily newspaper was still the only game in town. All of the national media is in town, and they are reading your story, so there is a lot of pressure in cases like this. There are two things that I remember specifically about that night. First, when the first pitch of the game was thrown, it was like a million fireflies lit up. There were so many flashbulbs going off, it felt like the stadium was a glistening diamond ring. The other thing was my deadline. World Series games start late as it is, but the game went 11 innings. Because of the deadline, at the bottom

Edgar Renteria runs to first after hitting the 1997 World Series-winning single in the bottom of the 11th inning. (AP Photo/ Hans Deryk)

of every inning, you basically have to have your game story written, and then figure out your lede after the game ends. You need to be able to hit *send* the second the game is over. So, for writing purposes, you kind of hope the visiting team wins, but in this case, the Marlins won on a single up the middle by Edgar Renteria. I just remember the misery in knowing everyone was in town and was going to read this game story, and I literally had around four seconds to file the most important story of my life. That was not fun.

Villanova at Duke, Cameron Indoor Stadium, Durham, North Carolina, December 10, 1997

I had just joined the *Charlotte Observer*, and this was my first trip to Cameron Indoor Stadium. I've been there around sixty times now, and after about ten of them, you realize it is the same game every time. The band plays the same songs, the students have the same chants, "Crazy Towel Guy" waves the same crazy towel. It is all the same. It is fun, but it is all the same. However, the first time you go, you don't know any of that, and it is magical. Even the drive to the arena is magical. At that time of year, the trees have lost all their leaves. There is a road, Wannamaker Drive, where you drive toward Cameron and these huge, tall trees with no leaves drape over the road like a big canopy and it is freaky. If you want you want to get cheesy about it, and actually think that nature can be scary, it is creepy.

When I got to Cameron, I parked my car and was walking near the library to the arena and asked a student where it was. The student pointed at the library and said that was it. It isn't that big from outside and looks like a library would. One of the beauties of Duke's campus is that all of the buildings are built out of stone and have the same kind of look, so it looked like everything else on campus. Once you go in, it looks like a library inside, too, with lots of brass and wood. But it is so loud, and it is so loud for so long, that when you leave the court area at halftime and after the game, and go into the tiny press room, your ears hurt. It's almost like getting the bends, but in your ears. It really is a special place to go to a game once.

UFC 68, Nationwide Arena, Columbus, Ohio, March 3, 2007

I went to this event to rip UFC. I wanted to write a hot take and call it barbaric. By the end of the night, though, I'd fallen in love with the sport and wrote a love letter to it instead. Within two weeks, I found an MMA gym where I lived in Cincinnati, walked in, and asked one of the UFC fighters there, Jorge Gurgel, to choke me out, just so that I would know what it felt like. He did, and I've been hooked on UFC since. You talk about a life-changing event, well, that changed mine. I'm in better shape than I've ever been in, I've got more confidence than ever before, and I'm not scared walking around anymore. And it is all because of covering that UFC event.

What hit me hardest were two things. First, it was the confidence each fighter walked into the cage with, knowing that if the referee didn't do his job, someone was dying. This isn't boxing, where you hit somebody and they go down and you leave them alone. When your opponent goes own, you keep hitting him until someone pulls you off. Both guys entered that cage thinking they were going to win (obviously someone was wrong, though). The other thing that got me was the camaraderie afterwards. I'd always hated watching fights, because they always scared me. You thought that these guys really hated each other. But these guys would literally beat each other half to death and then were hugging each other after it was over. I didn't get it until that night.

Ian Eagle

Broadcaster, CBS Sports/YES Network

1991 U.S. Open, Fourth Round, Jimmy Connors vs. Aaron Krickstein, National Tennis Center, Flushing, New York, September 2, 1991

Because I grew up in Forest Hills, the former home of the U.S. Open, tennis played a large role in my life. I played competitively as a kid and in high school and was also a ball boy for many years at the stadium in Forest Hills. Jimmy Connors actually chewed me out during a Tournament of Champions match one year in the early '80s. I was never a huge Connors fan, maybe because of that experience.

By the time 1991 rolled around, Connors's career was winding down, and on the only day I was able to get to the Open that year, he was taking on a young star named Aaron Krickstein in the fourth round. Connors had owned Krickstein during their careers, but the symbolism appeared to be pretty obvious that this was a passing of the torch. Connors had a love-hate relationship with the New York fans. I was there when he won the Open in 1982 and 1983 over Ivan Lendl, but Connors had never reached the level of adoration that others had in New York. In those matches, he had the backing of the fans more because of their dislike of Lendl.

It all changed against Krickstein. At the age of thirty-nine, Connors won over the crowd. He was trailing, 5–2, in the fifth and deciding set, and even I was feeling sorry for the southpaw, as all of his hard work and sweat in a grueling match would go for naught. Krickstein was ready for his signature win, but Connors had something up his sleeve and rallied to beat Krickstein in a fifth-set tiebreaker. I had been to a lot of tennis matches in my life but had never seen a crowd that was emotionally invested in a match like they were that day.

1994 Stanley Cup Finals, Game Seven, Vancouver Canucks at New York Rangers, Madison Square Garden, New York, New York, June 14, 1994

Growing up, I admittedly wasn't the biggest hockey fan, but I did have an interest in the New York Rangers. When they went to the Finals in 1979, I knew it was a big happening in New York, with the team having the potential of finally ending the "1940" chants.

In 1994, I was working at WFAN radio, which was the Rangers' flagship station. Living in New York City allowed me to get to the Garden frequently, and both the Rangers and Knicks were having banner years. When the playoffs rolled around, I finally got to see what hockey fans had always bragged about, experiencing the ambience of playoff hockey. I was doing some radio shows during the Rangers' run with Kenny Albert, who is as knowledgeable about hockey as anyone there is, while I helped provide the layman's perspective.

It is hard to look back now and not focus on Game Seven of the Devils series as the standout moment, and I was fortunate enough to be there for that, as well, but to watch the fans of New York react the way they did the night the Stanley Cup was won was almost a religious experience. I sat in the stands for the first two periods, and although I thought there was an air of overconfidence in the building that night, it quickly dissolved when the game started. All the die-hard fans in attendance were not taking anything for granted. In the third period, I moved over to the radio booth and watched from there with Marv Albert and Sal Messina calling the game. I had as perfect a view of the ice as you could possibly imagine. That is exactly where I was when time ran out, and I took a moment as the scene unfolded on the ice to absorb my surroundings and witness the pure joy on everyone's faces. Generations of Rangers fans finally had their moment in the sun, and that evening was an outpouring of emotion for anyone in attendance.

1998 NBA Finals, Game Six, Chicago Bulls at Utah Jazz, Delta Center, Salt Lake City, Utah, June 14, 1998

I did play-by-play at the 1998 Finals for a United Kingdom feed with former Nets broadcaster Mike O'Koren. There were rumblings at the time that this could be Michael Jordan's last go-around. In this series, it was the same old Jordan, and the Bulls looked like they were going to wrap up the title in five games, but Karl Malone had a vintage performance in Chicago to force a sixth game back in Salt Lake City.

Our location was literally in the stands among the screaming, rabid Jazz fans in the corner of the Delta Center. It was the loudest I had ever heard an arena in the NBA. If the Jazz could force Jordan into a seventh game, something he had never had to face before in the Finals, then maybe the Jazz could rewrite history. What people forget is that the final shot in this game

Michael Jordan holds up six fingers indicating the six NBA Championships the Bulls won after taking the 1998 NBA Finals. (AP Photo/Mark J. Terrill)

would never have happened if not for a defensive play by Jordan, who knocked the ball away from Malone on the previous possession.

During the timeout, there was no doubt who was getting the ball. We had seen the matchup all series long, with Jordan against Bryon Russell. Crossover dribble, a little shove, he drills the jumper, 87–86 Bulls. On tape, we all see the push, but at the time, as play was going on, there was no way any official would have called an offensive foul on Jordan. The way he did it made it feel as if it were part of the flow of the play. To this day, I have no memory of how I called it on the air (I never got the tape from Great Britain). The Delta Center went silent, and Michael Jordan's legacy was intact in what turned out to be his final game as a Chicago Bull.

2002 NBA Playoffs Opening Round, Game Five, Indiana Pacers at New Jersey Nets, Continental Airlines Arena, East Rutherford, New Jersey, May 2, 2002

This one is a personal favorite because of what it meant to the Nets organization, lifting them out of NBA Siberia and the shadows of the Knicks. When the Nets finished the regular season with the best record in the Eastern Conference, NBA observers looked at it as a fluke. The Nets had not been to the playoffs since 1998, and most people expected the team to fall on their faces once the postseason began. This was the last year of the best-of-five format in the first round, and the Nets were in a battle with the Indiana Pacers.

I worked the game with the great Bill Raftery, who had been calling Nets games for twenty years. The Jason Kidd era meant the beginning of a new persona, and that night it was truly born. The Nets had the game won in regulation, but rookie Richard Jefferson missed two free throws that could have iced it, and Reggie Miller made a desperation halfcourt heave off the glass as time expired to force overtime. The 20,000 fans in attendance thought, "This franchise is cursed." In the first OT, Indiana jumped out only to see the Nets respond, as Kidd willed the team into the second OT. Miller's heroics normally would take place just across the river against the Knicks at Madison Square Garden, but on this night, it was Kidd who created the lasting memory.

I had never felt tension for a sports team like I felt that night. All of the past failures, people who had worked for the franchise since their first day in the NBA, to see some of the looks on their faces at the end of regulation brought into focus just how much this night meant for an organization that desperately needed a highlight moment. When I got home that night, I couldn't sleep. I didn't realize until the next day what kind of impact that win had. It was, by far, the most reaction I had ever gotten after a broadcast—phone calls, e-mails, messages. For the first time, the Nets were the story, and they had a classic game to prove it.

2010 NCAA Men's Basketball Tournament Finals, Duke vs. Butler, Lucas Oil Stadium, Indianapolis, Indiana, April 5, 2010

I was hired to do play-by-play for the world feed with Pete Gillen. I think everybody jumped on board with the "Cinderella and mid-major getting respect" theme, along with the hometown narrative for Butler. I'm not sure anyone was convinced that the Bulldogs could actually play with Duke, though. The general consensus was that it was a nice story, but now they were taking on a college blue blood and the magic carpet ride would come to an end in their own backyard.

Lucas Oil Stadium was packed, and it was an electric atmosphere, with the fact that a local team was playing in the big game a big part of that. The Duke team was an experienced group, and they desperately wanted to win a championship for Mike Krzyzewski, since it had been a long time (relatively speaking) since their last title. There was something about that Butler team, however, and their head coach, Brad Stevens. Little did we know at that point that Stevens was going to be a hot commodity and eventually head coach of the Boston Celtics.

When the game started, you quickly realized that Butler could play with the Blue Devils and may be able to beat them. They hung around and went punch for punch with Duke. I remember the pressure building late in the game, and the Bulldogs weren't going away. Their chemistry was obvious and was on display the whole night. The Gordon Hayward heave on the last play of the game felt like it was in slow motion. We were in the second row, on the side of the midcourt line where Hayward was shooting, so I had a fantastic angle on the shot. Everything is happening and your head is spinning trying to process it, and I truly believed the ball was going in. I thought the ball had eyes. It came off the rim, and it strikes me that if that shot went down, I think that would have been the greatest ending in sports history. With everything at stake, with all of the storylines leading up to it, it would have been the biggest upset in NCAA history. To end in that manner, with the "Hoosier" backdrop all weekend, I think that would have catapulted it to the top of the list. It was still an incredible event and will be seared in my brain as one of the best sporting events I've ever called.

Mark Feinsand

Baseball writer, *New York Daily News*

Super Bowl XXV, Buffalo Bills vs. New York Giants, Tampa Stadium, Tampa, Florida, January 27, 1991

I was sixteen at the time, and my father had gotten us tickets as a birthday gift before we knew which teams would be playing. As a Redskins fan, I was a little disappointed that I was going to see the Giants play in the Super Bowl. I had never been to one, though, so I was excited nonetheless. Everywhere you went, there was security and insanity because of the Gulf War. Flying wasn't easy, and just getting into the stadium took three hours, so all you wanted to see was a good game to make it all worth it. It was the first Super Bowl for the Bills, so we had no idea they were going to go on this ridiculous four-year stretch of getting to the game. The atmosphere in the stadium was electric and was the most exciting thing I had experienced in my life to that point. We were sitting pretty high up, but in that stadium, there really weren't many bad seats. As great as the game was, the thing I remember above all else was Whitney Houston. People call that the greatest national anthem of all-time, and that night, every single person in the place stood straight up, with hats off, hands on their hearts, and sang along. You got the feeling that it meant something different to people because the country was at war. That set the tone for the night and the game we were about to witness.

I was rooting for the Bills and didn't hide that, while my dad was rooting for the Giants. It was a great game, but as is the case with many games, it is almost impossible to remember anything except for the kick. I remember Scott Norwood lining up for the 47-yard field goal, wanting him to make it so badly, if only because I didn't want to have to go home to New York on Monday and listen to all of my friends yapping about the Giants winning. It was like when a TV show has that big dramatic moment at the end, and it is all in slow motion. From where we were sitting, it was hard to tell whether the kick was good or not, so we were really watching the referees for their signal. When they signaled that it was no good, all of the Giants fans started celebrating, while the Bills fans put their heads in their hands. As we walked out of the stadium, though, it didn't matter who everyone was rooting for. All anyone could talk about was that it was the greatest Super Bowl ever played.

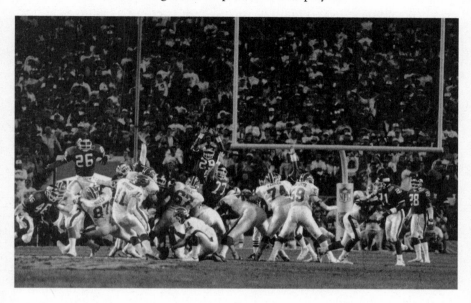

Scott Norwood gets ready to kick a potential game-winning field goal in the final seconds of Super Bowl XXV. (AP Photo/NFL Photos)

1996 American League Championship Series, Game One, Baltimore Orioles at New York Yankees, Yankee Stadium, Bronx, New York, October 9, 1996

Anytime you go to a game that takes on a title as the "(Fill in the Blank) Game," you know you've seen something memorable, and this game would become known as the "Jeffrey Maier Game." This was probably the best Yankees memory I have as a fan. I grew up in New York City and was a Yankees fan from birth. Being a Yankees fan growing up in the '80s wasn't all that great, but in 1996, after graduating from Boston University, I came home and had the chance to go to my first Yankees playoff game. As big as the Yankees-Red Sox rivalry is, in the mid-'90s, the Orioles were their biggest rival. I don't remember how we got the tickets, but they were on the lower level, in the last row right behind home plate. Yankee Stadium had an intimidation factor, because all of the seats were close to the field and this game was as intense as any I had ever seen. The Yankees were losing in the eighth inning of a close game, so we were all a little bummed but still into it, when Derek Jeter hits a ball to right field. From where we were sitting, you couldn't see whether it was gone, close, or caught, but we were feeding off the reaction of the rest of the stadium. All of a sudden, you could hear the roar, and you could see rightfielder Tony Tarasco didn't have the ball in his glove; our team's favorite rookie had just homered to tie the game. Then we see Tarasco arguing with the umpire, and we have no idea what is going on. Eventually word started filtering down from people that were listening to the radio in the stands that someone had interfered. We couldn't care less, of course, and said at the time that we would have reached out and grabbed the ball, too, if we had the chance. The fact that we all know Jeffrey Maier's name now is hilarious. He is the anti-Steve Bartman; he helped his team win. Even though it was only the tying run, it set the stage for Bernie Williams to hit a walk-off homer in the 11th.

2001 American League Division Series, Game Three, New York Yankees at Oakland Athletics, Network Associates Coliseum, Oakland, California, October 13, 2001

This was my first year on the Yankees beat for MLB.com. You expected this to be a good series, because both teams were loaded with great players. The Yankees lost the first two games at Yankee Stadium, and it didn't feel like the Yankees' year. With it being right after 9/11, it was almost like people didn't care, because there were bigger things to worry about. Game Three was Mike Mussina against Barry Zito and was a well-pitched game. Jorge Posada homered in the fifth inning, which ended up being the only run in the game, but that really just set the stage for what happened in the bottom of the seventh. After Jeremy Giambi singled with two outs, we assumed the A's were going to pinch-run with Eric Byrnes, but they didn't. It seemed strange, since it was a one-run game, and the Yankees had Mariano Rivera looming in the bullpen. Terrence Long comes up and hits a ball down the right-field line. Shane Spencer fields it, and you see Giambi being waved around third. It was going to take a really good throw to get him, but Spencer's throw sailed over Tino Martinez's head and it looks like Oakland is going to tie the game up. All of a sudden, Derek Jeter was there. I remember hearing someone in the press box yelling, "What the hell is Jeter doing there?" He got the ball, does his little flip to Jorge Posada, who tags Giambi on the leg, and they call him out. Everyone just had this stunned reaction and couldn't figure out what had just happened. No one had ever seen a play like it, including writers I talked to who had covered the game for forty or fifty years. The one thing nobody could figure out was what Jeter was doing there. You never see a shortstop make a play twelve feet from home plate on the first base line. What was he doing there? That play became symbolic of what Derek Jeter's career was. Right place, right time, incredible instincts and calm under pressure. Being there is one thing. Getting the ball on the overthrow is one thing, but having the mindset and wherewithal to turn and shovel-pass it to your catcher . . . I don't care if you are supposed to be there, that is not the play you are practicing for. He told us after the game that they practiced that play, and I said incredulously, "You don't practice that play. We've been at spring training and watched you guys do everything. You don't practice that play." The next spring, though, we were watching during drills, and, lo and behold, we saw that when the ball is hit to right, Jeter would move toward the first base line in case a throw got past the first baseman. Every time I've talked to someone who was on the A's in that game, though, they all ask the same two questions: why wasn't Eric Byrnes running, and why didn't Jeremy Giambi slide?

2001 World Series, Game Seven, New York Yankees at Arizona Diamondbacks, Bank One Ballpark, Phoenix, Arizona, November 4, 2001

The three games in New York in this series you remember for George Bush throwing out the first pitch before Game Three and the game-tying home runs in Games Four and Five. Normally it would be hard to top any of that, but Game Seven did. I was sitting in the auxiliary press box, which was way out in center field. When Alfonso Soriano homered in the eighth inning to give the Yankees the lead, you automatically assumed the Yankees were about to win their fourth straight World Series, because Rivera was coming in to pitch the eighth and ninth innings. I started to make my way from center field and got down to the clubhouse, where I was on line with around a hundred people, watching the bottom of the ninth inning on this little TV outside the clubhouse. We see the inning unfold, and when Arizona tied the game, the clubhouse door flies open, and you see these big pieces of wood being thrown out of the room. We later found out that because we were in Arizona, FOX was going to do the postgame show from inside the room, and when the Diamondbacks tied it up, George Steinbrenner went crazy and started yelling about everything being set up before the game was over. So, they were frantically trying to get everything out of the clubhouse at that point. As this was all going on, Mariano Rivera was giving up the series-winning hit to Luis Gonzalez. My first thought wasn't that the Yankees had lost the World Series, but what was I going to write about now? I had gone down there with "Yankees winning" stories planned out, but my boss tracked me down and we had to switch everything around. It was my first year on the Yankees beat, and that was the night where I realized that as great as it was to grow up a Yankees fan, this was now my job.

2003 American League Championship Series, Game Seven, Boston Red Sox at New York Yankees, Yankee Stadium, Bronx, New York, October 16, 2003

Whenever anyone asks me what the best game I've ever been to is, I say this one. Every year while I covered the Yankees for MLB.com, we picked a player at the beginning of the playoffs to do a postgame diary every day. Aaron Boone had come over at the trade deadline that season, and he and I hit it off, so I asked him if he would do the diary for us. He was having a dreadful ALCS, and I think he was a little embarrassed that I was talking to him every day for this diary. There was so much going on in that series, with the Yankees-Red Sox rivalry really at its peak. He was on the bench for Game Seven, and I knew that win or lose, he was going to be an awkward guy to have talk about the game after it ended. It wound up being an epic game, with so many different storylines from both teams, and the guy I was doing an exclusive thing with after the game wasn't taking part in it. He came into the game as a pinch-runner in the eighth inning and stayed in to play third from that point. He came up to lead off the 11th inning . . . and promptly homered off Tim

Wakefield to end the series. I remember sitting there in amazement at what had just happened, since it was a walk-off home run in extra innings of Game Seven of the ALCS, but also because it was the guy I had been working with all postseason. You couldn't have written a better script on how this worked out for me . . . and obviously for him.

Yankee Stadium was going bananas, and I never thought I would ever experience that stadium crazier than the two ninth-inning home runs in Games Four and Five of the 2001 World Series, but this was somehow louder and crazier. I was worried that the press box was going to collapse because of how much the building was shaking. Now, I had to do this exclusive interview with Boone and had to find a way to do it amidst the mayhem of the postgame champagne celebration in the clubhouse. I did all of my other interviews first, and happily I was writing for a website and not a newspaper, because there was no chance I would have made any sort of deadline. I basically wasn't allowed to leave until I got this diary done. It took two hours before I finally settled into a corner of the clubhouse with Aaron and his wife, Laura, and ended up doing the diary with both of them. You could see the joy and relief in his face, and even though it was a couple of hours after he hit the home run, it was really the first chance he had to breathe. I couldn't help but think that no athlete could be in a better place in their career than he was at that moment.

Bruce Feldman

Broadcaster, FOX Sports

ABCD Camp, Fairleigh Dickinson University, Teaneck, New Jersey, July 8-11, 1996

I used to cover the ABCD camp every year when I covered college basketball more. At the end of the camp, they would play the Outstanding Seniors Game. A lot of players would come into the camp with big reputations, and one of the guys that year was a local kid named James Felton. There was a transition play where the ball came free, and a lanky swingman from Florida got the ball and was out in front, and basically waited for Felton, who was a little bigger than him, to come back and play defense. He skied up, whipped the ball over his head and windmill-dunked on Felton. The dunk was so spectacular that fans literally ran onto the court and interrupted the game, because it was one of those amazing in-game moments. More than a decade later, I did a story on this game, because the guy who dunked it was Tracy McGrady. Nobody had heard of him in basketball circles until that week, and after that, he was the biggest star in high school recruiting. Obviously, he skipped college and went on to a long career in the NBA. Felton's career, though, went into a tailspin. He started at St. John's but ended up going to five different schools and, ironically, finished his career on that same court at Fairleigh Dickinson. You had two guys who met in midair, and after they met, their legacies flipped, where the guy who was the nobody became the big star, while the guy destined for stardom saw his career drift off into the margins.

USC Football Practice, Howard Jones Field, Los Angeles, California, August 6, 2003

USC had a highly touted freshman class coming in, with a bunch of five-star recruits. Reggie Bush had a pretty good reputation, but midway through his first practice in pads with the Trojans, after they went into their team drill, he broke off a run. Then he broke off another run. He was making crazy cuts all over the place. There were a lot of really good players on that team, and after the first time he did it, you thought it was great, but let's see it again. And it kept on happening, where he kept breaking these huge runs. I was talking to one of the USC assistant coaches, who had been around Marshall Faulk, and he said he had never seen anyone do the stuff that Bush was doing. As soon as practice ended, I remember calling the office at *ESPN The Magazine* and telling them they needed to find a way to work something in, even though the magazine's deadline to go to press had just passed. I knew that day he was going to be amazing, just from the stuff I saw him doing. It really was a "Stop the presses!" moment.

2006 Rose Bowl, Texas vs. USC, Rose Bowl, Pasadena, California, January 4, 2006

For days going into the game, ESPN was running a series comparing this USC team to the all-time greats. The hype around the Trojans was enormous, with Reggie Bush winning the Heisman Trophy that season and Matt Leinart winning it the year before. There were teams that had them on the ropes during the season, but, as was the case in games like the "Bush Push" game against Notre Dame, they always out-talented everybody by the time it was over. I remember walking into the Rose Bowl and seeing Leinart's dad in the parking lot, and him telling me it was going to be a boat race; he genuinely thought they were going to blow Texas out. At times, it looked like that was going to happen, but the Longhorns stayed within striking distance, and you would look down at the Texas sideline every time USC scored and see Vince Young just nod his head as if to say he was going to fix this. It seemed like he was the only one in that building who knew Texas was going to win, and he willed them to their first national title since 1970. This was the greatest game I've ever seen. There was so much happening throughout the game. On one play, Reggie Bush tried to lateral the ball to a walk-on receiver named Brad Walker, who wasn't even listed on any of the game cards or any rosters. No one knew who he was, which might explain why it turned into a fumble recovered by Texas. But Young put on a superhuman performance, one that I'll put against any game, especially when you consider what the game was for and the team they were playing.

Auburn at Alabama, Bryant-Denny Stadium, Tuscaloosa, Alabama, November 26, 2010

Cam Newton came into this game under so much scrutiny because of all of the rumors swirling around him. It was on enemy turf, and they were playing songs like "Take the Money and Run" over the P.A., while the students and the band were taunting him mercilessly. Alabama took a huge lead and were making Newton struggle like no one else had that season. What people forget is that while Nick Fairley was a great defensive lineman in college, Auburn didn't have that much talent around Newton. He was the kind of guy, though, who could put an entire team on his back, and he led that team back to beat their archrivals. ESPN did a *30 for 30* film on the Alabama-Auburn rivalry, and I spent two months chasing Newton to get a sit-down with him, because he had all of this drama going on with his dad and the NCAA, and the reports about whether he or his father had gotten money after leaving Florida and some of the problems he had there. So, he came into this game being vilified by a lot of people, and I thought the way he compartmentalized it and responded to everything was amazing.

Alabama at Texas A&M, Kyle Field, College Station, Texas, September 14, 2013

I had spent the week leading up to this game with the Texas A&M program for CBS and was behind the scenes with their staff and Johnny Manziel, so I had this remarkable access and saw all the drama and ups and downs. I was in the quarterback coach's office with Manziel and ESPN was on in the background, and in their list of upcoming topics, it seemed like every other one was about him, be it "Johnny Football" or "Johnny Drama" or some other "Johnny Something" reference. He was a larger-than-life story that season, having won the Heisman the year before. During that season (2012), the Aggies had gone into Tuscaloosa and won, but with the subplot that they had simply caught Alabama off-guard in that game. Now, Nick Saban and Kirby Smart had eight months to prepare for Manziel. I remember being with the team before the game and had never seen a team as hyped up as A&M was. They came out and went up, 14–0, but their defense was so shaky that they couldn't slow the Crimson Tide down and lost in a shootout, 49–42. Manziel, though, put up more yards (562 of them) than anyone ever had against Alabama. The Aggies coaches had talked about how they thought Alabama's cornerbacks were a weak spot and that Mike Evans, their best receiver, was too big for them and would destroy them. Everything they said and picked up during their preparation on offense played out exactly how they thought it would.

Scott Ferrall

Broadcaster, CBS Sports Radio Network

1987 NCAA Men's Basketball Tournament Finals, Indiana vs. Syracuse, Louisiana Superdome, New Orleans, Louisiana, March 30, 1987

I'll never forget Keith Smart's game-winning basket to win the national championship for Indiana. The play was set up for Steve Alford, but instead Daryl Thomas found Smart floating into the corner, and he nailed the shot to beat Syracuse and win the title. It was the last game that I ever covered at Indiana University, where I covered the team for five years. Strangely enough, I have never gone back once in all of these years. A lot of people go back to visit their alma maters, but for whatever reason, I've just never made it back to Bloomington. That was the greatest game I've ever been to, though, in college basketball. The Hoosiers were down eight points midway through the second half and should have lost the game, but what a comeback. After

Keith Smart follows through on the game-winning basket in the 1987 NCAA title game. (AP Photo/Bill Haber)

Derrick Coleman missed the front end of the one-and-one and the Hoosiers got the ball with the chance to win, the feeling inside that giant stadium, it was going to explode. When he hit that shot, it was euphoria. And after it was all over, I went down to Bourbon Street and got hammered!

1989 AFC Wild Card Playoffs, Pittsburgh Steelers at Houston Oilers, Houston Astrodome, Houston, Texas, December 31, 1989

This was the last NFL game played in the '80s and pitted Chuck Noll against Jerry Glanville in the Astrodome. Gary Anderson won the game with a 50-yard field goal in overtime, after Merril Hoge tied the game with a late touchdown. Rod Woodson caused a fumble in OT that led to the winning field goal. Here I am, a twenty-three-year-old reporter covering the Steelers, traveling with the team, and just in awe of Noll. I worked for Bob Knight and then worked for Chuck Noll, so I basically worked for God and Jesus. If you look at the video of the field goal, I'm the only guy standing under the goalpost as the ball sails through for the win. I'm also the only guy immature enough to be jumping up and down cheering because I was the only Steelers fan there. Everyone else was either a reporter or cameraman, or was from Houston. There was only one person jumping up and down, and that was me.

1996 Summer Olympics, Centennial Olympic Park, Atlanta, Georgia, July 27, 1996

I was broadcasting "Ferrall on the Bench" for Westwood One from the Atlanta Olympics in 1996 and was in Centennial Park doing the show one night when, maybe 300 yards away from me, a bomb exploded. We were broadcasting from right next to the Budweiser tent in the village, and when it went off, no one knew what it was, but everyone started running. The place emptied out, and what we did, as young guys tend to do, was start filling our equipment bags with beer. We ended up filling up three bags with ice-cold cans of beer before grabbing our equipment and running to the NBC media hotel where we were staying. Beer was expensive at the Olympics, so grabbing enough to last us for the rest of the Olympics was smart thinking on our part.

1997 NHL Eastern Conference Quarterfinals, Game Four, Philadelphia Flyers at Pittsburgh Penguins, Civic Arena, Pittsburgh, Pennsylvania, April 23, 1997

Mario Lemieux scored on a breakaway late in the game to give the Penguins a 4–1 lead in a series that they would eventually lose in Philadelphia, making the goal Mario's last one at home before his first retirement. Mario is my favorite athlete of all time and was always great to me when I covered the team every day. I would go to all of the practices and morning skates while working in Pittsburgh after working the morning drive for KQV, then go to the games after the afternoon drives. I loved the Penguins, so it was thrilling to see Mario break in from center ice, that huge 6-foot-4 frame barreling down the ice to beat the goalie, then going into a Pavarotti move, bending back and lifting his arms to the heavens to say, "There you go. That's it. I'm done, but this one was for you." The fans then stood for fifteen minutes and cheered him. It was orgasmic. I was standing with my dad and my two best friends and a guy I didn't know, and I poured a giant beer on him, and he still hugged me and didn't care.

2004 Aaron's 499, Talladega Superspeedway, Talladega, Alabama, April 25, 2004

I was hosting a show in Atlanta at the time, and some buddies had the idea to go to Talladega for the race and camp. We got an RV and drove to Alabama, and set up a tent and grills and spent the weekend there. We partied like rock stars from the time we got there on Friday night until the race on Sunday, which was won by Jeff Gordon. Talladega is an intimidating place. I'd never been there before and couldn't believe how many people shaved the number of their favorite driver into their chest hair, or how many people didn't shower for three days in 95-degree heat. People were chain-smoking cigarettes and pot, and drinking unbelievable amounts of whiskey and beer. The amount of debauchery that was going on was unlike anything I'd ever experienced before. It was the most chaotic sporting event I'd ever been to in my life. It was really hot on race day, just miserable. I had a loaded Ford Expedition then; they sponsored my radio show, so I drove a really nice truck. I needed to cool down, so my wife and I went into the air-conditioned Expedition, and, let's just say, we had relations. A month later, we went to the doctor and found out my wife was pregnant, and he figured out the day the baby was conceived was that day in Talladega. So ever since then, I've loved Talladega. To conceive a child there is humiliating for my wife but kicks ass for me.

Terry Gannon

Broadcaster, NBC Sports

Georgia Tech at Notre Dame, Notre Dame Stadium, South Bend, Indiana, November 8, 1975

Rudy Ruettiger is a life-long friend of mine, and our families have been close since I was born. My dad coached him in high school, as well as some of his brothers, who were champion wrestlers. My father had season tickets for Notre Dame football as long as I can remember, and I went to every game starting when I was five years old until the time I left to go to N.C. State.

We were living all of Rudy's story with him. When he was going to Holy Cross, my dad would give him twenty dollars every weekend so he could try to get into the games, and afterwards, we would go out to dinner, and he would constantly tell us (and anyone else who would listen) about how he was going to play football at Notre Dame. We would always humor him and say, "Yeah, yeah," just thinking it was one of those ideas that Rudy always had. Damned if he didn't make it happen, of course. I would actually stay with Rudy in what was a little closet at what is now the Joyce Center but was serving as his dorm room, during football weekends, and he would sneak me out and shoot hoops with me on the arena floor in the middle of the night when the security guard wasn't watching.

The weekend of the game he played in, I was there in the stands as the student body started chanting his name until Dan Devine eventually put him in the game, and, just like in the movie, where his family was going nuts, that was us, part of his extended family. Yes, he did sack the quarterback on the final play, just as the movie said it happened. If anyone wants to argue that, I would argue with them to the death. I witnessed it.

After the game, I went into the locker room, and Rudy said, "Here, take this with you." He then handed me a Notre Dame helmet, which I proceeded to take and wear around the neighborhood while playing sandlot football. Years later, it was stored in my mother-in-law's garage, and she called me to tell me she'd found this helmet that I had forgotten about. She was going to throw it out, but I made sure to stop her, and it is now on the mantel in my office at home. A couple of years ago, I called Rudy and told him about the helmet, so that he knew I still had it, but he told me that he had the helmet from the game and that mine was a different one. To be honest, though, neither of us really knows which the right one is. I'm not sure to this day. All I know is that he has a helmet and I have a helmet, and one of them is the one he wore in the game.

1996 Tour de France, Stage 17, Pamplona, Spain, July 17, 1996

I was hosting the Tour de France for what was then Wide World of Sports on ABC and would go to every stage and put together daily shows for ESPN and weekend shows for ABC. The Tour de France is the most incredible sporting event I've ever been to, because it is such a large part of the culture of France. It is like a Super Bowl that takes place every day at a different venue and moves from place to place across the country, with enormous compounds at the starting line and finish line of every stage.

Miguel Indurain was a beloved figure at that time in the sport and was the five-time defending champion. In 1996, one of the stages of the race went through the Pyrenees and passed through his hometown of Villava, and when the peloton arrived at the town, I've never seen such love from fans to an athlete as there was that day in that town. Every person who lived in the town was out on the side of the road. Every poster was a personal one, from cousins to friends. The route continued that day to Pamplona, which is not too far from Villava, and it was like a ticker-tape parade in Manhattan. People were hanging out of every window in every building. There were streamers and confetti. They were banging trash can lids for a good hour as they were waiting for the riders to arrive, singing his name. It was a scene that I'd never seen before, or since, in sports. There was so much love and respect for him welcoming him home.

1998 U.S. Women's Figure Skating Championships, CoreStates Center, Philadelphia, Pennsylvania, January 11, 1998

Michelle Kwan was the seminal figure in figure skating during my time covering the sport for ABC. She was a beloved figure for fans but could just never get it done at the Olympics. So, there was this respect for her and love for her, but also this sympathy for her because she had not been able to win that gold medal. In 1998, in the lead-up to the Nagano Games (where she lost to Tara Lipinski), at the National Championships in Philadelphia, it was one of those moments where a professional athlete has it all come together for them in one night, where you can take that performance and put it away and say that was what that athlete was about during their career. She ended up getting fifteen perfect sixes during the competition, everybody in the arena started standing midway through her free skate to cheer. It was very similar to the reception I saw with Miguel Indurain in 1996 that encapsulated the love for a professional athlete. In figure skating, the end of a performance is very abrupt, and, as an announcer, you are always looking for what to say in those moments, and I said very little. It just didn't need anything. It was one of those times where you look back and say, "Yeah, that was a moment."

134th Open Championship, Second Round, The Old Course at St. Andrews, Fife, Scotland, July 15, 2005

I was calling the early session from St. Andrews that day for TNT and got off the air when Jack Nicklaus was about midway through the back nine in what was his final round at the Open Championship at St. Andrews. Mike Tirico and Nick Faldo got off the air at the same time, and we were all standing there in the broadcast booth, which overlooks the first hole and the 18th hole. We all looked at one another and had the same thought, which was to get ourselves down to the 18th green. So the three of us, including a former British Open champ, ran like little kids down the stairs so we could get to the green. By that time, the crowd to see Jack had swarmed to the area, but we were able to get through everyone and were around fifty feet away from the green as Jack made his way up. He hit his approach to about fourteen feet.

What is unique about St. Andrews is that it is built right in the middle of town and is surrounded by buildings, so the 18th welcomes you right into the middle of town. People were sitting on ledges at every window in all of the buildings around the 18th green. When he got ready to putt, you really didn't think he was going to make it but then reminded yourself that this was Jack Nicklaus. And when he made the putt, the explosion from everyone there was

Jack Nicklaus waves from the Swilcan Bridge on the 18th hole of the Old Course at St. Andrews as he completes his final competitive round at The Open Championship. (AP Photo/Ted S. Warren)

one that I'd never heard on a golf course, even at Augusta, because the setting is just so different. It wasn't just the gallery cheering, but all of the people watching from all of the buildings. I still get chills thinking about that putt going in. And to be standing there with Nick Faldo, who knows what it feels like to win that event but was caught up in the moment like everyone else, made it even more special.

2007 Women's British Open, The Old Course at St. Andrews, Fife, Scotland, August 2-5, 2007

This was such a significant event, because it was the first time the women were allowed to play at St. Andrews, so early in the week, every golfer, regardless of stature, was giddy about the opportunity to play that course. Players were taking pictures of themselves on every hole and created a huge backup on 18 as they all took pictures on the Swilcan Bridge.

It was one of those final rounds that was windy and rainy, and just had that feel of something significant, with that mysterious fog rolling in. Lorena Ochoa was the number one player in the world at the time but had yet to win a major championship. Being from Mexico, she is a very important figure in her country for golf and for girls. And she was the first person to raise the women's version of the Claret Jug, right there, in front of the R&A. I think you can point to that event as the first step in paving the way for women to be finally accepted into the R&A, a decision that was only approved in September of 2014. It was a significant win for her, but also a really big event all week for women's golf.

I remember sitting with Judy Rankin after we got off the air one night at Rusacks Hotel, which is literally one hundred feet from the 18th fairway. Meg Mallon and Juli Inkster were still on the course, finishing their round on 18, and yelled to us at the bar, "Isn't this great? This is awesome!" They were like little kids playing St. Andrews.

Mike Garafolo

Broadcaster, FOX Sports

2003 NFC Divisional Playoffs, Green Bay Packers at Philadelphia Eagles, Lincoln Financial Field, Philadelphia, Pennsylvania, January 11, 2004

I was working for the Associated Press and covering the Eagles, who everyone expected to cruise through the playoffs. They were loaded that year and were the top seed in the NFC. Brett Favre led the Packers into Philly, though, and they executed their game plan perfectly for most of the game. The Eagles were faced with a fourth-and-26 late in the game, and everyone in the press box started to head downstairs to begin working on the team's obituary. But Donovan McNabb throws a pass to Freddie Mitchell over the middle, and there was no way you thought he was going to catch it. Mitchell, who was an absolute bust but had a bigger mouth than anybody, made the play, though. Because the game was in Philly, even the press box erupted. It was more bewilderment than anything. The next play was rushed, so you really didn't have much time to reflect on it, and everything happened so quickly that the next thing you knew, the Eagles had won the game. It was amazing to watch everyone regroup after the game ended, since most of the press box had gone downstairs with the assumption that the Packers were going to win.

Super Bowl XLII, New York Giants vs. New England Patriots, University of Phoenix Stadium, Glendale, Arizona, February 3, 2008

No one really gave the Giants much of a chance in this game, even though they had played the Patriots close in Week 17. I was in the press box at the corner of the field when the David Tyree catch happened across the field from us, so the view of the play wasn't great. The ball went up and it disappeared into a group of people, and the crowd down at the other end reacted, while the crowd at our end had a delayed reaction. When we saw the replay, Steve Politi, who was sitting next to me, started yelling, "He caught it on his head!" Of course, they still needed to score after that, but we knew we really needed to write great stories for this game. After the game ended, in the locker room, I remember Tom Coughlin doing session after session with the media, and Antonio Pierce was walking around the room grabbing media members and saying, "And you were wrong!" to each one. There was also a conversation between Peyton and Eli Manning that we were eavesdropping on, where they were talking about how you'd rather be down four than three, because it meant you had to go for the touchdown and weren't playing conservative.

Super Bowl XLIII, Pittsburgh Steelers vs. Arizona Cardinals, Raymond James Stadium, Tampa, Florida, February 1, 2009

It was the most subdued Super Bowl atmosphere I've seen for the week leading up to the game, and then a great game. The stock market had just crashed, so fewer people traveled to the game than usual. Steelers fans always travel well, but Cardinals fans don't, so it had the feeling of a Steelers home game. The week before the game was a lot more subdued than most Super Bowls, though. Then the game starts, and the first big moment was James Harrison's interception right before halftime. They say you aren't supposed to cheer in the press box, but there was this roar that came up as we realized he was going to score on the play. That play started a huge debate about which was better—that one or the David Tyree catch the year before. Steve Politi actually called Tyree during the game to get his opinion, and he said the Harrison play was better. Then the fourth quarter just explodes, and the teams are going back and forth. After a week where it felt like the air had been sucked out of all the excitement, it was ending with one of the best games any of us had ever seen, all culminating with the amazing catch to win the game by Santonio Holmes. I'll never forget watching Larry Fitzgerald's father, Larry Fitzgerald Sr., who was covering the game in the press box for the the *Minnesota Spokesman-Recorder*, showing no emotion on his face while watching the game, because he wanted to stay objective while doing his job.

Santonio Holmes makes the winning touchdown reception in Super Bowl XLIII. (AP Photo/Matt Slocum)

2010 Stanley Cup Final, Game Six, Chicago Blackhawks at Philadelphia Flyers, Wachovia Center, Philadelphia, Pennsylvania, June 9, 2010

I grew up a Flyers fan and knew that if they won the Cup, I wanted to be in the building. This was Game Six, though, and with them down three games to two, I knew it wasn't happening that night but went anyway. The Flyers tied the game late, and the place is going bonkers. Then, overtime happens, and we were sitting at the other end of the arena from where the Blackhawks scored the Cup-winning goal. It was the eeriest sound I've ever heard at a game. When Patrick Kane scored, nobody knew except two people—Patrick Kane and Flyers goalie Michael Leighton. The light didn't go on, and no one reacted. It went against everything you were trained to respond to at a hockey game. Your eyes were seeing something, but your ears were betraying you. Then the

Chicago bench reacted, and we all realized that he scored. They had to go to video to make sure it was a goal, and as the Blackhawks bench found out that it was, they were reacting before everyone else knew that it was official. The Stanley Cup Final was ending, but what we were hearing didn't match up to what we were seeing. I stayed for the Cup presentation just to see it but wasn't happy about it.

Super Bowl XLIX, Seattle Seahawks vs. New England Patriots, University of Phoenix Stadium, Glendale, Arizona, February 1, 2015

I was in the tunnel leading to the field, getting ready to go out for postgame interviews and planning on which Patriots I wanted to talk to. Then Jermaine Kearse's catch happens, and the whole plan changes. The monitors in the tunnel are on delay, so as I am watching the replay of next plays, the crowd roars. The crowd was split pretty much down the middle, so it was tough to tell from the noise what was going on. We had to wait for the play on the monitor, and as the ball disappears, it was hard to tell what had happened. First it looked incomplete, then we realized it was an interception, and, within a couple of minutes, we were all rushing out on the field. Because he wasn't the most well-known player, we didn't even realize that Malcolm Butler was running right past us, but once we did, we immediately grabbed him for an interview. You could see in his eyes that he didn't have any feel for what had just happened, and the reality hadn't come close to setting in for him. I remember seeing Patriots defensive coordinator Matt Patricia on the field and he was going to give us an interview, but he was so emotional and had tears in his eyes. His mother had come down to the field and someone for some reason had thrown an American flag over him, and you could see that his mother had never been prouder of him. It was just an incredible scene. These are the moments we all get into this business to be a part of.

Jason Gay

Columnist, *Wall Street Journal*

The Tour de France

The Tour de France has been described as three weeks' worth of Super Bowls, but that's not completely accurate; a better way to describe it is three weeks' worth of Super Bowls and also three weeks' worth of Super Bowl parades. Because that's what it pretty much is: one of the planet's most demanding sporting events sandwiched in between a near-daily Mardi Gras partying. You do not have to be a cycling fan to love it; I suspect a good number of people on the roadways of France are casual fans at best. But it's a pretty glorious way to spend a day. This is the part where I remind you that you're in France, so you do not have to worry about the food and wine situation. It's basically impossible to screw that up. If you're lucky, you find yourself in the mountains, hopefully the Alps, which are almost comical in their scale and beauty, and punishing on anyone who's chosen to ride up. I've been fortunate enough to ride an Alpine stage before the race, and it does give you real perspective on how truly brutal the sport can be. Cycling has a bad rap because of the drug scandals, and this is mostly deserved; it's a self-inflicted mess. But it hasn't diminished a reality that becomes very clear on the side of the road in France in July: it is one of the most staggeringly beautiful sporting events on the planet. It passes by in just a couple minutes, but those couple of minutes are unforgettable. Then there's more wine, some cheese, maybe some chocolate, and a slow return down the mountain.

2011 NCAA Wrestling Championships, Wells Fargo Center, Philadelphia, Pennsylvania, March 17-19, 2011

I am not a wrestler. I did not grow up following the sport. In high school, the wrestling room was a pungent place I quickly walked past on the way to basketball practice. And yet I know it's an extraordinary sport with a rich history and tradition, and in 2011 I found myself at the NCAA Division I championships in Philadelphia to watch a wrestler from Arizona State named

Anthony Robles. Robles was born without a right leg, but had become an elite high school and collegiate wrestler and was now on the verge of a national title, his first. Along the way, he'd become an inspirational figure with a national following. But on this night, in the concrete of the Wells Fargo Center, he just wanted to win. His opponent was a wrestler from Iowa named Matt McDonough, the defending champion in the 125-lb. weight class, who was in difficult position of standing in the way of a conclusion mostly everybody wanted. Robles came out very hard and took an early advantage, and that was really that. McDonough managed only one point. Robles took the national title, his last goal as a college athlete. I remember talking with him in the corridor afterward and seeing his quiet joy. In that moment, Robles wasn't an inspiration or a heartwarming story or a media sensation. He was a champion. Which is what he'd worked for, and what he really wanted.

2012 Summer Olympics, Men's Tennis Semifinals, The All England Lawn Tennis Club, London, England, August 3, 2012

I grew up watching Wimbledon with my dad. Because of the time difference, the tennis championships at the All England Lawn Tennis and Croquet Club are televised in the morning in the United States, of course—right around the time I usually ate my Cheerios. This was in and of itself a treat: my dad letting me watch TV before noon. This was also the late 1970s and '80s, an apex for tennis; the game was dominated by true originals like Bjorn Borg, John McEnroe, Jimmy Connors, Chris Evert, and Martina Navratilova. Long, hot mornings were spent inside the house, watching icons play on manicured grass in this jewel box of a stadium that looked like something out of an impossible fantasy. It wasn't until 2012 that I got to Wimbledon myself, and it wasn't technically Wimbledon, but the Olympics in London, which were using the All England Club for the tennis competition. But it was still the same palace. Wimbledon is one of those places that appears magical on TV even if TV doesn't fully render all of its magic. When I walked into Centre Court—I'm trying not to say, "It took my breath away," but it took my breath away. As it happened, my wife was pregnant with our first child, and she sent me a sonogram photo on my phone just as Roger Federer was about to play Juan Martin del Potro. This was a first picture of our son-to-be, and I immediately thought of all the hours I'd spent watching tennis from this court with my father. Federer wound up winning, 3–6, 7–6, 19–17, in what is considered one of the greatest best-of-three-set matches of all time. But I don't remember the match very well. What I remember most was wishing I was there with my dad.

2012 Summer Olympics, Men's Keirin, London Velopark, London, England, August 7, 2012

I guess this means I am listing two events from the same Olympics, but I love the Olympics for a very straightforward reason: every single day, you see one of the greatest moments of someone's life. I'm a bit of a cycling fanatic, and the Scotsman Chris Hoy is considered one of the greatest track riders ever; before the 2012 Olympics even happened, he'd won multiple gold medals and been knighted by the Queen. London was supposed to be a grand climax to Hoy's extraordinary career, but there was also astonishing amount of pressure on him, as there was for all of the UK favorites. The Velopark in London had been rocking all week, and on the final day, Hoy found himself in the Keirin final. The Keirin is an eccentric race in which the riders pace themselves behind a tiny motorbike for a few laps until the motorbike peels away, and then it's a mad sprint to the finish. Hoy managed to get out in front until the final lap, when Germany's Max Levy pulled on his right and got almost a full wheel on him. If you're sprinting a bike and someone gets a full wheel on you, it's awfully hard to get back in front. Hoy himself admitted as much later—he thought he was doomed. Somehow, miraculously almost, Hoy managed to pull back in front. It was like watching Superman pry a truck off of a bridge. Hoy won the race—his sixth gold, making him the most successful British Olympian of all time—and the arena just exploded as if someone had released a valve. A few minutes, that's all it was. But one of the greatest sports moments I ever saw.

2013 World Series, Game Six, St. Louis Cardinals at Boston Red Sox, Fenway Park, Boston, Massachusetts, October 30, 2013

By now, we're used to the idea of the Red Sox as winners—after more than eight decades of suffering, they went out and won three World Series in nine seasons. I am old enough to remember when the Red Sox didn't win—or rather, they won enough to put themselves in a position to lose, and not just lose, but to lose in dramatic and tragicomic fashion, to the point where the suffering was expected, a ritual for anyone who dared to put their heart behind this star-crossed team. I doubt I'll remember any of the Red Sox twenty-first century championships in the way I remember October 1986, when Bob Stanley came in to replace Calvin Schiraldi in Game Six, and the Great Meltdown Unfairly Pegged to Bill Buckner began (I was at Amy Hanson's house in eighth grade, I think her parents were away, she had a small party; if the Hansons read this, please don't ground Amy). That kind of agony sticks with you much longer than the joy, and yet in 2013 the Red Sox managed to do something they'd not done since 1918, which was to win a Series at home. Fenway Park is a much different place than I remember it from my teenage years—there are seats atop the Green Monster, tickets cost as much as Cape vacations, and people are nice to one another in the bleachers. Satisfaction has now replaced anxiety; the whole thing is super-weird and foreign and a little unsettling to me. I'm far more comfortable when the Red Sox are in free fall. And yet, this night against St. Louis was something only a handful of living Bostonians could claim to have experienced, a World Series clincher at home, and the Sox made it easy, jumping out to an early lead and turning the evening off Landsdowne St. into a three-hour coronation. When it was over, there was no shock or sentimentality or even an impromptu throng in Kenmore Square. It was just . . . happiness. And history.

Doug Gottlieb

Broadcaster, CBS Sports

1988 World Series, Game Two, Oakland Athletics at Los Angeles Dodgers, Dodger Stadium, Los Angeles, California, October 16, 1988

My best friend growing up was Miles Simon, who played basketball at Arizona and won a national championship there. We had a friend who had season tickets for the Dodgers, and he went to Game One, while Miles and I went to Game Two. I remember watching Game One at Miles's house, and he turned to me and said Kirk Gibson was going to hit a home run. I looked at him and said he couldn't even walk, and of course, he hit a home run. That got us even more excited to go to Game Two the next night, when Orel Hershiser was pitching for the Dodgers. He was so completely and thoroughly dominant that night. I might be hokey this way, but I always try to take a message from big sporting events I've seen. The message here was that, despite what anyone says, there is a carryover from one game to the next. The A's went out there thinking they had no chance. They were facing the most dominant pitcher in baseball, and the night before, the most dominant closer in baseball had given up a game-winning home run. It was one of those things where they were playing, but the game was basically over before it even started. You couldn't help but get the idea that the Kirk Gibson home run, followed by Hershiser starting Game Two, completely deflated the A's.

1990 NCAA Men's Basketball Tournament First Round, Loyola Marymount vs. New Mexico State, Long Beach Arena, Long Beach, California, March 16, 1990

This was Loyola Marymount's first game after Hank Gathers passed away during the WCC semifinals. I was in eighth grade at the time, and the summer before, I had played in a pickup game at Cal State Northridge with Gathers. He was such an incredible specimen and looked like he was chiseled out of stone. There were a couple of Orange County guys on that team, and they were a cool story, with Bo Kimble and Gathers and the obscene number of points they scored every game. I was watching the game when Hank died. I actually had a friend who had died suddenly earlier that year, as well. So I went to the arena to watch them play. I'd been to that arena many times, since my dad had been an assistant at Long Beach State, and had seen it full, but not like it was this day. Everywhere you looked, there were signs for "Hank the Bank," which is what they called Gathers. Everything was adorned with 44s and LMU's colors of maroon and baby blue. When the Lions came out, there was a hum and a murmur through the crowd, and they ran up and down the floor as usual, making lots of shots. Then Bo Kimble got fouled and went to the line. He took a couple of dribbles with his right hand, then switched to his left hand. Not only did he switch to honor his friend Hank, but he made the free throw. Grown men and women started crying, and he pointed up to the sky. It was such an emotional moment. I've grown up around college basketball and will never forget what it was like to see that connection not just between a team and their fans, but maybe everyone's mortality, too. I've always loved the NCAA Tournament and have been to twenty Final Fours, but this moment was the coolest one of all of them.

USC at UCLA, Rose Bowl, Pasadena, California, November 23, 1996

USC scored midway through the fourth quarter to go up seventeen points, but UCLA came back to force the only overtime game ever between the two teams. The Rose Bowl is very difficult to get out of after a game, and my brother and sister, who had both gone to UCLA, were in town at the game, while I was in junior college after going to Notre Dame the year before. Our pregame drinks were starting to wear off, and we were getting a little tired and cranky and didn't feel like sitting in traffic. We were so disgusted with the way the Bruins were playing when they fell behind by seventeen, we decided to leave and didn't even think twice about it. When we got to the car, a cheer went up, and we figured USC had scored again. I didn't even turn on the radio in the car, drove an hour to get home, played basketball, and then turned on the TV after eating dinner, only to find out UCLA won the game in two overtimes. It was the first time in my life where I had been bitten by that bug to beat the traffic. Of course, I could have said I was at the comeback and that it was amazing.

2003 NBA Western Conference Finals, Game Six, San Antonio Spurs at Dallas Mavericks, American Airlines Center, Dallas, Texas, May 29, 2003

Tony Parker was in his second season that year, and at the time, there was talk about the Spurs either trading Parker or trading for Jason Kidd. So often, we focus on stars, and for good reason. Tim Duncan was incredible, but Steve Kerr won that game. He didn't play a minute in the first half, but at halftime, I was down near the court and saw him and Steve Smith come sprinting out of the tunnel, and they were clearly trying to get loose for the second half. Kerr came into the game late in the third quarter and a couple minutes in made his first shot—a three-pointer. He ended up making four threes and played flawless basketball. He didn't play a lot, but one of the greatest skills in sports is being able to sit on the bench for most of the game, and then come in and make a shot. That's talent and years of being able to groove your shot. The reason guys want to start isn't because they want to hear their name called, it is because you can get acclimated to the flow of the game easier. Coming off the bench, though, is hard, especially at the NBA level, when most of the players are used to being starters all their life. I marveled at this guy in his mid-30s coming in completely cold and dominating a game. I've asked Steve about it, and he said he didn't know the call was coming. He just went out there with Steve Smith to get ready in case it did.

2008 NCAA Men's Basketball Tournament Finals, Kansas vs. Memphis, Alamodome, San Antonio, Texas, April 7, 2008

I was working for ESPN at the time. It was a really close game, and Kansas coach Bill Self went to a triangle-and-two, which is guarding the best two players on the other team, while playing a zone and daring the other three players to shoot. So the Jayhawks were guarding Chris Douglas-Roberts and Derrick Rose man-to-man and weren't guarding the other players, but Memphis then goes and makes a bunch of shots. Guys that weren't shooters were making them pay. The two narratives in the game were John Calipari potentially winning his first national championship, while Bill Self couldn't win the big game (even though I thought he made the right call by going to the zone). As the game went on, though, when you looked at Memphis, they looked tired. The Final Four is a long weekend for the players, coming at the end of a four-week stretch filled with travel, practices, media sessions, and games, and there is never a time to catch your breath. That means the coaches need to be mindful of fatigue, and I remember watching the Memphis players at the free throw line and thinking that they were dead tired. Even though they were making shots and winning, they still looked like a fighter who was just about to tip over. Sure enough, Kansas makes a couple of plays, and Mario Chalmers sends the game into overtime after a couple of missed Memphis free throws. I just think it was mental fatigue. Calipari was telling his guys to foul in the backcourt, but they didn't. Kansas ran the same play they always ran in that spot, and almost screwed it up, but still came away with the game-tying three. Not only was Memphis exhausted, but the moment that ball went in, after they thought they had the game and the championship won, that game was over. The overtime was just a formality at that point.

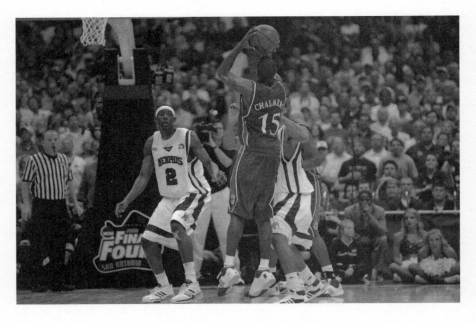

Mario Chalmers makes a three-pointer to send the 2008 NCAA title game into overtime. (AP Photo/Mark Humphrey)

Mike Greenberg

Broadcaster, ESPN

Indiana at Northwestern, Welsh-Ryan Arena, Evanston, Illinois, January 11, 1988

I went to Northwestern in the mid-'80s, and like everyone else, I supported the sports teams there. The football teams weren't very good, and I went to the games and rooted for them, but I really loved the basketball team. My roommates and I went to every game. One of the nice things about going to the games there was that our seats were directly behind the visitors' bench, so every time I've encountered Bob Knight or Gene Keady or Lou Henson or any of the Big Ten coaches who were there during those years, I've had to apologize to them for the things I screamed at them during those games.

Northwestern always played these great Big Ten teams tough but always lost. It was heartbreaking. They were a scrappy, hard-working team that was very easy to root for, and they always came up just short against teams that were clearly better than them. Indiana was the defending national champion, and this was the beginning of what ESPN called Big Monday, where every Big Ten team was guaranteed one home game on ESPN, and this was that night. It was a close, hard-fought game, but Northwestern finally won. I still remember one of our guards, Terry Buford, dribbling the clock out to close out a 66–64 win, and we just went crazy. I think my roommates and I were the first ones out on the floor as the crowed stormed the court. I was standing behind head coach Bill Foster as Dick Vitale was interviewing him after the game, and my roommate, Craig Isaacs, went over to the scorer's table and grabbed Dick's game notes . . . and still has them to this day. It was the most excited I've ever been to see a team win in my life. I've seen teams win more significant games, but I've never been happier to see a team win a game.

Super Bowl XXVII, Dallas Cowboys vs. Buffalo Bills, Rose Bowl, Pasadena, California, January 31, 1993

This was significant to me, because it was the first Super Bowl I ever attended. Like most people in my generation, I grew up with the Super Bowl being the biggest event of the year. I was covering the game for WSCR in Chicago, and it was the thrill of a lifetime. I was in Pasadena for the week and covered all of the events leading up to the game. Showing just how little I really know, I picked the Bills to win, saying that they had been in the Super Bowl the year before and had experience being there, while the Cowboys were this young, upstart team. Of course, Dallas ended up winning, 52–17.

There were a lot of memorable things about that game. The halftime show was Michael Jackson, and it was without question the greatest halftime show I've ever seen. The game also had the legendary Leon Lett play, where he was going in for what really would have been a meaningless touchdown after recovering a fumble, but Don Beebe came running up from behind him to knock the ball out of his hand before he scored in what was one of the greatest hustle plays ever. But what I remember most was the National Anthem, which was sung by Garth Brooks. A military flyover went by, the sun was just starting to set over the mountains in the distance, and I started to think about all of the times I watched the Super Bowl with my family and that I was finally at one. It really felt, more than anything in my life, that my dream of working in the sports business had really come true. I might not have wept, but I certainly had tears in my eyes as those planes went overhead. I've been to seventeen Super Bowls, and this one is still the most memorable experience I've had at any of them.

Minnesota Twins vs. Chicago White Sox, Ed Smith Stadium, Sarasota, Florida, March 14, 1994

When Michael Jordan left basketball after his father was tragically killed, he tried his hand at a baseball career with the Chicago White Sox and attended spring training in Sarasota, Florida. The radio station I was working for sent me to cover it, and I spent the entirety of spring training covering Michael Jordan, who was ultimately assigned to the team's AA affiliate in Birmingham, Alabama (where he was managed by future Red Sox and Indians manager Terry Francona).

The White Sox were a very good team at the time, with guys like Frank Thomas and Robin Ventura. I was a huge Jordan fan, especially after watching him succeed like he did in the NBA, and found it excruciating to watch him play baseball, because he struggled so mightily. I would sit in the press boxes in these tiny little stadiums as he traveled up and down the west coast of Florida, and I can't count how many times he would be playing the outfield and off the crack of the bat, he would be running in the wrong direction. It was just awful to watch, and I felt sick watching him. He was 0 for his first five games, just an incredibly long, depressing streak of hitless at-bats. Then, on a rainy night in Sarasota, when the rain was hard enough that most people assumed the game wouldn't be played, Jordan hit a little dribbler up the third base line and beat it out for his first hit. There couldn't have been more than a thousand people in the stands and only around five reporters in the press box. After the game, we went into the clubhouse to talk to him, and all of his teammates were giving him a beer shower in celebration, as though he had just won the World Series. After we were done, I started to leave, but something inside of me made me turn and look at him one more time, and he was sitting there covered in cheap beer, with just his pants on, no shirt, and a look of satisfaction and joy on his face that was the equivalent of anything I'd ever seen from him when he was a basketball player. I'd probably seen him more excited, but never more satisfied. That expression on his face has just stayed with me forever. I have endless and undying respect for Michael Jordan, and that night made me respect him even more, for some reason that I just can't put my finger on.

Chicago Bulls at New York Knicks, Madison Square Garden, New York, New York, March 28, 1995

I covered Michael Jordan through a good part of his early career, including the first three championships with the Bulls. When he came back after playing baseball, he was wearing number 45 instead of his famous 23 and didn't look quite himself, which made sense, since he rejoined the Bulls late in the regular season. He just looked a little rusty and a little off for the first few games, until he got to Madison Square Garden in the fifth game of his comeback to play the Knicks.

The Knicks and the Bulls had a great rivalry at the time, so the spotlight was really on him in his first game in New York. Of course, it ended up being the night that he scored 55 points and then won the game with a gorgeous pass to Bill Wennington for an uncontested dunk after taking an inbounds pass and having the entire Knicks team chase him before he passed to Wennington.

I remember walking in the media entrance, and a guy approached me and offered me $5,000 for my media pass. I was in the building for four of the six championships that Jordan won, yet Madison Square Garden that night, on that stage, was as electric as any of the nights he won a title. He might not have fully regained his form until the next season, when he would win another championship, but that was the night I knew he was back. I grew up in New York City and was a Knicks season ticket holder as a kid, and for me there is something different about Madison Square Garden than any other building, so for this to happen there just magnified it. Reasonable or not, it just made it feel bigger. That night, it felt like the biggest sporting event in the world.

Atlanta Falcons at New Orleans Saints, Louisiana Superdome, New Orleans, Louisiana, September 25, 2006

Sometime after the tragic events of Hurricane Katrina, my radio partner Mike Golic and I went to New Orleans. I remember walking around the city and having people come up to us and ask us to tell everyone during our shows how great they were doing and how great the city was doing. Only the city didn't look great; it was like a million bombs had gone off. Then, the Saints came back, and we went back again for their first game back in the Superdome, which was on a Monday night. Since ESPN does Monday Night Football, it was a huge event for us as a company, and they sent Mike and me down to do our show from there. At the game, U2 and Green Day came out to perform. Steve Gleason blocked a punt that turned into a touchdown to beat the Falcons, a play that has been immortalized with a statue in front of the stadium. Out of all of the sporting events I've been to, I've never been in a stadium that was louder than the Superdome that night.

Mike Hill

Broadcaster, FOX Sports

1999 AFC Wild Card Playoffs, Buffalo Bills at Tennessee Titans, Adelphia Coliseum, Nashville, Tennessee, January 8, 2000

I was working for WKRN in Nashville, and it was my first chance to cover an NFL team, and it ended up being a new team (they changed their name from the Oilers to the Titans starting with the 1999 season) in a new stadium that went on one of those magical runs. I remember how quiet the stadium, which was one of the loudest in the league at the time, got after Buffalo scored to take the lead with just a few seconds to go in the game. I was on the sideline behind the Titans bench and was looking up at the Jumbotron as the Titans received the kickoff and the play developed. After Frank Wycheck lateraled to Kevin Dyson, from that sideline, you could see that the Bills were fooled and Dyson was in the clear. If you took a wide-angle shot of that stadium from up high, you could see me running down the sideline, cheering Dyson as he scored. The stadium just erupted to epic proportions. Of course, they first had to review the play to make sure the lateral was legal. When the referee went under the replay hood, I remember telling my friends that I didn't care if it was a legal lateral or not. Today, it was going to be a lateral because if it wasn't, the refs might not have gotten out of the building with their lives. It was really intense while everyone waited, and the booth was right up against the stands, where there were people sitting wearing hunting gear, yelling to the ref that he better get it right. It was so close that I just don't think they had any choice but to let it stand.

Super Bowl XXXIV, St. Louis Rams vs. Tennessee Titans, Georgia Dome, Atlanta, Georgia, January 30, 2000

The game was kind of boring for the first three quarters. As I headed down from my seat up high in the Georgia Dome to the field, the Titans scored on an Al Del Greco field goal to tie the game. Then Kurt Warner answered on the Rams' first play from scrimmage with a bomb to Isaac Bruce to regain the lead. I was en route to the field, so I missed both of those scores. They wouldn't let any media on the field until the game was over, so I watched the final drive of the game with a few dozen media members on a TV monitor in the tunnel leading to the field. After the Titans were stopped on the final play of the game, I went into the team's locker room, and it felt like a morgue. The team was devastated, and I'll never forget the looks on the faces of guys like Frank Wycheck or Kevin Dyson, who stretched out on that last play but was stopped just short of the end zone. To see a team that you covered all year long come up one yard short of possibly winning the Super Bowl, it actually still hurts to this day, even though I'm not a Titans fan.

Mike Jones tackles Kevin Dyson just before the goal line on final play of Super Bowl XXXIV. (AP Photo/Kevin Terrell)

2000 World Series, New York Mets vs. New York Yankees, Shea Stadium, Flushing, New York, and Yankee Stadium, Bronx, New York, October 21-26, 2000

It was my first year working in New York for FOX Sports New York and MSG Network. I grew up across the street from the old Yankee Stadium on 158th Street and Gerard Avenue, so to be in New York, covering the team for the first time as they played in the World Series, was an unbelievable thrill. What made it even more memorable, of course, is that it was against the crosstown, hated rival Mets. I remember the city being electric—everyone was so hardcore about the Series starting. At Game One, the atmosphere was incredibly tense, and there were so many unforgettable moments throughout the entire series, from Timo Perez being thrown out at home to Roger Clemens throwing the bat at Mike Piazza to Derek Jeter's heroics. At the Series clincher, which was Game Five at Shea Stadium, I was sitting up in the grandstand above home plate in the media area. When Piazza made the final out, I could see Mariano Rivera's face on the mound. For a split second, he thought he had given up a game-tying home run on the pitch. Then the celebration started, and I got the chance to be on the field during it while doing interviews. To be down there with my favorite team of any sport, it was a magical moment for me.

Seattle SuperSonics at New York Knicks, Madison Square Garden, New York, New York, February 27, 2001

I didn't get a chance to cover Patrick Ewing while he played for the Knicks but did get to cover the game in which he made his return to Madison Square Garden after being traded to Seattle. I had always heard how Patrick could be belligerent or ornery with the media. He never brought a championship to New York, and the fans would get on him at times because of that, but I still think he is the greatest Knick of all time. When he came back with the Sonics, it looked so weird, but it was the first time I had ever gotten to see him in person. The ovation he got from the fans that night, even while wearing that other uniform, was amazing. He only scored 12 points, but just him coming back onto that court at the Garden, and that ovation he got, was unforgettable.

Bernard Hopkins vs. Felix Trinidad, Madison Square Garden, New York, New York, September 29, 2001

I had a chance to interview Bernard Hopkins ahead of the fight and liked him after talking to him. His backstory really was amazing. I went to the fight as a fan, not a member of the media, and will never forget how divided the arena was that night. The Puerto Rican fans of Felix Trinidad outnumbered the African-American fans of Hopkins probably around 80–20, and sitting there in the arena, I was a little nervous. I remember seeing at least ten fights in the crowd. There were actually better fights outside of the ring than inside it, and they were right down racial lines. I was there to cheer for Hopkins, who would pull off an incredible upset, but I don't think I stood up and cheered once the entire night. The night wasn't necessarily memorable for the most positive of reasons, but it was definitely unforgettable. I grew up in the Bronx, but I was very afraid that night in midtown Manhattan.

E.J. Hradek

Broadcaster, NHL Network

1977 World Series, Game Six, Los Angeles Dodgers at New York Yankees, Yankee Stadium, Bronx, New York, October 18, 1977

I was seventeen years old and sitting in the bleachers at the old Yankee Stadium, and being a huge Yankee fan, it was exciting to be there. I camped out overnight outside the stadium to get the tickets, so just getting the tickets was a memorable experience. The Yankees hadn't won a World Series since before I was old enough to understand and were swept the season before by the Reds, so it was an exciting time for Yankees fans. Reggie had hit his first two homers, and when he hit the third homer off of Charlie Hough, from my spot in the right field bleachers, the ball looked like it went straight up in the air. It wasn't one of those that, from our angle, we knew was gone. It just went high in the air, and when it reached its highest point, it just took off. Maybe it was the spin of the ball after hitting a knuckleball, but it landed in the old black area at Yankee Stadium, where not many homers went. Only a few minutes later, the Yankees won the game and the World Series, which was another emotional release. I've experienced a lot of events while in the media, but I think it is a lot more fun to be there as a fan, when you can just let it out and have that emotional tie to it.

1980 Stanley Cup Finals, Game Six, Philadelphia Flyers at New York Islanders, Nassau Coliseum, Uniondale, New York, May 24, 1980

It was an afternoon game on a warm May day, and I scalped a ticket for $75 to get in, which was basically all the money I had at the time. I had gone to all of the Islanders' home playoff games that season except one, and there was no way I was going to miss a potential Stanley Cup-clincher. I was sitting about halfway up the upper bowl behind the net in which the Islanders would eventually score the winning goal. The Islanders led, 4–2, but gave up two late goals, and the game went to overtime. Obviously, everybody was on pins and needles, because the Islanders were a team that had teased their fans for so long and had a disappointing loss in the playoffs to the Rangers the year before, so blowing that lead caused a lot of tension for the fans. I don't think anybody was really eager to have to play the Flyers in a Game Seven. I remember the play unfolding in overtime, and Bobby Nystrom was able to get his stick on a pass and deflect it past Flyers goalie Pete Peeters. It was absolute pandemonium in the building after the goal. Security wasn't quite what it is today, so the place went bonkers, and fans were leaping over the glass and running out onto the ice. Then they brought the Cup out, and, also unlike today, there wasn't the pomp and circumstance of an announcement and presentation. It just came out of the tunnel and you could see it on the ice, and the next thing you knew, Islanders captain Denis Potvin was skating around with it. At that time, the Rangers were the big team in the New York area but hadn't won a Cup since 1940, so for the Islanders to win one in just their eighth season was unbelievable. It was a crazy party, and I couldn't speak for a couple of days after from yelling so much.

1996 NFC Championship Game, Carolina Panthers at Green Bay Packers, Lambeau Field, Green Bay, Wisconsin, January 12, 1997

I grew up a Green Bay Packers fan, even though I lived in New York. I was a kid during the Vince Lombardi era, so some of the first games I saw on television were big Packers games, including the Ice Bowl. I had never been to Lambeau Field, though, until this game. The Packers had been so bad for so long to this point that I couldn't have imagined them playing for a spot in the Super Bowl. I ended up getting tickets to the game and went with a friend of mine. On the day before the game, when we got to Green Bay, we drove over to Lambeau and got out of our car and got on our knees in the parking lot in front of the hallowed stadium. Before the game, they had a video of Reggie White saying "Amazing Grace," and it stuck with me how different the atmosphere was at a game there. We were sitting near one of the goal lines and I remember Dorsey Levens catching a pass right in front of us for a touchdown, which was great. Usually at an NFL game, you'll see a number of fans from the other team, but there weren't many Panthers fans that day. I might have seen just one guy in a Carolina jersey. That's it. Just one. He didn't get too many chances to get very excited, though. But even though he was a Panthers fan, unlike in most other cities, the Green Bay fans actually embraced him being there and didn't pick on him, showing just how different it is to go to a game there.

2001 World Series, Games Four and Five, Arizona Diamondbacks at New York Yankees, Yankee Stadium, Bronx, New York, October 31 and November 1, 2001

I was at both games as a fan, and it is impossible to separate them because of how similar they were. It was in the aftermath of 9/11, and I had been in Manhattan that morning; I got through the Lincoln Tunnel around 8:45, and one of the buildings had already been hit. I think this World Series resonated with me even more, because I'm a New Yorker and was there when it happened. Less than two months after 9/11, New York was hosting the World Series, and, like most New Yorkers, my emotions were frayed. Just the littlest thing could get you teary-eyed. They brought out Ronan Tynan to sing "God Bless America" during the seventh-inning stretch, which was emotional, but you went from crying at the song to saying, "We need a hit!" because they were losing. Tino Martinez homered off of Byung-Hyun Kim in the bottom of the ninth to tie the game, and everyone was just emotionally spent. There was just so much more to it than the game, given the circumstances. For that game, I was sitting in the upper deck behind home plate, which is a place I love to sit. The next night, for Game Five, I was sitting down the first base line and was with a very close friend of mine and my mom. And again, the same thing happened. The Diamondbacks brought Kim in for the ninth inning again, which we couldn't believe after he gave up the homer to Martinez the night before. This time, it was Scott Brosius who homered, and I remember almost crushing my mother when we were jumping up and down and hugging. For all of this to happen in New York, just weeks after 9/11, was so emotional.

2002 Winter Olympics, Men's Ice Hockey Finals, United States vs. Canada, E Center, Salt Lake City, Utah, February 24, 2002

I covered the Olympic hockey tournament in 2002 in Salt Lake, and when you are covering the Olympics, you are completely immersed for two weeks.

Over the course of time, I ended up having a lot of conversations with Herb Brooks, who was coaching Team USA that year. It was really special for me, because, being an American hockey fan who watched the Miracle on Ice in 1980, he held a special place in my sports heart, to the point where my first son is named Brooks. The Americans made it to the gold medal game, where they faced Canada, which hadn't won Olympic gold since 1952. The Americans, though, had won the last two Olympics on home soil, in 1980 and 1960. Canada ended up winning the game, and it was a fun game to watch that was close for a while. The moment for me, though, and I think it might be my most memorable in my career, was seeing Brooks afterwards. I went over to him to thank him for his time during the tournament. He would just sit and engage us and talk hockey throughout the two weeks. I thanked him for that and congratulated him on winning silver, and he turned to me and thanked me for the questions that I asked, and told me how much he enjoyed talking with me. At that point, I almost fell over, because here was Herb Brooks complimenting me. It is a moment I'll always treasure because of how much I love the game. I had always meant to make my way up to Minnesota and meet him for lunch one day and talk, but sadly, he passed away in a car accident before I had the chance. My son was born right around the time of his passing, which is why we named him Brooks.

Jerry Izenberg

Columnist, *Newark Star-Ledger*

Elected to National Sports Media Association Hall of Fame, 2000

1970 NBA Finals, Game Seven, Los Angeles Lakers at New York Knicks, Madison Square Garden, New York, New York, May 8, 1970

The Knicks had starved for a championship for so long and were still looking for their first one despite being an original NBA team. Willis Reed hurt his leg in Game Five of the series and flew with the team from New York to Los Angeles in the hopes of playing in Game Six. They tried everything they could to get him healthy enough to play but weren't able to, so they put him on a plane home so that he could try and get ready for Game Seven. It was a muscle injury, and by the time he got back to New York, his leg hurt so badly after the long flight that he almost crawled off the plane. I got to the arena early for the game, and the Lakers were out on the floor shooting around. Wilt Chamberlain came over to me to ask if Willis was going to play, and I told him that if anyone was capable of playing, it was Willis, but I don't think he'll be able to.

During warmups, Chamberlain kept looking over at the Knicks, and there was no Willis. Just before the pregame horn blew to end warmups, here comes Willis limping out of the tunnel to the floor. The Lakers heard the roar and didn't want to look, except for Wilt, who stood there with his hands on his hips. He watched Reed walk all the way out of the tunnel onto the court and over to the bench. Right at the start of the game, the Lakers were shooting a free throw, and Knicks coach Red Holzman tried to get Reed away from the lane and the collision that was going on for the rebound, but he stayed there and banged away and got the rebound. He passed the ball, got it back, and made his little soft jumper. It was like V-J Day, and I swear I could see the roof bouncing up and down. In the second half, he finishes the job. He would lean on Chamberlain, more to help himself stay up than move Chamberlain away. Willis just kept leaning and leaning, and Wilt looks over his shoulder, because you knew when he got the ball, he was going to shoot. He took one look at Willis's face, and when he did, Walt Frazier ducked in and stole the ball. Reed went down again, and his courage being out on the court in so much pain just captured me.

1973 Belmont Stakes, Belmont Park, Elmont, New York, June 9, 1973

Secretariat is one of my favorite athletes of all time. I really loved that horse. There hadn't been a Triple Crown winner since Citation in 1948. Belmont was packed, it was hot, and there was a feeling of rain in the air. Secretariat's big rival in the Triple Crown races was Sham, who had finished ahead of Secretariat at the Wood Memorial earlier that year (although both horses finished behind the winner, Angle Light). Right at the start of the race, though, he destroyed Sham. Belmont is one of the biggest racetracks in the world, as well as one of the widest; you can get lost on the track, and jockeys who didn't ride it much did get lost, thinking they were at the three-quarter pole when they weren't. After the first turn, Secretariat just took off. I turned to the late Bob Hardy and said I thought the horse was going to break down. He agreed, because we had never seen a horse take off like that. In the owner's box, trainer Lucien Laurin was screaming for someone to stop jockey Ron Turcotte and slow the horse down before he killed him. Secretariat kept getting farther and farther ahead, and when they started coming down the stretch, Turcotte was getting upset because he couldn't hear anything behind him. He started to see something on his left, and he looked over, and it was Secretariat's shadow. Turcotte then committed the cardinal sin, which is turning around in the saddle, but when he looked back, he couldn't see the rest of the field. Secretariat was in a world of his own, and as they went down the stretch, Turcotte looked up and said, "God, just don't let me fall off this horse." Later that day in the press conference, the first thing Turcotte said to me was, "I wasn't a jockey. I was a passenger."

Muhammad Ali vs. Joe Frazier, Araneta Coliseum, Quezon City, Philippines, October 1, 1975

I had a lot invested in this fight, because both Muhammad Ali and Joe Frazier are friends of mine; Ali is probably one of my five closest friends in the world. By the time the fight arrived in Manila, nobody thought Frazier could fight any more. I actually thought he was going to win, though. A couple of months before the fight, Frazier's trainers knew they needed to teach Frazier how to throw rights, since he almost always threw lefts. I didn't even think he could tie his shoes with his right hand. It was a steaming hot day, with no air conditioning in the arena. Once they turned on the television lights, it had to be 110 degrees. The fight started, and Ali was pop, pop, pop while Frazier was plod, plod, plod. Frazier's legs were getting wobbly and it looked like he was going to go down, and this went on for two or three rounds. Then in the fifth round, Frazier hit Ali with a right hand. It wasn't the Hammer of Thor, but it was a good punch. Ali looked at him and started saying, "You ain't got no right hand." Frazier told him to go ask his trainer, George Benton, about it, and then hit him with another right. The fight turned on that, and now Frazier is in command. I can see it like it was yesterday. The reason that it was the greatest, most barbaric, and most emotional heavyweight fight I've ever seen was because the ebb and flow of the fight was so up and down. Ali was ahead, then Frazier was ahead, then Ali, then Frazier. It was anybody's fight.

I always keep my own scorecard, and I had a draw going into what would have been the 15th round but knew the fight had to stop. I was sitting next to the late Jerry Lisker, who was the sports editor of the (New York) *Post*, and Frazier was standing there with his hands at his sides and his legs looking like wet spaghetti. All Ali had to do was go three feet and push him, and the fight would be over, but Ali could not go the three feet. I turned to Jerry and told him that it didn't matter who won the fight, they had to stop it. Then all hell broke loose. Maybe it was God that decided the fight, maybe it was genetics. Frazier was a small man compared to Ali, and his eyes were closing. His whole fight was spent in a crouch, and he had to straighten up to see Ali. That is when Ali really hurt him. Before the 15th, Eddie Futch turned to Benton and told him to cut off Frazier's gloves. Frazier said that if they did that, he wouldn't speak to either one of them again. At the same time, Ali is in his corner sprawled out in his stool trying to get up the energy to go out for the last round. But Benton cut off the gloves, and I was told later by Futch that he told Frazier that his eyes were too important and this was just another fight. When they were announcing the winner, Ali fell to the floor, and there is always going to be a debate about why. These were two beaten fighters, and I'll always remember Ali coming over and leaning out to us and saying, "Fellas, that is the closest you'll come to watching death." You just don't forget a fight like that.

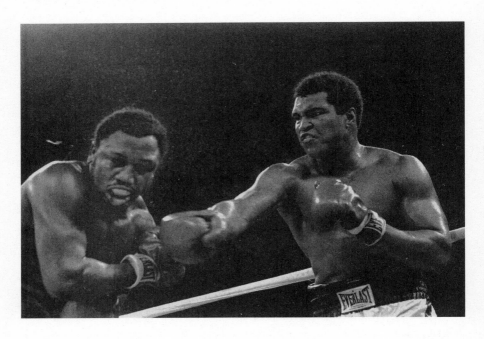

Spray flies from the head of Joe Frazier as heavyweight champion Muhammad Ali connects with a right in the ninth round of the "Thrilla in Manila." (AP Photo/ Mitsunori Chigita)

1984 Summer Olympics, Greco-Roman Super Heavyweight Final, Anaheim Convention Center, Anaheim, California, August 2, 1984

I know as much about Greco-Roman wrestling as I do about the tea ceremony. While I was in Los Angeles for the Olympics, someone told me the best story of the games was going to be Jeff Blatnick, although I had no idea who he was. He had beaten Hodgkin's lymphoma to make the team, so I realized I needed to go check it out. I met with him, and he told me about how he found out he was sick, and that the doctor told him he could beat it, but that there was no chance he could compete at the Olympics because he wouldn't have the strength to compete after going through the treatment. He vowed to his parents that he wouldn't just wrestle in the Olympics but would win win gold. He moved out of his house into a YMCA so that he could focus on beating the disease and training for Los Angeles.

That is exactly what happened. After he won the gold, he celebrated by running around with the American flag and the flag of his hometown. It was a great moment, but just one year later, the cancer came back. Of course, he beat it again. His wrestling career was over, but he triumphed over everything that touched him before he eventually passed away in 2012 from complications related to heart surgery.

2001 World Series, Game Seven, New York Yankees at Arizona Diamondbacks, Bank One Ballpark, Phoenix, Arizona, November 4, 2001

This was more about the setting than it was the about being the seventh game of the World Series. It was in Arizona, but there were plenty of Yankees fans there, as there are across the country. Usually Yankees fans are hated by opposing fans, but they weren't on this night. It didn't matter where the Yankees went after 9/11, the opposing fans would stand up and cheer them, and that is really what motivated everybody. I had bought an FDNY hat and was wearing it while having breakfast one morning in Arizona, and three people came over to me thinking I was in the fire department to thank me for what we had done. Wearing the hat was my way of showing my appreciation for them. That is how much everyone was aware of what was happening in New York. For the Diamondbacks, though, it meant that they weren't even the sentimental favorites in their hometown.

Then, baseball took over, and this is what the seventh game of the World Series is supposed to be. It was Roger Clemens against Curt Schilling, and they owned the game. The Yankees were ahead late, when all of a sudden, it started to rain in the desert. It was like God decided to give everyone a little more background to remember the night. By the ninth inning, the pitching matchup had become Randy Johnson against Mariano Rivera. It felt like I was back at Ali-Frazier, with two guys who always refused to lose. The Diamondbacks scored two runs against Rivera in the bottom of the ninth, which was remarkable because he was so unhittable in the postseason, to win the game and the series. After the game, when the players were talking out on the field, you could sense that they were saying to one another that the series was so good and the events of the world were so big that it didn't really matter which team won.

Dave Kindred

Columnist

Recipient of Basketball Hall of Fame's Curt Gowdy Award, 2000
Elected to National Sports Media Association Hall of Fame, 2007

The 1967 Masters, Third Round, Augusta National Golf Club, Augusta, Georgia, April 8, 1967

My first Masters was in 1967, and I've been to every one since except for 1986 when Jack Nicklaus won (because my son got married that weekend). In 1967, I went to Augusta with two goals in mind—to see Ben Hogan hit golf balls and see Red Smith type. I checked in at the press center, and after they gave me my credential, I asked where Smith was. They pointed him out to me, and I stood at the back of the room and watched him type. Then I went out and watched Hogan hit balls on the range. I thought Hogan's hands were thick and strong and reminded me of my father's hands. Hogan was fifty-four, and Saturday, he shot 36 on the front and 30 on the back for a 66. As he is making birdies on the back nine, we decided we needed to go watch this. At that time, they had a standing bleacher on the 18th green, where you could look down on the green. Hogan was there and had to make a putt for 30 on the back—it was about eighteen to twenty feet downhill. I can still see him standing there. The yips were there, and it was almost like he was afraid to hit the putt. He finally touches it, and it rolls down the hill and in for the 30. What I remember most about that day is that Hogan came into the room where the players changed shoes and was sitting on a window seat, his back to a window that has a white lace curtain on it. The sun was coming through that curtain, and it looked like a halo around Hogan's head. He was as happy as he would allow anyone to see him. He didn't think he could do much on Sunday, because he was aching and tired and had limped his way around the course while shooting the 66. I don't remember anything he said, but while we were all asking him questions, sitting in one of the seats behind us was Arnold Palmer, who, like all of us, understood that he was sitting in the presence of something majestic. Twenty years later, on Wednesday of Masters Week, I needed to write a story and decided to write about the twentieth anniversary of that round. A few weeks later, I got a letter in the mail from Fort Worth with Ben Hogan's name on the back of the envelope. In the letter, he thanked me for writing about the round and bringing back all of the great memories. I told my wife about the letter, and her reply was "Who's Ben Hogan?" I told her it was like getting a letter from God. I have saved that letter ever since.

Muhammad Ali vs. Joe Frazier, Madison Square Garden, New York, New York, March 8, 1971

My first real newspaper job was in Louisville at the *Courier-Journal* in 1966. Muhammad Ali was already the world champion and came back to Louisville. I was a kid writing headlines and little stories that we were slipping into the sports section, and someone told me that Cassius Clay was in town and I needed to go find him (the Louisville paper still called him Clay). It wasn't hard to find him, and I would end up spending the day with him. My four-year-old son was with me and Ali carried him around to all of his boyhood haunts, and I wrote a story about it and have been writing about him ever since. I went to seventeen of his fights and did a dual biography of him and Howard Cosell called *Sound and Fury*. I didn't see him fight in person, though, until his comeback fight against Jerry Quarry. The Frazier fight was the third after his return and was billed as "The Fight of the Century." It was the greatest event that I have ever seen. One thing I learned in covering a lot of boxing is that it is hard to watch both fighters, because you are emotionally invested in one of them. Ali held all of my emotions at the time; I was still relatively young and came through the '60s as a liberal and was always on Ali's side on almost every issue. He was also the greatest athlete I've ever seen or ever will see. So all I see at that fight is Muhammad Ali. I sat at ringside and remember early in the fight, he was back against the ropes and looked down at me. I don't think he was specifically looking at me, but we definitely made eye contact, and while Frazier is pounding on him, he is leaning over the ropes shouting to the people in the first row, saying, "No contest!" That is when he gave up rounds that he later regretted giving up. Because you can only see one guy in the ring, I thought Ali won the fight, even when he was knocked down in the 15th round, which was stunning. I didn't count that as much of anything, but now it is one of the great moments in fight history. The whole thing was so stunning to me that, even though I was on deadline, I couldn't write. Fortunately, I was writing that story for the *Louisville Times*, which was an afternoon paper, so I had all night to finish it.

1973 Belmont Stakes, Belmont Park, Elmont, New York, June 9, 1973

I was actually a political writer for the *Courier-Journal* at the time. The paper would send a writer to Washington for a year, then you'd come back and do your old job. I had been a sports columnist, but wasn't sure I wanted to do that forever, and loved politics. I went to Washington for a year, and, coincidentally, at the end of that year was the Belmont. I didn't see the Kentucky Derby or the Preakness but went to the Belmont because I was the closest writer to New York from the paper. It was the most amazing thing I've ever seen. Secretariat was coming down the stretch, and he was five lengths ahead. Then he was ten lengths ahead, then twenty lengths, then thirty. He became the first Triple Crown winner since Citation, and there was never a doubt whether he would win that day. It was as if all of the other horses were running uphill while he was running downhill. I was standing beside Joe Falls, who was a columnist at the *Detroit News*, and as Secretariat reached the finish line, Falls nudges me and says, "Citation, my ass." It was one of those surreal

Jockey Ron Turcotte turns and looks at the field racing behind Secretariat in the 1973 Belmont Stakes. (AP Photo/Dave Pickoff)

moments, like a team winning the World Series in four games by 14–0 scores in each game—an otherworldly experience that didn't seem possible.

1976 Daytona 500, Daytona International Speedway, Daytona Beach, Florida, February 15, 1976

Richard Petty and David Pearson were the Ali and Frazier of stock car racing. They were the two best drivers at that time. The Daytona 500 was still a relatively young event, and I went every year because I wanted to. I liked racing and the people. Petty was as personable a guy as you could ever want to meet, while Pearson was more of a salt of the earth, down-home country guy. Petty was more popular among the fans, although everybody liked them both. This ended up being the greatest finish to any sports event I've ever seen. After almost 500 miles, it was down to the final mile, when Pearson passes Petty on the backstretch and goes under him into the third turn. The two cars were basically side-by-side, with Petty outside Pearson. Pearson ends up in front and Petty's only chance to win—and what makes this a moment is that everyone knows what he is going to do—is to go under him. If Petty went under Pearson going into the fourth turn, though, physics wouldn't allow him to stay on the bottom of the track. He was going so fast that the car was going to move up the track, and that would make him hit Pearson. So you know he is going to go low, and that physics won't allow it. So you know they are going to collide. That is exactly what happens as they come out of the fourth turn, and they both go spinning into the infield grass. Pearson had the wherewithal to push in his clutch and kept the engine running, while Petty didn't and crossed the finish line going around 15 miles per hour. I remember Petty coming into the press area after the race and saying, "Well, this assures that we'll have 100,000 people here next year."

1991 World Series, Game Seven, Atlanta Braves at Minnesota Twins, Hubert H. Humphrey Metrodome, Minneapolis, Minnesota, October 27, 1991

I was working for the *Atlanta Journal-Constitution*, and thought and wrote that this was the best World Series of all time. Five games were decided by one run, four games were decided in the last at-bat, and three of the games went to extra innings, including Games Six and Seven. The home game won every game in the series, and there was tension the entire time. Kirby Puckett won Game Six with a home run, and Bobby Cox walked him every time he could after that, because he wasn't going to let the other team's best hitter beat them. The series ended with Jack Morris pitching one of the great games in baseball history and Dan Gladden scoring in the bottom of the 10th to win it. I hated the Metrodome because it was so loud, and it was never louder than after that win. I was intimately involved with the Atlanta organization and knew how it had been shaped and formed by Stan Kasten and Bobby Cox, so I was very much a hometown columnist, but for seven games, you couldn't get better baseball.

Andrea Kremer

Broadcaster, HBO/NFL Network/CBS Sports

1980 NFC Championship Game, Dallas Cowboys at Philadelphia Eagles, Veterans Stadium, Philadelphia, Pennsylvania, January 11, 1981

My family had season tickets to the Eagles from the year Veterans Stadium opened, so I'd been going to games there my whole life. My dad's best friend was from Dallas and was a huge Cowboys fan. Every year, when the Cowboys and Eagles would play, he would come up for the game but was smart enough to always be very reserved in the stands. It ended up being a dominant Eagles win, and I remember the euphoria of the idea of the Eagles finally going to the Super Bowl. I was there as a real fan, which I don't get to do any more. Even my dad's friend was happy for us, since we had waited so long to get to the Super Bowl.

1992 NBA Finals, Game One, Portland Trail Blazers at Chicago Bulls, Chicago Stadium, Chicago, Illinois, June 3, 1992

When I first started with ESPN, I was based in Chicago and covered Michael Jordan a lot. I ended up covering all six of his championships. We've all seen Jordan take over games, but something felt different that night. His shot was dropping, which wasn't a surprise, but he wasn't a three-point shooter. But he starts hitting these threes, and he keeps making them. It was as though someone took an electrical cord and plugged it into the socket, and the electricity was beamed around the entire arena. That is what it was like in that building. Not only are you seeing something that you've never seen before, but you got to see what it was like when someone was in the zone. That is what it was like. You felt like every time he had the ball and shot from three, he was going to make it. He made six of them in the first half. There are a number of famous shots of Jordan from his career, but the shrug might be the best of them all. It was almost like he was saying, "Even I have no clue what is going on here." I was sitting right behind the basket when the Bulls played the Lakers in the Finals and he made the layup where he switched hands in midair, and it felt like we had just seen a man fly. We were used to seeing Jordan do incredible things. But the ability to hit shot after shot, especially when that shot wasn't his forte, was just amazing.

Miami Dolphins at Philadelphia Eagles, Veterans Stadium, Philadelphia, Pennsylvania, November 14, 1993

I grew up in Philadelphia, but my favorite team was the Miami Dolphins. I was so into them that when Bob Griese broke his leg during the 1972 season, I sent Don Shula a letter saying how sorry I was about it. He sent back an autographed picture, which I put up on my wall. Fast forward to my career, where I had the chance to cover the Dolphins a lot and got to know him a bit. I actually brought the picture with me to a practice one day to show him and said, "I'll bet you didn't really sign that picture." He pulled out a piece of paper and signed it, and the autographs matched. He really did sign it. Over the years, I got to know his entire family, which was special because he was an idol of mine growing up, but I've always tried to comport myself with the utmost sense of professionalism and propriety, so I never really let any of that on. When Shula was in the position to win his 325th game and pass George Halas to become the most winning coach in history, the game was in my hometown of Philadelphia. I went to countless games at the Vet, but this one was different, because it was my hometown team, my father was in the stands, Shula won the game and they carried him off, and it was as if all of my worlds had come together—football, family, the Eagles, the Dolphins, Coach Shula. When you are a kid growing up, you never think in a zillion years that you are going to cover the team you grew up loving, and this is where it all came together.

2008 Summer Olympics, Men's 4x100 Meter Medley Finals, Beijing National Aquatics Center, Beijing, China, August 17, 2008

The morning of the event, when I was getting ready after waking up, I remember thinking to myself that I could be a tiny part of history that day. I was going to be on the pool deck, feet from where Michael Phelps was going to get out after having potentially accomplished the momentous event of winning his eighth gold medal of the 2008 Olympics. The race was far from the most exciting one of the eight—that one was the seventh race, when he won the 100-meter butterfly by one hundredth of a second. That one was a better story, but winning number eight in the 4x100 medley relay was more historic. When you are at the

Michael Phelps holds up his eighth gold medal after the men's 4x100-meter medley relay final at the 2008 Olympics. (AP Photo/Mark J. Terrill)

race, you aren't a fan because you are working, but you can't help but marvel at the athletic accomplishment. You literally are seeing something that no one has ever seen before and that no one may ever see again. You see how Michael reacted and how his teammates reacted. You didn't need to be a fan of America or swimming; if you were a fan of sports, you had to marvel at the accomplishment. Without any hyperbole, in my opinion, there have been few places that were more electric, exciting, historic, or monumental to be than on the pool deck at the Beijing Olympics. It was, by far, the top moment of my career.

Super Bowl XLIII, Pittsburgh Steelers vs. Arizona Cardinals, Raymond James Stadium, Tampa, Florida, February 1, 2009

There were two transcendent plays in the game. First was the James Harrison interception return for a touchdown at the end of the first half, when it seemed like the half was over and everyone was going to head to the locker room and get ready for the Bruce Springsteen halftime show. We were getting ready for halftime interviews, and then all of a sudden, this play comes out of nowhere. Then there was the Santonio Holmes game-winning touchdown catch, which was one of the greatest catches ever. When they went to look at the replay to make sure he caught the ball, you couldn't help but think that there was no way in the world that any referee was going to overturn that call unless there was something so blatant that they had no choice.

Keith Law

Writer, ESPN.com

Cleveland Indians at New York Yankees, Yankee Stadium, Bronx, New York, September 4, 1993

It was right before my senior year of college, and most of my friends had gone back to school. My mom wanted us to do one big family thing before I left, so she got us all tickets to a Yankees game. It was a gray day, and there weren't a lot of people in the stadium. Jim Abbott started for the Yankees and wasn't that great through the first three innings. He was still Jim Abbott and was famous for obvious reasons, but he was past his peak at this point. After the third, though, I remember looking up at the scoreboard and noticing he hadn't given up a hit but also knew he had thrown a lot of pitches already. Then, he started rolling, and it started to become evident that something was happening. I'm not a believer that you knew someone was going to throw a no-hitter that day, but he was clearly having a pretty good day. He was starting to throw more strikes, and Cleveland players were not making good contact. None of us were saying anything about it, though. In the late innings, there was a dad in front of us who told his son that Abbott was pitching a no-hitter, and we all yelled at him to not talk about it. I mock that superstition now but believed it back then. The last few outs were electric. It was one of the few times I've been in a baseball stadium where the crowd wasn't made up of individuals but were all together as one unit. It was an amazing feeling that I always hope I'll get again at a ballpark. I'm not usually at the stadium as a fan, but if there is a chance I'm going to see a no-hitter, I'm rooting for a no-hitter. I want that feeling again. They say there is no cheering in the press box, but the guy who said that is dead, and I'll cheer in the press box for something like that.

Arizona Diamondbacks at Pittsburgh Pirates, Three Rivers Stadium, Pittsburgh, Pennsylvania, September 3, 1998

When I was a grad student in Pittsburgh, I used to skip class sometimes and go to Three Rivers Stadium to see the Pirates play. They weren't very good and the crowds were usually small, so it was easy to get tickets at the last minute. One afternoon, I went to this game, and the pitching matchup was Francisco Cordova against Brian Anderson, and the game was played in two hours with a 1–0 final score. I basically had a section in the mezzanine entirely to myself. Neither team was great, but both pitchers were really on that day and threw a ton of strikes. A minor defensive miscue by a Pirate infielder led to the game's only run; otherwise, it probably would have gone into extra innings as a scoreless game. I wish all games were like this. It was fun, it was nice out, everyone there was into the game, and it was quick and crisp, with just that one mistake in the entire game. That is my kind of game.

Detroit Tigers at Toronto Blue Jays, SkyDome, Toronto, Canada, September 6, 2003

Roy Halladay threw 99 pitches in the single best-pitched game I've ever seen. I've always been a fan of the well-pitched game, but this was the best individual performance I've been to. Halladay was completing overmatching the Tigers and took a no-hitter into the eighth inning, until former Blue Jay Kevin Witt broke it up with a two-out double. The Blue Jays didn't score either, though, and the game went into extra innings. It wasn't just that aspect that was special, but also that he could do that in under 100 pitches. He was so dominant. The Tigers couldn't hit him or work the count against him—they were completely befuddled by what Halladay brought that night. I've seen a no-hitter and seen a bunch of other near misses, but this was a better-pitched game than any of them.

Tampa Bay Devil Rays at Toronto Blue Jays, SkyDome, Toronto, Canada, September 25, 2003

I was working for the Blue Jays, and it was a home game late in the season. I'm not a believer in premonitions, but I had one that day, and it was right because Carlos Delgado hit four home runs in the game. I remember turning to my wife after the second homer and telling her that he might hit four in the game. His swing was perfect, and they didn't know how to pitch to him. What was even more incredible was that three of the four homers either tied the game or gave the Blue Jays the lead, so they were really significant in the game. When he came up in the ninth inning looking for his fourth home run, the atmosphere in the stadium was like the final out of a no-hitter, but when it is a pitcher, you are concerned that something bad is going to happen. When it is a hitter, though, you are more optimistic that something great is going to happen. The moment he hit it, you knew it was gone. I love when a player's teammates pour out on the field, because it makes the moment seem more real. To see the players flying out of the dugout and celebrating because the little kid in them remembers what that feeling is like, I love seeing moments like that. You don't get enough of them.

2004 Eastern League Championship, Game Three, Altoona Curve at New Hampshire Fisher Cats, Gill Stadium, Manchester, New Hampshire, September 18, 2004

I've been to one championship game. I was with the Blue Jays, and it was the first year our AA team was based in New Hampshire. They were playing in a municipal stadium while their new ballpark was being built in Manchester. It wasn't an elimination game, but a win that night would give them the championship. I was living in Boston at the time and it was only an hour drive, and it was a good thing for there to be someone from the front office there if they won, so I decided to make the trip. You don't think of minor league championships the same way as in the majors, but the players still celebrated the same way. They poured out of the dugout and did the dogpile, and there was still a champagne celebration in the clubhouse afterwards. Then, the manager announced that a couple of players were being called up to the big leagues, and everyone erupted all over again. It was a recognition that this stuff counts, too. For many of these kids, it is the only time they'll get to experience it. It is easy to dismiss because it isn't the World Series, but that is the worst possible way to look at it.

Steve Levy

Broadcaster, ESPN

1981 AFC Wild Card Playoffs, Buffalo Bills at New York Jets, Shea Stadium, Flushing, New York, December 27, 1981

Up in the mezzanine in the enclosed end zone at Shea, the wind really whipped and hit you right smack in the face. Shea was rocking that day. I always thought it was a great football stadium. It was the Jets, and I thought they always had a great home-field advantage. It was never a nice day for a Jets game weather-wise, and this was no exception . . . gray, cold, and ugly. The place was a dump then, but it was my dump, and there was no place on earth I'd rather have been.

Prior to the opening kickoff, the place was literally shaking. The Jets won the toss and received. Little, exciting Bruce Harper received the kick and took off, only to fumble the football. With that, all the air was sucked out of the stadium. Of course, the Bills went on to score and score and score. My Jets were down, 24–0, in the second quarter and 31–13 with ten minutes left in the game. And then, all of a sudden, Richard Todd got the team back in the game. Two touchdowns later, down four, at the Buffalo 11 with 14 seconds left. Once again, the stadium is literally shaking. We were on the verge of witnessing a great comeback when Buffalo's Bill Simpson stepped in front of a Todd pass and picked it off at the 1-yard line. Ballgame.

To this day, that's the best football game I ever attended. I remember thinking I must really be a sports fan. Even though my team lost in heartbreaking fashion, I was still able to appreciate what's great about sports . . . the drama that's often involved, even when the wrong team wins.

1986 World Series, Game Six, Boston Red Sox at New York Mets, Shea Stadium, Flushing, New York, October 25, 1986

Thanks to some good parenting, my folks let me come home from college. I had tickets to Games One and Seven at Shea Stadium and wrangled a press credential for Game Six, which I got from Steve Malzberg of WABC Radio. I had interned for him the previous summer, and he wasn't going to the game, so he let me take his pass. My seat was in the auxiliary press box. We are talking really auxiliary, since, while I was on the press level, I was also out by the right-field foul pole.

The Mets were obviously in big trouble, so I called to commiserate with my buddy, Jeff Levick, who was so annoyed he turned the TV off. Anyway, the game appeared to be over, and all the other members of the press seated in my area had already gone downstairs to be near the clubhouse to get quotes. Their stories were already written, because this game was over. Or not. Mookie Wilson chops one through Bill Buckner's legs, and I am screaming my head off. I learned a few years later about "no cheering in the press box," but not yet. The kicker to the story is, I am jumping up and down yelling all by myself. There is not another person within a hundred feet of me. I call my pal back to tell him the news, since he really had kept the TV off. By this time, all the other members of the media were scrambling back to their seats in my section. They had to rewrite their ledes.

1994 Stanley Cup Finals, Game Seven, Vancouver Canucks at New York Rangers, Madison Square Garden, New York, New York, June 14, 1994

It was my first NHL postseason working at ESPN, and I served mostly as a reporter during the Stanley Cup Finals. It was Game Seven at the Garden. Now, this building always has a buzz—I think it has something to do with the ceiling. But it has a different buzz during the playoffs for both the Knicks and Rangers. It has always been a special place for me, and you can imagine the electricity buzzing through the building for a Game Seven of the Stanley Cup Finals. What I remember most is that, after waiting my entire life (twenty-nine years at that point), even though I was in the joint, I never really got to see the Rangers carry the Cup.

Let me explain. ESPN was a rights holder, meaning we had first crack at the best location in the winning dressing room. But because that positioning is such a big deal, you have to be all set up and ready to go really early. So, with five minutes left on the clock in the third period, I'm already all hooked up with microphone in hand on the podium in the Rangers room and have to watch those final five minutes on a little TV monitor. My mind is in the stands, but my body isn't. So the Rangers win, the celebration is underway, and there is craziness one hundred feet from me, yet I might as well have been in Vancouver. After what seemed like an eternity, the Rangers start to trickle in from the on-ice celebration.

I got Adam Graves to stand next to me, and we're ready to go. By this time, we've already finished the game broadcast and thrown to *SportsCenter*, and they're going to throw it back to me for locker room reaction. So Graves, a super guy, was being unbelievably patient. It seemed like we waited fifteen minutes, although in reality it probably was much shorter than that. Graves and I are watching in disbelief as *SportsCenter* is showing Cleveland Indians highlights, even though I've got the Rangers' 50-goal scorer standing by, idling his celebration engine. I've already apologized numerous times, he's already messed up my hair with the champagne shower, and, with ESPN producer Tom McNeeley trying to keep me calm, Graves bends over and says to me, "I know how important this was to you, too."

To this day it blows me away that in the middle of the best night of his life, he remembered that I was a native New Yorker and that it was the best night of my life, too. They finally came to us, we did the interview, and I thanked him and let him go. Hours later, after the final few people had finished lingering, someone offered me the chance of a lifetime. Professional?

Probably not. But you know what? I drank from the Stanley Cup that night.

1996 NHL Eastern Conference Quarterfinals, Game Four, Pittsburgh Penguins at Washington Capitals, USAir Arena, Landover, Maryland, April 24, 1996, and 2000 NHL Eastern Conference Semifinals, Game Four, Philadelphia Flyers at Pittsburgh Penguins, Mellon Arena, Pittsburgh, Pennsylvania, May 4, 2000

I've been privileged to broadcast the three longest Stanley Cup playoff games on television (there have been longer games, but they took place before hockey was televised). In April of 1996, we were at the old Cap Centre, which was a dark and dingy building, for the Penguins and Capitals. By the time the fourth overtime rolled around, we had already witnessed Mario Lemieux getting kicked out of the game and a penalty shot in the second overtime. At some point in the third overtime, I was running out of words. I was just using the last names of players (Pivonka, Miller, Johnson, etc.), and at some point in the fourth OT, I just stopped speaking as play was going on. Fortunately, the game was on TV, not radio. My partner, Daryl Reaugh, looked over at me, and on the air I just said, "What?" and we started to giggle. It was late, my mind was fried, and my chest was tight after broadcasting so long at such a high excitement level.

Petr Nedved finally ended it at around 2:30 a.m., and you know what? He came on live with us and did an interview. I remember walking out to the parking lot and seeing Washington coach Jim Schoenfeld going to his car. He was always so positive about everything, but even he was having a tough time swallowing this loss.

I also remember the awful Holiday Inn right near the arena. They lost my laundry that night, so I was prepared to handle a five-overtime game like the one in Pittsburgh in May 2000, against the Flyers. The Igloo ran out of coffee in the second overtime, there was food in the truck during the third overtime, but there was no way to get it to us upstairs in the broadcast booth because it was so late that our runner's mother had come to pick him up and take him home. It was a school night! It seemed like every 30 seconds, I was being passed a note that said we just passed another game on the list of the longest games of all time. Keith Primeau was the hero on this night/morning. Afterwards, since we hadn't had anything to eat since the awful press meal at 6 p.m., my faithful sidekick Darren Pang and I made our way to Pittsburgh's legendary late-night sandwich place, Primanti Brothers. It was after 3 a.m. now, and we walked in and were met with a standing ovation, which was good because with everyone standing, we were finally able to sit down.

2001 GMAC Bowl, Marshall vs. East Carolina, Ladd-Peebles Stadium, Mobile, Alabama, December 19, 2001

The amount of preparation that goes into broadcasting a college football game is mind-boggling, and as is the case in prepping for any sporting event, only about 25 percent of what you have ready ever actually makes it on the air. Well, on this night I used 100 percent and could've used more. East Carolina led, 38–8, at halftime, and this baby was over. We were in garbage time from the start of the third quarter and started using the A, B, C, D, E, and F material, trying to keep it somewhat interesting for whoever was still watching this blowout. Thousands of fans that were at the game left the building . . . and missed a pretty good second half.

Marshall came all the way back to tie it at 51 on a touchdown in the final seconds of the fourth quarter on this crazy night and just needed to hit the extra point to win. Of course, they missed it. The game had four defensive touchdowns. Byron Leftwich had his fifth 400-yard passing game of the season and finished with 576 yards passing and a 64–61 Marshall win in double overtime. It was the highest-scoring bowl game in history and at the time the second biggest comeback in college football history behind only Frank Reich at Maryland in 1984 against Miami. Lesson learned? Never leave a sporting event early.

Bob Ley

Broadcaster, ESPN

Chicago White Sox at New York Yankees, Yankee Stadium, Bronx, New York, June 8, 1969

I was fourteen and grew up in Northern New Jersey, where you become a Yankees fan simply by osmosis. At that time, you also became a Mickey Mantle fan. I remember trying to hit left-handed, just because The Mick was a switch-hitter. There was this great fascination with Mantle and what he represented . . . the iconic American hero, years before we learned more about him in Jim Bouton's book *Ball Four*. It was a very different media time, so the hagiography of Mantle was very much intact.

When I found out this was going to be the day that the Yankees were going to retire Mantle's number, I got my money together and bought tickets. I went with a friend from school, his father, and his grandfather, and we had seats on the third-base line in the mezzanine. Even at that age, I had heard about the ceremonies for Gehrig and Ruth, so being at this one was a little eerie. The Yankees brought out every living legend they could, and, while Frank Messer started the ceremony, Mel Allen came out to do the final introductions. Of course, the penultimate introduction was Joe DiMaggio, which brought the house down. Then they brought out The Mick. I have never in my life, to this day, experienced a crowd reaction like that. It was over 60,000 people, standing and cheering for eight minutes. In retrospect, you realize there was so much emotion wrapped up in those eight minutes—the recognition of the lineage of Yankees moments like this one, the fact that the Yankees were sliding into a period of irrelevancy, plus just what Mantle meant to people. Then he started speaking, and if you go back and look at his remarks, he says that he never knew how a man who knew he was going to die could stand here and say he was the luckiest man on the face of the earth, but now he knows how Lou Gehrig felt. It got a great ovation, but I remember wondering if that meant he was telling us that he was sick. That was my initial reaction. Then the Yankees gave him some gifts, they retired his number, they showed him the plaque that they were going to put out in center field, and he got into a golf cart and they drove him around the perimeter of the field in the old Yankee Stadium, with the huge center field, and he waved and said goodbye to the fans. That day left a powerful impression on me.

1985 NCAA Men's Basketball Tournament Finals, Villanova vs. Georgetown, Rupp Arena, Lexington, Kentucky, April 1, 1985

Georgetown was the defending national champion. Patrick Ewing was an incredible presence on the floor and an awesome talent who had played in the national championship game as a freshman and was about to play in his third title game. This Hoyas team coached by John Thompson was equal parts feared and admired for the relentless, suffocating defense they played. They just rampaged through the season. The Final Four was in Lexington, Kentucky, but it was the Big East Final Four, with three of the four teams coming from that conference. At one point during the Saturday semifinals, the crowd started chanting "Big East," and it was eerie being in Rupp Arena while the Final Four was basically turning into a Big East tournament game.

Villanova lost to Georgetown twice during the season but played them tough; I actually did one of the games that season that went to the buzzer. But Georgetown was Georgetown, and Ewing was a senior and Player of the Year. He was at the height of his abilities, and all Rollie Massimino had was his match-up zone and a bunch of guys who might be able to shoot. The outcome was a foregone conclusion, but we all know what happened. I was sitting in the second row, and you watch this play out right in front of you, and everyone around you is saying the same thing, "Can you believe what you are seeing?" And what we saw was one of the greatest upsets in the history of college sports. In the din afterwards on the floor, I remember Tommy McElroy, one of the associate commissioners of the Big East, turning to me and saying, "Just another Monday night in the Big East." Indeed, it was. As it plays out, I couldn't believe what I was seeing. Villanova played the perfect game. The teams had played twice during the season, and the players told us afterwards that they went back and watched those two games and learned what to do from watching them.

1989 World Series, Game Three, Oakland Athletics at San Francisco Giants, Candlestick Park, San Francisco, California, October 17, 1989

It has been over twenty-five years, and any time I talk about it, I try and remind whoever has asked the question not to forget the sixty-three people killed and the more than 3,000 people injured in the Loma Prieta earthquake. It was as beautiful a day as you could imagine, and it was as surreal a moment as you could ever have. I heard it before I felt it. We were five rows from the top of the stadium in the auxiliary press seating, and at 5:04 p.m. you hear what you think is a beer truck backing up beneath you. You hear it and then you start to feel it, and you think that you shouldn't be feeling a beer truck. Then you suddenly realize and come up out of your chair a little bit, because the structure that you are now standing in is starting to feel like the mattress of a waterbed. That is when you process it and realize that it is an earthquake. I looked around in my field of vision, and the handrail at the bottom of the deck is doing the wave. People ask how long it lasted, and I tell them it lasted long enough to start a Hail Mary, but not long enough to finish it.

After it ended, it was kind of a stunned moment, and the crowd went nuts. They started cheering. It was a "Welcome to California" feeling from the fans, and since it was the Giants against the Athletics in the Series, it was only appropriate for there to be an earthquake. But I turned to my producer, John Hamlin, and we looked at each other and realized the lights were out, the scoreboard was out, and our TV monitors were out. There was no power, so we needed to get back to the truck. We start making our way out of the stadium, but they were still letting people in. No one really knew what was going on, and the police radios weren't working because the towers were down.

ESPN was not a rights holder for MLB at that point, so our TV truck was in a very disadvantageous position out past center field, and there was no power out there, so we had to be on generator power even before the earthquake. That turned out to be the most fortunate occurrence of all, because since we were on generator power, we still had two phone lines. We gave one to the police in San Francisco because their phones were out, and we used the other. Within eighteen minutes, we were on the air telling people what we knew from there and were the go-to outlet for several hours, because no one else had any power.

There was footage rolling into Bristol and being played out so that we could see the breadth of the damage. When we saw the footage from the Bay Bridge and the smoke from the Marina District, it became apparent immediately that we weren't going to be playing baseball. There was some video being shot from our camera up near the top of the stadium of the grounds crew out on the field when a tremor hit, which was magnified by the telephoto effect of the lens. As that picture is shaking from the tremor, the members of the grounds crew were picking up the bases. That was the most apocalyptic moment; there wasn't going to be any baseball for several days. You can call it surreal, but it was even wilder than that.

1998 FIFA World Cup Final, Brazil vs. France, Stade de France, Saint-Denis, France, July 12, 1998

Seamus Malin and I lived in Paris for a little over a month during ESPN and ABC's World Cup coverage (which doesn't stink, by the way) and traveled throughout France doing matches. Any host nation has a built-in advantage, but there was a curious reaction to this French team. The nation was very slow to warm to them, but as they progressed through the tournament, the nation slowly got more comfortable. A lot of this was because the team was playing a lot of black players—players of African heritage or dual citizens from old French colonial nations in Africa that were having a huge impact on the team. The star of the team was Zinedine Zidane, who was of Algerian heritage but was born and grew up in France.

The Cup final saw France face Brazil, and the anticipation was through the roof. There was some question about whether Ronaldo would play for Brazil, because when the team sheet came out before the game, he wasn't on it. Apparently he was having some sort of seizure downtown, and that's how we came on the air. Then a new team sheet came out, which is almost unheard of at a World Cup final, saying that he is going to be in the game. When the teams come out, the moment was almost indescribable. If you've seen the movie *Casablanca*, when they sing "La Marseillaise" at Rick's Café, it is one of the most stirring scenes in cinema. So to stand in Paris and hear 80,000 Frenchmen sing "La Marseillaise," I get goose bumps just thinking about it. And then France goes out and lays a 3–0 licking on Brazil. Out of the blue,

French teammates Zinedine Zidane, Marcel Desailly, and Laurent Blanc hold the World Cup after France defeated Brazil to win the championship in 1998. (AP Photo/ Michel Euler)

they just kicked their derriere up and down the pitch. It was as convincing a win as you will ever see. On the press bus back to the hotel, all you saw were people starting a several-day party to celebrate. People were riding on the hoods of cars, waving bottles of champagne, and you realized they were trying to keep up with the bus, which was probably going around 50 miles per hour. It was just an incredible moment.

2014 FIFA World Cup Qualifier, United States at Mexico, Estadio Azteca, Mexico City, Mexico, March 26, 2013

In August of 2012, the United States was invited to Mexico to play a friendly at Azteca in Jurgen Klinsmann's first trip south as coach of the American team. It was just a friendly, but the U.S. won the match, 1–0, marking the first time ever that the American team had won a game on Mexican turf. Mexico was celebrating their Olympic championship from London that night, so losing that match was horribly received by the Mexican fans. People started blaming the Mexican Federation for allowing a young American team to learn how to play at altitude in Mexico City, amidst the poor air and hostile environment.

A year later, American qualifying had gotten off to a bad start, with a loss at Honduras. The U.S. then beat Costa Rica in the snow in Denver before heading back to Mexico City for a very important match in which they had to get some points. To complicate things, American goalkeeper Tim Howard couldn't play due to injury, and the U.S. was starting a very young defense pairing. Cynics who want to pick on soccer like to ask how you can have an exciting scoreless draw, but this was an exceptional performance. To do it in the Azteca, to Mexico, during World Cup qualifying at a time of utter necessity was as good as it gets.

Stewart Mandel

Broadcaster, FOX Sports

2003 Fiesta Bowl, Ohio State vs. Miami, Sun Devil Stadium, Tempe, Arizona, January 3, 2003

The buildup to the game was that Miami was unbeatable, while Ohio State was undefeated but had gotten a reputation for being lucky. I always felt like Ohio State was being taken too lightly. The Big Ten that season was very strong, and Ohio State did go undefeated. The Buckeyes had Maurice Clarett at running back, but you didn't realize just how much talent was on that team until the NFL Draft. Even with that, Miami had this aura of invincibility around it, having come into the title game on a 34-game winning streak. Ohio State outplayed them early, however, and Miami was lucky just to get the game to overtime on a late field goal. Everyone remembers the late pass interference call, which puts a bit of a stain on the game and overshadows how competitive it was, but there were so many twists and turns in the game, from Miami intercepting a pass but losing possession when Clarett stripped the ball away from Sean Taylor, to the Willis McGahee knee injury. I actually remember two plays from overtime more than the pass interference penalty—Craig Krenzel completing a fourth-and-16 pass and the last play of the game, when the Buckeye defense got to Hurricanes quarterback Ken Dorsey and made him force up a pass. At that moment, you realized that Ohio State had just pulled it off and ended the Miami dynasty. I was going back and forth between sidelines late in the game and was on the Miami sideline for the pass interference call, but was on the Ohio State sideline for the end of the game and got to see those players celebrate up close.

USC at Notre Dame, Notre Dame Stadium, South Bend, Indiana, October 15, 2005

I had a very interesting vantage point for the infamous Bush Push play. I was down on the sideline with my then-*Sports Illustrated* colleague Austin Murphy. That final drive for USC was so riveting. You could feel the tension in the air, and they had so much at stake—the Trojans' winning streak was on the line and everyone was expecting them to go play for the national championship, but not only was it all in serious danger, but it would be their archrival Notre Dame that stopped it. Matt Leinart completed a 61-yard pass to Dwayne Jarrett on fourth-and-9, and you couldn't believe that had just happened. Then, Leinart fumbled the ball out of bounds and there were all zeroes on the clock, and fans started rushing the field. Everyone thought the game was over. We were standing next to a monitor down on the field and could see that time was going to be put back on the clock. I can't say that on the winning play you could tell from watching it in person that Bush pushed Leinart; that would only become obvious afterward. I do remember vividly after it, though, Leinart coming back to the bench and breaking down in tears from the emotion of it all.

2006 Rose Bowl, Texas vs. USC, Rose Bowl, Pasadena, California, January 4, 2006

Both teams were undefeated, but USC was being hyped up a lot more than Texas, to the point where ESPN ran a week-long series debating whether the Trojans were the greatest team of all-time. The funny thing, though, is that they weren't even the best team of the Pete Carroll era; the team the year before had all of the same stars on offense, but a better defense. There were some warning signs with this defense—both Fresno State and Notre Dame gave them problems during the regular season. It is hard for me to remember at this point why Texas was so discounted going into the game, and even though I don't make a lot of good predictions, I did pick Texas to win this game. The hype around USC had gotten so high that Texas got the feeling that USC was taking them lightly and wasn't totally focused on this game. As we later learned, there were agents buzzing all around that program. There was a bizarre play during the game where Bush tried to lateral the ball and USC ended up losing possession, and I remember turning to someone in the press box and saying, "See, this is what I was talking about." All that being said, USC could have and should have won that game. All they had to do was convert that late fourth-and-2, but they didn't, and it basically gift-wrapped the win for Texas, who just had to go down the field and score. I was standing just off the side of the end zone when Vince Young came scrambling around and ran right past me for the game-winning score. It was one of the all-time memorable plays, and it happened right in front of my eyes.

2006 NCAA Men's Basketball Tournament Regional Finals, George Mason vs. Connecticut, Verizon Center, Washington, DC, March 26, 2006

We have all become a little desensitized to mid-majors making runs in the NCAA Tournament, after teams like Butler and VCU have done just that in recent years. But before them, the notion of a school like George Mason making it to the Final Four seemed preposterous. The Patriots had upset some name-brand programs earlier in the tournament, but everyone assumed this was where the road would end, against the top seed and a team where all five starters would eventually end up drafted by the NBA. UConn jumped out to an early lead, but Mason made a run and got back into the game. Because the game was being played in Washington, DC, there were already a lot of Mason fans there, but unless you were a Connecticut fan, you ended up rooting for the Patriots.

The longer George Mason hung around, the longer you believed this actually could happen, but everyone just expected the Huskies to go on that run eventually and put the game away. Connecticut was able to send the game into overtime with a last-second layup, and once they did that, it felt like it was just a formality that they would win. Mason ended up winning in overtime, though. I had covered Mason for two rounds at this point, so I had gotten the chance to know the vibe of that team pretty well, and it wasn't nearly as giddy as you thought it would be. The team had held onto the notion that they belonged there at that point. I then went over to the UConn locker room, and you could get a feeling for how something like this could happen. It was an incredibly talented team, but as talented as they were, they always felt a little "off" during the season, and you got the feeling that everyone was more interested in getting to the NBA than winning a national championship. It showed after that game; they weren't devastated and were more matter-of-fact about losing. Once it all sunk in, though, it was hard to believe that a school like George Mason, that barely anyone had heard of, was going to the Final Four.

Folarin Campbell reacts as he cuts the net after George Mason's win to advance to the 2006 Final Four. (AP Photo/Lawrence Jackson)

2014 BCS Championship Game, Florida State vs. Auburn, Rose Bowl, Pasadena, California, January 6, 2014

After so many years of bad BCS championship games, it was great to finally have one that wasn't a blowout and over in the first quarter. A lot of people thought this game was going to go that way beforehand, because Florida State had been so dominant all season, but Auburn went up, 21–3, early. You knew it wasn't over, simply because of how good the Seminoles had been all season.

You always try to time the trip downstairs from the press box to the field at games like this so that you don't miss anything important. I don't even think I was in the elevator that long, but I come out and hear people screaming, because Florida State had just returned a kickoff for a touchdown. That was the first time I can ever remember missing a touchdown while in an elevator. Fortunately for me, it wasn't over at that point, though, because Auburn came back to score and retake the lead. But Florida State came back one more time, and it was just like 2006 for me, because I was standing in the same spot by the same end zone when Jameis Winston completed the game-winning touchdown pass. I covered just about all of the BCS championship games, and it was cool that the last one ended in such dramatic fashion.

Hal McCoy

Writer, FOXSportsOhio.com

Recipient of Baseball Hall of Fame's J.G. Taylor Spink Award, 2002
Elected to National Sports Media Association Hall of Fame, 2015

Philadelphia Phillies at Cincinnati Reds, Riverfront Stadium, Cincinnati, Ohio, June 23, 1971

I actually wasn't even supposed to be at the game that day. I didn't become the regular beat writer until a couple of seasons later and was just a backup writer at this point. Our regular writer, Jim Ferguson (who later became the Reds PR person, leading to me getting the beat), was supposed to cover the game, but his wife was sick, so our editor called me that afternoon to cover the game. And I ended up seeing history. Rick Wise not only pitched a no-hitter against the Reds, but hit two home runs in the game, as well. When he hit the first homer, it was special. Then he hit the second one, and he still has the no-hitter going, and the whole press box gets excited, because we knew that if he finished that no-hitter, we were seeing history.

1975 World Series, Game Six, Cincinnati Reds at Boston Red Sox, Fenway Park, Boston, Massachusetts, October 21, 1975

Carlton Fisk's game-winning home run capped what was simply an amazing game. I've covered thirty-five World Series, and of all of the Series games that I've covered, that one stands out above them all. There was so much drama, with the game going back and forth and ending the way it did. I remember Pete Rose saying after the game that during the game, when it was tied, he turned to Carlton Fisk while batting and said, "Isn't this a great game?" There was all of this drama and tension, and Rose was having the time of his life. I was sitting in the main press box at Fenway Park, and my seat was almost directly down the left-field line, so I had the perfect seat to watch the flight of the home run. I could see the ball was hooking a little bit and looked down to see Fisk jumping up and down, signaling for it to stay fair, then looked up just in time to see the ball hit the foul pole. As he was running the bases, I remember looking out to left field and seeing George Foster pick up the ball and put it in his pocket; he later auctioned it off.

A few years ago, the History Channel did a documentary on baseball beat writers, asking them to pick out one story they remember writing. In 1975, I was in my second year covering the Reds and had to write this dramatic story while on deadline. So during the taping of the documentary, they pulled out a copy of the story and asked me to read the first two or three paragraphs. All I could think about was how young I was, and how I was covering what turned out to be one of the most historic events in baseball, and just hoped that I got it right. When I saw the documentary, I'm proud to say I nailed it and described it just as it had happened.

1975 World Series, Game Seven, Cincinnati Reds at Boston Red Sox, Fenway Park, Boston, Massachusetts, October 22, 1975

Everybody talks about Game Six, and it makes people forget that the Red Sox didn't actually win the Series. Game Seven was almost as dramatic as Game Six, except for the way it finished. The Red Sox went ahead, 3–0, and players told me afterward that Sparky Anderson was back in the tunnel, nervously smoking cigarettes. Eventually, he sat back down, and Johnny Bench walked by him, patted him on the knee, and told him not to worry about it, that they would win the game for him and to just stay out of the way.

Tony Perez then hit a two-run homer off of a Bill Lee blooper pitch; earlier in the game, Lee threw that pitch to Perez, and he swung and missed it. Perez went back to the dugout and told Sparky that if he threw that pitch again, he was going to hit a home run off it, and he did, to make it 3–2. The Reds eventually tied it at three, and then Joe Morgan drove in Ken Griffey Sr. in the ninth inning to put them ahead, 4–3, and that is how it all ended.

San Diego Padres at Cincinnati Reds, Riverfront Stadium, Cincinnati, Ohio, September 11, 1985

This might have been the defining moment of my career, seeing Pete Rose break Ty Cobb's all-time hits record. It was such a memorable night. Jerome Holtzman wrote a book *No Cheering in the Press Box*, but the only time in my career I saw writers stand and cheer during a game was this night. When Pete got that hit, the entire press box stood and applauded.

Knowing it was going to be a historic moment, I had my headphones on and was listening to the play-by-play, and when Rose hit the blooper off Eric Show, I remember Joe Nuxhall screaming, "Get down! Get down!" as the ball landed in front of Carmelo Martinez. I looked and saw Pete standing on first base, and Steve Garvey, who was the Padres first baseman at the time, took his glove off and applauded. In all of the years I covered Pete Rose, it was the only time I saw him cry. His son, Pete Rose Jr., came out on the field to celebrate with him. And through it all, Show was just sitting on the mound, just waiting for the celebration to end.

Los Angeles Dodgers at Cincinnati Reds, Riverfront Stadium, Cincinnati, Ohio, September 16, 1988

The start of the game was delayed by rain until 10 p.m., and my deadline was midnight. Fortunately, Tom Browning pitched the perfect game fast enough for me to hit the deadline. I only had around five minutes, though, to write a story about a perfect game, but my paper was very benevolent and gave me an extra five minutes to get it done. I'm very proud that I've never missed a deadline in my life, and it is a good thing, because this story ran on the front page of the paper the next morning.

It was raining so hard that night that no one thought the game would even be played. Browning had even taken off his uniform and was getting ready to go home until the equipment manager stopped him and told him he needed to start warming up because the game was going to be played. So Browning had to get dressed again and run down to the bullpen and get warmed up. The pitcher for the Dodgers that night, Tim Belcher, also had a no-hitter through the first five and two-third innings, so we actually had a double no-hitter going for a while. They only sold 16,000 tickets for the game that night, and by the time the game ended, after being delayed at the start for so long, there were probably only around 2,000 people left.

Jiggs McDonald

Broadcaster

Recipient of Hockey Hall of Fame's Foster Hewitt Award, 1990

Colorado Rockies at Atlanta Flames, The Omni, Atlanta, Georgia, March 1, 1980

I was involved with the media relations department of the Atlanta Flames during my time calling games there. The Flames had the rights to Jim Craig, who had just won gold in the Olympics as part of the "Miracle On Ice" team. There were a lot of rumors flying around that the team would be sold, and Craig was being viewed as the savior to help keep the team in town and not be moved as part of the sale. It was set up that he would come into town on a Friday and sign his contract at center ice at the Omni in a big public event. On Saturday afternoon, I was scheduled to do a game in Boston for the NHL Network, and my producer called to ask me to bring footage of the contract signing with me and fly to Hartford where the network was doing a Friday night game, so I scrambled to the airport to get the footage there in time for the telecast that evening. Then after the Saturday afternoon game in Boston was over, I had to get right back to Atlanta for the game that evening, which was Craig's debut. In the day I was away, though, Atlanta had an ice storm. I threw my stuff in the car, grabbed the ice scraper, started the car to get the defroster going, started scraping . . . and locked myself out of the car. I left the car running, walked back to the terminal, and got a cab. The driver was overly cautious about driving in the ice, and by the time I got to the arena, it was in the middle of the first period (Skip Caray had started the game in my place). I went to where my wife was sitting and told her the car was at the airport, running and locked, and waiting for her to pick it up, but we ultimately decided to get it after the game. I then went to take over for Skip, who had no idea whatsoever about who anyone was or even which team was the home team. I think most of the players he named were old college buddies or people he grew up with in Missouri. When the game ended, I first had to shoot an ad in the locker room with Jim, which took another hour, and my part ended up getting cut. Finally, after a bite to eat, we went to the airport, and there was my car, still running.

1983 Stanley Cup Finals, Game Four, Edmonton Oilers at New York Islanders, Nassau Coliseum, Uniondale, New York, May 17, 1983

My last radio job before being hired by the Los Angeles Kings was in Orillia, Ontario, which is the same hometown as Gordon Lightfoot. We have become good friends over the years, and he was convinced that Edmonton was going to end the Islanders' Stanley Cup run in 1983. We made a wager on the series, and he came to the Coliseum that night as the Islanders won their fourth straight Cup. After the game was over, I brought him down to the locker room to celebrate with the players, and then to the after-party at the Marriott across the street. It was the first time he was around the Cup, but it was also the first time my mother was. She was at the game with my wife, as well, and partied well into the night with us. My daughters babysat for Duane Sutter's kids, and a couple of days later, they hosted the Cup and invited my family over. My mother came with us, and I don't think I'd ever seen her happier than when she had her arm around the Stanley Cup.

1987 Patrick Division Semifinals, Game Seven, New York Islanders at Washington Capitals, Capital Centre, Landover, Maryland, April 18, 1987

At the end of the second OT, after five periods of hockey between the Islanders and the Capitals, with Stan Fischler doing interviews and myself and Eddie Westfall calling the game, we thought it was never going to end. You could see how fatigued the players were getting, but I had bigger concerns. I started thinking that if I didn't get to a men's room, there was going to be a problem. The press room was right across the concourse behind us, and when I got there, the line was coming out the door. Neither Eddie nor I ever did make it to the front of the line before we needed to get back to the booth.

After Pat LaFontaine scored the goal in the fourth overtime, the first thought that went through my head was "Thank God!" Any play-by-play announcer is cognizant of redundancy, and after more than six periods of play, it was getting increasingly difficult to describe the action without repeating yourself. It was time for that game to end. It was a classic, but it was almost two in the morning! Every so often, I run into Bob Mason, who was the goalie for the Capitals that night, and we talk about the goaltending matchup that night between him and Kelly Hrudey, and how it was just save after save after save. It was a classic game to be involved with and was loaded with scoring chances for both teams.

Los Angeles Kings at Edmonton Oilers, Northlands Coliseum, Edmonton, Canada, October 15, 1989

Wayne Gretzky was chasing Gordie Howe's all-time scoring record, and SportsChannel America assigned me to call the game with Herb Brooks. The Islanders played at home on Saturday, and I had a 7 a.m. flight booked the next morning to Toronto, connecting to Edmonton. When I got to LaGuardia, though, the flight was canceled, and I ended up getting to the booth in Edmonton around ten minutes before the game started. Gretzky ended up breaking Gordie's record with the game-tying goal late in the game (for good measure, he would also score the game-winner in overtime), all with Howe in attendance to see it. It was a record that many of us growing up as kids never thought would be broken, but along came Gretzky to rewrite the entire record book. It is the thrill of a broadcaster's lifetime to be able to call something like that, and to be there as they stop the game and do all of the presentations. Just a great memory, made even more memorable in getting to know former NHL referee Ron Hoggarth, who officiated that game. Being in the booth, you often wonder about conversations between players and officials. I'd noticed that on one particular faceoff, Wayne backed out of the faceoff area and was laughing after a conversation with Hoggarth. Turns out Wayne had asked Hoggarth why he was staying so close to him all game long. Hoggy's reply was that he knew tonight was the night and he was going to be in the picture. Sure enough, any photos of that historic goal show referee Ron Hoggarth signaling goal.

1993 Patrick Division Semifinals, Game Six, Washington Capitals at New York Islanders, Nassau Coliseum, Uniondale, New York, April 28, 1993, and 1993 Patrick Division Finals, Game Seven, New York Islanders at Pittsburgh Penguins, Civic Arena, Pittsburgh, Pennsylvania, May 14, 1993

I had never seen a more vicious play than when Dale Hunter hit Pierre Turgeon after he scored late in the game to put the game away for the Islanders. Turgeon scored in the goal to our left and skated toward the near corner with his arms raised in celebration, when Hunter came from behind and cross-checked him into the boards, separating his shoulder. As it unfolded, you could see Hunter space out and come after him, and it felt like it was happening in slow motion. With one eye, I saw Turgeon celebrating, and with the other, I saw Hunter skate across the ice, ready to nail him, which he did. My heart was in my mouth, and I couldn't believe what I had just witnessed. The words kept coming, but you struggle with what words to use, because you know what you've just seen was totally wrong and should never be part of the game. It was just horrifying. After the game, you felt great for the team winning, knowing they had just advanced in the playoffs to face the two-time defending Cup champs, but you also know that the team just lost its best player in the process. The next day, at the airport, I was talking to Al Arbour and asked him, hypothetically, that if the league were to allow him one player from the team they just eliminated to replace Turgeon, who would it be? Without any hesitation, he said Dale Hunter. I reminded Al that he had just maimed the team's star, and he replied that all Hunter wants to do is win, and that he would do anything to do that, so that's the guy I would want.

To the surprise of everyone, the Islanders went to a seventh game against the Penguins in the next round. Most people predicted a four-game sweep, but that Islanders team had a group of personalities that complemented each other perfectly, with guys like Ray Ferraro and Glenn Healy, who are both now among the top hockey analysts on TV in Canada. They could hit and hurt, and did in that series. Rich Pilon had a huge hit on Kevin Stevens in Game Seven, and Darius Kasparaitis kept Mario Lemieux off his game the entire series. The team was on a mission and used the injury to Turgeon as motivation, and shocked the hockey world by getting to Game Seven. That game went to overtime and, to this day, I can still see the pass from Ferraro to David Volek, and he just unloaded. The puck is in the net, and you try to figure out how this just happened. Volek was in Al's doghouse most of the season and was only in the lineup because the Islanders had so many injuries at the time, so Al had no choice but to play him. The team just went bananas, and we did in the booth, as well. The Islanders had no right to win that series, but they took it to another level and, more important, believed. It was very special, and that entire playoff run in 1993 was unforgettable.

Liam McHugh

Broadcaster, NBC Sports

Massachusetts at Syracuse, Carrier Dome, Syracuse, New York, May 1, 2004

I was in grad school at Syracuse, where lacrosse is immensely popular. While I was there, the Orangemen had a player by the name of Mike Powell, who was one of three brothers that starred for 'Cuse. The first two were both four-time All-Americans, and word was that Mike was better than both of them. Leading up to the UMass game, Powell had promised to do something that had never been seen before. There was a buzz building on campus in anticipation of something called "The Move." As the game started, Powell clearly stood out. He was the tiniest guy on the field, but he was easily the most dynamic athlete. It was like watching Barry Sanders or Allen Iverson play lacrosse. He had unbelievable skill and elite quickness, a combination that could make defenders look like fools. At one point during the game, he put a move on a guy behind the goal that caused the other player to trip over the net, and he stopped and looked at him before scoring. That was sick, but we were all still waiting for him to deliver on his promise to unveil something new. He wouldn't disappoint. Late in the game, with his team in the lead, Powell got the ball, and the defenders immediately gave him a little room, just like scorers get room in other sports. He started cradling the ball and stutter stepping, creating space, when all of a sudden, he jumped in the air and did a full flip while shooting the ball. He didn't hit the target, but it didn't really matter. It was one of those moves you wish you were watching on TV, because you wanted to see the replay a few times. Even though he didn't score on "The Move," you still knew you'd just witnessed greatness (he did score six goals in the game). He was so much better than everyone else on the field, even though everyone out there was playing at the highest level of that sport. He wasn't bigger or stronger, he was just better. It was one of those rare moments in sports where you get to be in attendance to see genius.

2004 Belmont Stakes, Belmont Park, Elmont, New York, June 5, 2004

This was the year Smarty Jones was going for the Triple Crown, and it was mayhem. Back then, people went to the Belmont every year, even if there wasn't a Triple Crown contender, because it was a giant party. There is the grandstand, where you have to pay for a ticket to get in, but there is also a picnic area behind the grandstand, where at that time, you could bring in as much food and drink as you wanted, and you would watch the race on big screen TVs. Things sometimes got a little out of hand back there, which is why they no longer let you bring your own beverages. In fact, I think that was the last year of the policy, because half of Philadelphia came up to the race to watch Smarty Jones, and it was wild. Hunter S. Thompson once wrote a fabulous story about how the Kentucky Derby was decadent and depraved, and this could have been a follow-up. People were drinking heavily, passing out, fighting, and in the midst of this, there was a huge sporting event. But then, the race started, and everything froze. It was pin-drop quiet as the horses entered the gates. And a moment later, when the horses were off, Belmont erupted. The picnic area just went ballistic. At the end, after Smarty Jones lost, there was a feeling of utter disappointment for every single person there. The party had ended. The hangover had begun. We didn't get to witness history. In a matter of minutes, the day went from debauchery to anticipation to electricity to depression, and that roller coaster ride is something I'll never forget.

Texas Tech at Oklahoma State, Boone Pickens Stadium, Stillwater, Oklahoma, September 22, 2007

The Cowboys won the game in a high-scoring affair, but what makes this event memorable for me has nothing to do with what happened on the field. This was the day Oklahoma State coach Mike Gundy walked into his press conference and delivered his "I'm a man! I'm forty!" rant, and I was lucky enough to be standing about fifteen feet away from him. Gundy was furious about an article that was written by Jenni Carlson of *The Oklahoman* that was critical of quarterback Bobby Reid. It focused on his character and implied he was soft. Gundy burst into the press conference holding the paper, and he clearly did not want to talk about the game. Instead, he proceeded to produce around three-and-a-half minutes of YouTube magic. The catchphrase "I'm a man, I'm forty!" is what everyone remembers, but there were so many golden lines in that outburst. It got weird instantly, when Gundy began by saying, "This article was brought to me by a mother!" followed by a pause, and then "of children." I remember looking back at my producer and wondering what other kind of mother there was. Right there, we knew this thing was going to be epic. Gundy finished his rant in strong fashion, with the unforgettable walk-off line: "Makes me want to puke!" I was working for KOKH, the FOX affiliate in Oklahoma City, and I remember calling back to the station and telling them we were probably going to lead the news with this, we were probably going to run it a million times, and in the sports report, we were going to run the entire clip start to finish. People were going to want to see this over and over. I'll never be in another press conference as strange as that one, where you knew within minutes it was going to go viral. Deep down inside, I'm really hoping for an updated version when Gundy hits fifty.

Toronto Maple Leafs at Detroit Red Wings, Michigan Stadium, Ann Arbor, Michigan, January 1, 2014

There were over 105,000 fans packed into the Big House to watch two Original Six teams play in blizzard conditions. At the beginning of the day, I was out on the field, next to the rink, freezing and waiting to do a pregame TV hit. I was to take a throw from Al Roker, who was hosting the Rose Parade in California. I could barely see the monitor but was able to tell that Al was wearing short sleeves and it was beautiful and sunny in Pasadena. Meanwhile, I was wearing a huge coat, scarf, gloves, a winter hat, and was trying to focus while the wind whipped snow everywhere. The temperature was in the teens, but the wind chill made it feel like single digits. When we got up to our booth upstairs, it was open-air, so there was little relief. You could see most of the Big House, and it looked like we were inside an enormous snow globe and someone had just shook it up. The game went to a shootout, with Toronto beating Detroit, but the result was secondary to me. The imagery that I'll take away from the game was of two hardcore fan bases sharing a major moment, but somehow getting along. There were no fights,

The Detroit Red Wings and the Toronto Maple Leafs skate during the third period of the Winter Classic at Michigan Stadium. (AP Photo/Carlos Osorio)

people were standing and dancing during breaks in the action (although I don't think they were cheering as much as they were simply trying to stay warm). It was the biggest outdoor sports celebration I've ever been to, and it was spectacular. Bitterly cold, but spectacular.

2014 Winter Olympics, Men's Hockey Preliminary Round, United States vs. Russia, Bolshoy Ice Dome, Sochi, Russia, February 15, 2014

This was the game in the Olympic tournament everyone had circled on their calendar. It might have only been group play, and I've been to bigger events, but I don't think I've ever seen, or will ever see, a more unique contest. The atmosphere was electric right from the start. Vladimir Putin was in attendance, the crowd was fired up, and the United States and Russia took things to a shootout. Unlike the NHL, in international hockey you can use the same shooters over and over if you want, and the U.S. clearly had a ringer in T.J. Oshie, who was named to the team in large part because of his shootout ability. His moves were mesmerizing. No one could believe what he was doing with the puck. He badly fooled Russian goalie Sergei Bobrovsky several times and scored on four of six attempts to lead Team USA to victory. Oddly enough, on the attempt that most baffled Bobrovsky, Oshie actually missed the net. While it was happening, my NBC colleagues and I were openly wondering how many tricks he had up his sleeve, and Oshie himself would later say that he was running out of moves, but he had enough to deliver the win. In a hostile environment, with all eyes upon him, with all of that attention and pressure, Oshie was in complete control. It was exhilarating to see a guy whom most Americans had probably never heard of before turn into an instant international star. It was unlike any other finish to a great game I have witnessed.

Chris McKendry

Broadcaster, ESPN

Morgan State at Georgetown, Capital Centre, Landover, Maryland, November 30, 1994

I was a sports anchor with WJLA-TV in Washington at the time. It was right after Allen Iverson's stay in prison, and he was now John Thompson's prodigal son, after Thompson answered Iverson's mother's request to help save her son. We had heard the stories about him on the court out of Newport News, Virginia, but to see him play in person was absolutely phenomenal. His speed and quickness was unlike anybody's I'd ever seen. He was so explosive and such a dynamic scorer, and that is what coach Thompson needed on that team. He would say, "Allen, go win me this game. Go score my points." He went on to be the Big East Rookie of the Year that season. When they made it to the Sweet 16, Thompson was so excited after winning that second-round game. He didn't have a great team, he had a great player (although Jerome Williams eventually developed into a great player, as well). But to see Iverson play in person that first time is a moment I'll never forget. In the tournament that season, one of the opposing coaches made a comment before playing Georgetown that they could play up-tempo, too, and I couldn't help think to myself that he had no idea what up-tempo meant to Iverson. He was a freshman in college and was probably already better than half of the point guards in the NBA. It was the first time I got the chance to cover a real phenom and someone who transcended the sport.

1999 Women's World Cup Final, United States vs. China, Rose Bowl, Pasadena, California, July 10, 1999

I was the sideline reporter for ESPN for all Team USA games, and it was magical. No one knew it was going to be as big as it was, so I was lucky enough to be given the assignment, which I really wanted to do. I just had a feeling it was going to be special. I had done some work during the World Cup in 1994 while working in Washington, so I had a feel for how it worked and wanted to be a part of it. It was something to watch that team grow. There were probably only around twenty media members at their practice before they opened at the Meadowlands, but they sold out Giants Stadium to open the tournament. From there, it kept growing and growing, until we got to the final game at the Rose Bowl, where I had to fight to get my microphone into the media scrum around players. I had to nudge aside crews from shows like *Entertainment Tonight* to get my interviews and sound bites. At this point, it became about more than just soccer. I'm a child of Title IX, and I've written in the past about how much I owe to people like Billie Jean King. That is why I could play soccer growing up, and all of these players on this team were Title IX women, as well.

That match against China was so intense. Team USA's defense was considered its weak link, and China was really testing it, but it held up. You could see China pack the box and start playing for a tie and a shootout, and they were going to take their chances there. After the match ended, people would ask me about why I didn't ask Brandi Chastain about ripping her shirt off. First, that is a very traditional soccer thing to do, and, being a woman, I really didn't think it was that big of a deal seeing a sports bra. Also, it was so hot that during every commercial break, quite a few players were taking their shirts off. I'm always amazed at how that came to signify something so big. There was no gender barrier when it came to this team; you would look into the crowd and see ten-year-old boys cheering for Team USA. It made me realize that the next generation was growing up with that mindset. To me, this game is a symbol of my whole generation, and hopefully it stays fresh in everybody's mind.

2012 Australian Open, Men's Final, Rafael Nadal vs. Novak Djokovic, Rod Laver Arena, Melbourne, Australia, January 29, 2012

This was the longest championship match in Grand Slam history, running five hours and fifty-three minutes. I was hosting for ESPN with Brad Gilbert, and our booth was located in a suite above the court for almost six hours of tennis played at its highest level. Rafael Nadal and Novak Djokovic were just beating on each other the whole time. It wasn't a match loaded with big serves and short points; it seemed like every point was a long rally, and as it went on and on, you wondered how long Nadal and Djokovic could sustain that level of play. One guy would have a peak and you thought he was going to pounce, but the other would bounce right back. They were so cramped at the end of the match that they were basically hanging on the net for the post-match presentations. Everyone out on the court was sitting in chairs for the speeches, but no one thought to bring out chairs for the two players. One person talked for about fifteen minutes, and you could see Nadal kneeling and bending over while Djokovic was using the net to help him stand. But I'll never forget this match for the sheer length of it. Tennis is a rare sport where it is mano a mano, with no subs coming in, and when it is at its best, it is two players going at it like these two did. There are only a handful of matches that help define a Grand Slam event in tennis, and this was one of them.

2014 Little League Baseball World Series, Lamade Stadium, Williamsport, Pennsylvania, August 14-24, 2014

It was a treat following Mo'ne Davis as her team advanced in the Little League World Series. There was so much to like about her—her beautiful face, her eyes that just captivated everyone, her stare on the mound, her attitude and swagger. There wasn't anything cocky about it; she was just a supremely confident and mature girl and the perfect person to handle the moment and her teammates loved her. She was a girl just like me. I also grew up in Philadelphia and played on the playgrounds there, so I totally got her. It was so much fun to watch, and it was absolutely Mo'ne Mania.

2014 U.S. Open, Women's Final, Caroline Wozniacki vs. Serena Williams, Arthur Ashe Stadium, Flushing, New York, September 7, 2014

It was a thrill to be there when Serena Williams won her eighteenth career Grand Slam title, and then do the interview with her afterward with Chris Evert. I think Serena is the greatest women's player ever, just for her athleticism alone. It was an incredibly difficult Grand Slam season for her in 2014, and she went to the Open just hoping to get out of the fourth round. All season long, she had carried what seemed like a burden as she tried to reach Evert and Navratilova's mark. It went from everyone assuming she'd get to twenty championships that season to just hoping to get to eighteen. I think she had so much respect for Chris, and I know they have a very nice relationship. There was something about reaching eighteen, though, that made it more than just a number. It was personal to her. She so desperately wanted to be in that group and reach the same level as those greats. It was interesting to see someone who seemed so invincible struggle personally to reach an accomplishment. When she finally got it, we talked to her around twenty minutes after the match ended, and she was still in a daze. The crowd was screaming behind her, but it didn't feel like she was completely with us. I'll never forget that moment when she fell back on the court and celebrated after going through everything she went through to get there.

Serena Williams hugs the championship trophy after winning the 2014 U.S. Open for her eighteenth Grand Slam title. (AP Photo/Darron Cummings)

Bob Miller

Broadcaster, Los Angeles Kings

Recipient of Hockey Hall of Fame's Foster Hewitt Award, 2000

1967 NFL Championship Game, Dallas Cowboys at Green Bay Packers, Lambeau Field, Green Bay, Wisconsin, December 31, 1967

In those days, if the network of the station you were working for did not cover the game, you didn't get highlights from the other networks. I worked in Madison, Wisconsin, for a station (WKOW-TV) that was not covering the game, so we had to go to Green Bay to film it. The first thing I heard on the radio when I woke up that morning was, "It is seven-thirty in Madison and twenty-six below zero." My wife couldn't believe I was going to a football game in that cold, but I had to, because it was the NFL Championship and the winner was going to Super Bowl II. We drove two-and-a-half hours to Green Bay, believing we were going to be sitting in the press box, but the press box was small and there were so many credentials given out that they told us we had to sit on the Lambeau Field roof. And that is where we stood for the whole game. They put some canvas around the back to keep some wind off of us, but it was still sixteen below at kickoff time. There were big cauldrons of coffee and soup to keep us warm, and we needed to keep heat lamps on our cameras to have them run at the right speed. When you went to thread the film, it was so brittle that it would break apart in your hands. I remember running to the locker room after the game to do interviews, and, from my knees down, I really could not feel my legs. I'll never forget that I was going to interview Ray Nitschke, who had his jersey off. It looked like someone took a razor blade and slashed him all over his arms after he fell on the frozen turf all game. It was a great game to be at, but there were multiple times during the game where I had to ask myself what I was doing standing outside in the cold like that.

1982 Smythe Division Semifinals, Game Three, Edmonton Oilers at Los Angeles Kings, The Forum, Inglewood, California, April 10, 1982

The Oilers were climbing to the height of their domination of the NHL, and, with all of the great players they had, no one gave the Kings a chance in this series. At that time, the opening round series was best-of-five, and the first two games were in Edmonton. The teams split, with the Kings winning a classic offensive battle, 10–8, before the Oilers won the second game. The series moved to Los Angeles, and everyone was excited because the Kings came back with the series tied . . . until the Oilers took a 5–0 lead after two periods. I was so upset and disappointed, because the Kings always got their fans so excited that they might advance, then would come home and lay an egg. The Oilers were just toying with the Kings, and everyone figured there was no way the Kings would come back in this one. Even team owner Jerry Buss had left. But the Kings came back and scored five goals in the third period, the last one coming with just five seconds left. I remember thinking after the first goal that at least it wouldn't be a shutout. After the third goal, though, the feeling in the Forum was that Kings might just have a chance to come back. With around four minutes left, they made it 5–4, and it was complete bedlam in the arena. The Oilers had a couple of opportunities to increase their lead on breakaways, but Mario Lessard made the saves. A lot of people forget that my current partner on TV, Jim Fox, made one of the great plays with about 10 seconds left in regulation. Wayne Gretzky, who was with the Oilers at the time, had the puck and just needed to clear it to center ice and the game would be over, but Jim stepped in front of him, took the puck away, centered it to Mark Hardy, who took a shot that was saved, but Steve Bozek got the rebound and scored. As I hollered "Bozek scores!" I looked at the scoreboard and there were five seconds left. During the intermission before overtime, the Zambonis were resurfacing the ice, and the fans were going crazy yelling and screaming. In OT, the Oilers had a great chance to win, but Mark Messier shot high and over the net with Lessard way out of the net. Later in overtime, Daryl Evans fired a laser over the shoulder of Grant Fuhr to complete the Miracle on Manchester, and the place just erupted. I remember Evans doing an Ice Capades pirouette all the way down the ice in celebration, with his teammates chasing him.

Los Angeles Kings at Edmonton Oilers, Northlands Coliseum, Edmonton, Canada, October 15, 1989, and Vancouver Canucks at Los Angeles Kings, The Forum, Los Angeles, California, March 23, 1994

We knew Wayne Gretzky was going to break the all-time points mark, because he only needed six points at the start of the 1989–90 season. We get to, of all places, Edmonton. His career was like a Hollywood script, you just wondered how things can happen like this because you'd never believe it otherwise. I was doing radio and TV that night, and told my partner that when Wayne was on the ice, just point toward the ice and when he gets off the ice, point back toward us. I didn't want him to sneak on for a line change and not pick it up, because he came into the game needing just one point, and it could be on an assist that you don't always see. Whenever he came onto the ice, I told everyone he was out there, and when he left the ice, I told everyone he was on the bench. Fans later told me that whenever I said he was on the ice, they were on the edge of their seats, and then when I said he went to the bench, they all sat back and caught their breath. The Kings were losing, 4–3, with less than a minute left when Gretzky scored the goal for the points record. The previous summer, a friend asked me what I was going to say when he broke the record, and I told him that I was going to do the play-by-play and hope I got it right, because people were going to hear that call forever. He then asked if I had something special planned to say, and I started thinking about it and jotted down some things I might say. I told our producer that night that I knew he wanted to get crowd noise but asked for six seconds to say something. I'm glad I did that, because I got to say, "The Great One has become the greatest of them all with his 1,851st point. The all-time leading scorer in the history of the National Hockey League." There was nothing profound about it, but it put a capper on the play. They stopped the game and had a ceremony with Gordie Howe on the ice, along with Kings owner Bruce McNall and NHL Commissioner John Ziegler. The game was tied, though, and eventually went to overtime . . . where Gretzky scored the game-winner. It was that Hollywood script once again. You couldn't believe something like that would actually happen.

A little over four years later, Gretzky was going for the all-time goal-scoring record, and now I'm thinking I have to come up with something else to say. The great thing about that game was that he did it at home, so all of the Kings fans had the chance to enjoy it. Luc Robitaille and Marty McSorley had the assists on a goal scored against Vancouver's Kirk McLean, who was way out of position when McSorley got the puck over to Gretzky for the goal. I just said, "Wayne Gretzky's NHL record book is now complete. He is the all-time leader in points, assists, and now in goals with number 802." Moments like these are nervous times for play-by-play announcers because you don't want to mess it up, but there is no place else I would rather be than doing those games.

1993 Campbell Conference Finals, Game Seven, Los Angeles Kings at Toronto Maple Leafs, Maple Leaf Gardens, Toronto, Canada, May 29, 1993

The Kings had a mediocre season, with Wayne Gretzky missing a good part of the year with a herniated disc in his neck, so when the playoffs started, I don't think anyone thought the Kings had a chance to go to the Finals. They actually opened every series on the road, and it came down to Game Seven in the Campbell Conference Finals in Toronto. It was a great series, and everyone in Toronto wanted the Leafs to play the Canadiens (who had won the Prince of Wales Conference) in the Finals. The Kings had a 5–3 lead, thanks to a hat trick by Gretzky, but the Maple Leafs scored with just over a minute left to make it a one-goal game. They then pulled the goalie and were buzzing all around the net for the last 55 seconds of the game. I thought they were going to tie it up and was so nervous while doing the game that I was shaking. Finally, Marty McSorley knocked a puck out of the zone, and time expired, ending the series.

2012 Stanley Cup Final, Game Six, New Jersey Devils at Los Angeles Kings, Staples Center, Los Angeles, California, June 11, 2012, and 2014 Stanley Cup Final, Game Five, New York Rangers at Los Angeles Kings, Staples Center, Los Angeles, California, June 13, 2014

The two Los Angeles Kings Stanley Cup wins were so different. The first one is always significant, because I thought I'd never, ever see the Kings win a

Cup, and I don't think I was alone. The 2012 season wasn't a great one for the Kings, and they just got into the playoffs as the eighth seed in the West. From there, though, they went on an unbelievable run that none of us could have seen happening. They had a three-games-to-none lead in every series, which had never been done before, won ten straight games on the road, which had never been done before, and the eighth seed had never won the Cup before. But they steamrolled through everyone. In the Final against New Jersey, I remember getting to the arena before Game Four around noon, and there must have been 5,000 people there already, all yelling to me that this was the night. Sure enough, New Jersey won, and then won Game Five back at home, making the series 3–2 coming back to Los Angeles.

In Game Six, the Kings jumped out to a lead following a five-minute major against Steve Bernier of the Devils, where they scored three goals on the ensuing power play. I thought at the time that the third goal was really the killer for the Devils. After the Kings scored again, New Jersey made it 4–1, but two late goals made it 6–1 with three-and-a-half minutes to go, and everyone knew it was over. The greatest thing for me was looking around that arena and seeing Kings fans celebrating with that much time left because they knew this was it. This was what they were waiting all of those years for. I thought I better have something to say, so I tried to time it to the final whistle and said, "This is for you, Kings fans, wherever you may be. The forty-five-year drought is over. All the disappointment and frustration of the past is gone. The Los Angeles Kings are indeed the Kings of the NHL. They are the 2012 Stanley Cup champions." My partner, Jim Fox, played ten years for the Kings and had tears in his eyes. I think he had always followed the tradition of not touching the Cup until winning it, so he was so emotional. It was a great scene when the Cup came out on the ice and the fans finally had something to celebrate.

It was much different two years later. Even the players said that when they won it in 2014, this is the way it had to be won. It was so much tougher the second time. The Kings played twenty-six games in the playoffs that season out of a possible twenty-eight. There were seven overtime games, three of them going to double overtime, and they came back from a 3–0 series deficit in the first round against San Jose. That set the tone right there. In the Final against the Rangers, the first game in L.A. went to overtime, while the second went to double overtime, meaning they could have been down, 0–2, going back to New York. Instead, they were up, 2–0. They split the two games at the Garden, to come back to Los Angeles up three games to one. It is so great to win at home, but even that game was so close, going to double overtime again. Everybody was on the edge of their seats, unlike the first time around when the result of the game wasn't in doubt. When Alec Martinez scored the winning goal off of a rebound, the place exploded. I think everyone expected it to be a long time after the first Cup before it would happen again, but two years later, we got to experience it all over again. Any time you win, it is tremendous. Personally, though, I don't think anything can beat that first one, after you have waited so long for it to happen.

Alec Martinez scores the winning goal in overtime of Game Five to give the Los Angeles Kings the 2014 Stanley Cup. (AP Photo/Mark J. Terrill)

Jon Morosi

Broadcaster, FOX Sports/MLB Network

2002 NHL Western Conference Finals, Game Seven, Colorado Avalanche at Detroit Red Wings, Joe Louis Arena, Detroit, Michigan, May 31, 2002

I had just turned twenty, and that was the year at Harvard where I decided I wanted to be a sports journalist and had covered the hockey team there that season. During the summer, I was working as a news intern for my hometown paper, the *Bay City Times*, and they let me do some stringing at the Red Wings' playoff games for other papers. I got an assignment from the *Colorado Springs Gazette* to be the third person of their coverage team writing sidebars for the series. This series was the culmination of the Red Wings-Avalanche rivalry that had been going on for many years and was one of the fiercest rivalries I remember while growing up, so to cover it as one of my first assignments was really powerful for me. It was a great lesson about how to keep your emotions in check while working at games.

We were all expecting a tight, close-checking, emotional game, since every series between these two teams in all of their postseason matchups was that way. But the Wings came out and scored, then scored again, and again, and now Joe Louis Arena is coming off the screws, because not only are the Wings winning and headed to the Stanley Cup Finals, but they were embarrassing the villain that had been their chief rival and adversary. Claude Lemieux might have been more hated because of his hit on Kris Draper, but Patrick Roy represented his team for Detroit fans in a way that no athlete had since Michael Jordan represented the Bulls. The way he played that day, it was like Jordan going 3-for-25 in a Game Seven. There was a feeling of *schadenfreude* for the fans because of this dismantling of Roy. They finally pulled him after he gave up six goals, and I've never heard a combination of booing and cheering at the same time by the fans as I did then. I've also never seen a player that great vanquished like he was that night.

Milwaukee Brewers at Detroit Tigers, Comerica Park, Detroit, Michigan, June 12, 2007

The big story entering this game was that it was the first game in Detroit for Prince Fielder, who had grown up in the city. I was writing for the *Detroit Free Press* at the time and had done a big story about his return to the city where his father had done so much. There was also an issue with insects in the grass at the ballpark and these insects were a very popular food for seagulls, so for a period of a few days, Comerica Park was dealing with seagulls swarming everywhere. If you look at footage of the game, you can see seagulls scattering everywhere as Magglio Ordonez chases down the final out. It had actually reached the point where while I was writing the game story, John Lowe was there to write a story about the seagulls. As the game went along, though, we realized John might need to change the focus of the story, because Justin Verlander was in the process of throwing a no-hitter. It was fun for me to watch this game, because I had been covering the team since he came up from the minors. The chance to watch the culmination of his first true masterpiece was special. Sometimes during a no-hitter, you wonder whether the pitcher has the stuff to finish it off. There was no question that night that Verlander had everything he needed and was so masterful that left fielder Craig Monroe didn't touch the ball the entire night. If he had given up a hit, it would have been a total shock.

Cleveland Indians at Detroit Tigers, Comerica Park, Detroit, Michigan, June 2, 2010

It was only Armando Galarraga's fourth appearance (and third start) of the season, and although he was facing a less-than-stellar Indians lineup, there wasn't even a hint that this could be a special outing for him. He just cut through the Indians with incredible efficiency, and I remember looking up around the seventh inning, realizing he was throwing a perfect game, and thinking, "Was this really happening?" When he got through the eighth, I thought the most dangerous hitter he would face in the ninth was Mark Grudzielanek, a veteran hitter who wouldn't be afraid of the moment. Grudzielanek got a pitch to hit and crushed it to the warning track, where Austin Jackson tracked it down and made an unbelievable catch against the wall in center field. Now, you start thinking Galarraga is going to do it. He retired Mike Redmond to bring up a young infielder named Jason Donald representing the final out.

Donald hit a grounder to the right side, and there are a couple of things about the play. If first baseman Miguel Cabrera had let the ball go, I think second baseman Carlos Guillen would have made the play and thrown Donald out. That being said, I understand why Cabrera made the play, since with two outs in the ninth inning in a perfect game, you don't want to let the ball get through the infield for a hit. And he did make the play and threw Donald out at first. Galarraga wasn't really struggling to find the bag or set his feet, but clearly, on all replays, Donald was out. Jim Joyce missed the call, though, and called him safe, ending the perfect game and no-hitter. Even Donald's reaction on the field looked like he thought he was out. No one will ever know what was going on in Joyce's brain circuitry at the time. We'll never know, though. None of us were making the call, but even to the naked eye, he was out.

You always want to see history at a sporting event, even when you are in the press box, so I think on a certain level, we all wanted to see a perfect game. Then it hit us that now we were covering something that might have been more important than a perfect game, and possibly even more memorable than a perfect game. This game was going to be talked about longer and across more walks of life, because it struck people so deeply. Galarraga had achieved something, and it was taken away from him unjustly, albeit accidentally.

I was one of three reporters to interview Jim Joyce after the game, and it was the worst I felt in a sports context for anyone I've ever interviewed. You could see the pain on his face and tears in his eyes, and that he was physically and emotionally sick about what had happened. He hadn't seen a replay of the play until he got to the umpire's room after the game and left the field thinking he had gotten the call right, and I was standing outside the room when he watched it. He let out a guttural wail, as if he had been given a piece of devastating news. I heard the sound through the wall of the umpires' room. It was that loud. It was that immediate reaction of not even realizing what you are seeing, or saying or feeling in reaction to seeing it. The lasting legacy of that day, however, is that it was one of the moments that led to instant replay being instituted in Major League Baseball.

2011 World Series, Game Six, Texas Rangers at St. Louis Cardinals, Busch Stadium, St. Louis, Missouri, October 27, 2011

It felt like the Rangers had fate on their side after Game Five, where Tony LaRussa made a mistake with his bullpen, which is like Yo-Yo Ma missing a note on his cello. Texas had the lead, 7–5, after eight innings in Game Six, and it felt like they were going to close St. Louis out to win the Series. I still don't understand why Rangers manager Ron Washington kept a possibly injured Nelson Cruz in right field instead of replacing him with Endy Chavez, who was a superior defensive player and had made the last out in the top of the ninth inning as a pinch- hitter; it felt like 1986, when Bill Buckner stayed in the game for the Red Sox in Game Six instead of Dave Stapleton coming in for defense. I was watching the bottom of the ninth inning with Mark Kriegel, who was covering the game with me for FOXSports.com, from a walkway behind home plate, so that we had a head start to get downstairs once the game ended. We were surrounded by nervous, anxious Cardinals fans who were watching their team lose the World Series.

Then the comeback started, and the noise was ear-splitting. They were giving Albert Pujols a standing ovation with one out in the ninth because it might be his last at-bat as a Cardinal, and he doubled. Lance Berkman walks, then Allen Craig strikes out, bringing up David Freese. With two out and two strikes, he hit the ball well, which you could tell the moment he made contact. Cruz had a chance to catch it but couldn't get there, and it looked like he wasn't moving right because of that possible injury. Freese ends up on third base with a triple, and the game is tied. Josh Hamilton homered in the top of the tenth to put the Rangers up by two again, and again, everyone thinks the Rangers are going to win. For some reason, Washington brings in Darren Oliver, rather than send Neftali Feliz back out after he gave up the two runs in the ninth, and before you knew it, the tying runs were on base. They got one run across on a Ryan Theriot groundout, bringing up Berkman with two outs and the tying run on second. With two strikes, Berkman fights a pitch into center field to tie the game again. In the 11th, Freese does it again, this time homering for the win.

I covered the Rangers clubhouse after the game was over, and it was a mixture of despondence and shell shock. It was almost impossible to process everything in the immediate wake of what had just happened and I don't think the gravity of all of it had hit them yet. I remember being at Hamilton's locker, and it was one of the most memorable postgame interviews I've seen in my career. We all know his story, and he tells us that God himself had told him he was going to hit the home run in the 10th inning. Whatever your religious beliefs are, the fact that he is saying what he said was tremendously compelling. It was very real to him, and when I asked him exactly what God had said, he told me, "God said I was going to hit the home run. God never told me we were going to win the game." In many respects, that was the story—not that the Cardinals had won, but that the Rangers had lost, and lost in such a difficult manner.

David Freese hits the game-winning homer in the 11th inning of Game Six of the 2011 World Series. (AP Photo/Jeff Roberson)

2014 National League Division Series, Game Two, San Francisco Giants at Washington Nationals, Nationals Park, Washington, DC, October 4, 2014

This was the first playoff series I ever worked as a sideline reporter, so there is a lot of personal significance for me, as I did the series with Matt Vasgersian and John Smoltz for FOX. On top of that emotion is what became a historic game. It was an incredible ballgame, and it is a shame that Jordan Zimmermann's performance that day really gets lost in the shuffle. As the game went along, it looked like he was going to throw a complete-game shutout. In the top of the ninth, with the Nationals up, 1–0, I was talking with our producer, Brad Zager, to discuss whether the postgame interview was going to be live or taped. Brad decided that if Zimmermann completed the shutout, I would get him on the field as quickly as possible, and we would do it live. As I was trying to figure out what to ask him, the Giants rallied, and he was pulled with two outs. The Giants tied the game off Drew Storen, and we were off to extra innings. Now, we had to be ready to do a walk-off interview at any moment when Washington was hitting, because the game could end on every pitch. It got to be where I had questions for every player on the Nationals ready to go, because the game just went on and on, with no one scoring. I also had to be careful every time they sent it down to me for a report whenever the Nationals were hitting, because I didn't want to get caught in the middle of a story while something happened on the field to end the game. I was stationed near the Nationals dugout, and, in the top of the 18th, I had noticed they had swapped out the propane tanks on the heaters in the dugout for the second time. We decided to tell the story after Brandon Belt hit that inning, but I never got to tell it, because Belt homered to give the Giants the lead. In between innings, I ran over to the Giants' side of the field, so that we could be there to interview him as soon as the game ended. I was on one side of the field for 17-1/2 innings, then the other for the final three outs. When the game ended, I remember saying to Belt that it almost looked like he was relieved that he homered, and he started talking about how tired he was, as we all were. And for the record, I ended up using the men's room once, somewhere around the top of the 14th or 15th inning.

Chris Myers

Broadcaster, FOX Sports

1989 World Series, Game Three, Oakland Athletics at San Francisco Giants, Candlestick Park, San Francisco, California, October 17, 1989

I was with Joe Torre, who was between managing jobs at the time and was doing some work with Chris Berman, Bob Ley, and me at ESPN, and we were in the auxiliary press box at Candlestick Park, ready to file reports. Then we heard this noise, a loud rumbling. I live in California, so I've experienced minor earthquakes before. You could almost see the noise, and you thought that a plane had hit the stadium because of the shaking and the noise. Then, you could see the field almost ripple. The stadium was built on bedrock, so it didn't crumble, but you certainly could feel the vibrations. For people around us who had never been through something like this, you could see them turn pale and wonder exactly what was going on.

After things started settling down, you could see players come out on the field and start looking for their families and collecting them so they could make sure they were okay and get out of the stadium. I remember talking to Tony LaRussa after the Series ended and his A's swept the Giants, and realizing how bad we felt for guys who played their whole career to make it to a World

Members of the Oakland Athletics look into the Candlestick Park stands for family and friends in the aftermath of the earthquake that struck Northern California just before Game Three of the 1989 World Series. (AP Photo)

Series and for this to happen, where the games were nothing more than an afterthought and so unimportant.

1990 West Coast Conference Semifinals, Portland at Loyola Marymount, Gersten Pavilion, Los Angeles, California, March 4, 1990

I was the West Coast ESPN reporter, and it was my night off. I was out watching the movie *Born on the Fourth of July*, when I checked my messages and found out that I had gotten a call from the assignment desk telling me to get to the gym at Loyola Marymount because something had happened to Hank Gathers. I rushed over to the gym and found out that he had collapsed on the court and was being rushed to a medical center in Marina Del Rey, which was the first indication to me that this was a very serious situation.

When I got to the hospital, Gathers was being rushed inside. As I stood there, coach Paul Westhead and all of Gathers's teammates began to arrive and go in, but my camera crew and I waited outside. ESPN went on the air with *SportsCenter* at this point, and given the fact that I was totally unprepared physically to go on the air (I was in such a rush to get to the gym, I hadn't shaved or gotten dressed for TV), I borrowed a coat from an AP reporter for my report.

A medical representative came out to tell us that the family and coaches were being informed that Gathers had passed away and that it was believed to be from a heart attack. I confirmed the story with someone else who was inside and broke the story live on *SportsCenter* once I knew that the family was, in fact, informed of his death. All this happened literally within minutes of the doctors telling the family, so it was almost as if we were passing the story along as it was happening. At that point, a medical center spokesman came outside, and I pulled him into the shot, where he confirmed everything and gave more details. Then Loyola Marymount's athletic director came out, and we did the same thing. I've always been proud of the way we handled the story, not just by breaking it accurately, but with the sensitivity it warranted.

1996 Summer Olympics, Centennial Olympic Park, Atlanta, Georgia, July 27, 1996

I was on the rooftop of the Commerce Center in downtown Atlanta, right in the thick of all the Olympic activity that night, and was taping a wrapup for *SportsCenter* when we heard a loud "BOOM." I paused for a second but then kept going on the report, thinking it was just fireworks or something like that coming from Centennial Park. Then I turned around and saw the lights and people scrambling and realized that it was something serious. We had a pretty good view of the park but didn't know exactly what was going on.

As security told us to evacuate, and more information became available, I stayed with a camera crew and was able to get security to let me stay and finish the reports. I was able to move around with the security people and interview medical people and others about the situation as the National Guard came in to clear the area. We ended up being the only ones there to feed any information from inside that evacuated area. It looked like a vacated war zone, and we stayed on pretty much through the night giving reports.

2001 Daytona 500, Daytona International Speedway, Daytona, Florida, February 18, 2001

This was the first Daytona 500 broadcast for FOX. Dale Earnhardt was the face of his sport and was actually in a blocking position for his teammate Michael Waltrip at this point in the race. When he hit the wall in the wreck, at the time it didn't look pretty, but everyone assumed it was just another crash— Earnhardt had walked away many times from worse-looking accidents. But the way the car hit the wall, along with the way the seat belts were adjusted, led to his unfortunate death. You could see in the way some of the track personnel and drivers ran over to his car that something was terribly wrong. When they all stepped away the way they did, you could see they knew by the look on their faces. On the broadcast, of course, you can't say anything of that nature until you have absolute medical clearance to do so, so people questioned our delay in reporting his death. Unfortunately, there was nothing we could do in that situation. Just like that, the face of racing was gone.

2004 American League Championship Series, Game Four, New York Yankees at Boston Red Sox, Fenway Park, Boston, Massachusetts, October 17, 2004

I was the field reporter for FOX starting with Game Four of the ALCS, when the Sox were down three games to none. It was a rainy night in Boston for Game Four, and I remember Derek Lowe coming out of the dugout before the game, seeing the rain and gloom, and commenting that it felt like everyone was coming to a funeral. That really was the feeling at Fenway that night, from the fans and from both teams. After the Red Sox pulled out the game that night, though, you really could feel the shift in momentum. The Sox just felt like a different team after that—usually a day off will stop any shift in momentum, but it didn't in this case. After they finished off the Yankees by winning Games Five, Six, and Seven, beating the Cardinals was almost an afterthought.

Jim Nantz

Broadcaster, CBS Sports

Recipient of Basketball Hall of Fame's Curt Gowdy Award, 2002
Recipient of Football Hall of Fame's Pete Rozelle Award, 2011

The 1986 Masters, Final Round, Augusta National Golf Club, Augusta, Georgia, April 13, 1986

My first broadcast from Augusta happened to coincide with Jack Nicklaus's epic and historic sixth victory at the Masters. I was twenty-six years old and frightened out of my mind, trying to exude nothing but confidence and warrant being a part of the tapestry of the broadcast.

What unfolded that day many consider to be one of the greatest moments in the history of sports. Nicklaus shot 30 on the back nine, including a tee shot on 16 that very nearly went in the hole. I was stationed right behind the green and tried to get my mind around the enormity of the event. I was determined not to say something unworthy of the moment and risk CBS never inviting me back to work the Masters again. After Jack made a putt at 16 for birdie, I said, "There's no doubt about it. The Bear has come out of hibernation." After the tournament ended, I was walking back to the compound when a cart pulled up next to me. It was Ken Venturi. Little did I know then that he would eventually be my on-air partner for seventeen years in the tower at 18. He asked me how old I was, and I told him twenty-six. He said, "Jimmy, I'm going to make a prediction. Someday, you are going to be the first broadcaster to lay claim to broadcasting fifty Masters tournaments. But I will tell you this: you are never going to live to see a day greater than this at Augusta National."

1987 NCAA Men's Basketball Final Four, Louisiana Superdome, New Orleans, Louisiana, March 28-30, 1987

I had lived in New Orleans for three years when I was a kid, and the first game I ever attended was the old Sugar Bowl Basketball Classic when I was eight years old. My dad took me to see the University of Houston play because of his respect for their great coach Guy Lewis, who would later become a central figure in getting my career launched while I was a student at the school. In 1987, the Final Four was in New Orleans; it was my second Final Four. It was a great memory for me because my mom and dad came to it. They got to sit off to the side and watch their son host the broadcast from the Superdome. The year before at my first Final Four in Dallas, my dad drove up from Houston to attend the open practice on Friday and watch me rehearse for the broadcast the next night. He saw all of these people make a big fuss around his boy, and his eyes never really left me. He never even turned to watch the teams practice. When the practice was over, we said our good-byes, and he drove right back to Houston the same day. That night, our director, Bob Fishman, came over to ask where my dad was sitting for the games, and I told him he had driven home because he didn't have a ticket. He couldn't believe it and said, "Did you ask anybody for a ticket?" When I asked, "Who?" he replied, "CBS. You know, the people you work for." I didn't know we were allowed to ask, and he read me the riot act. He said, "Jim, you are working for the network now and hosting the Final Four. Don't ever let an opportunity like that go by again. For your family and your father, CBS would have found a way to get a ticket for him. All you had to do was ask." I was so new to this, I didn't know we were entitled to ask for tickets, so my poor dad drove five hundred miles round-trip, just to sit off to the side and watch his son rehearse. That made the 1987 Final Four so sweet for me, because I was coming back to New Orleans, where I had first gone to a basketball game. It all came full circle for me, and I got to introduce my folks to network television and this life that their son was just embarking on.

The 1992 Masters, Final Round, Augusta National Golf Club, Augusta, Georgia, April 12, 1992

Fred Couples and I were suitemates at the University of Houston. We arrived on campus on the same day in 1977 and roomed together until Fred left after his junior year to turn professional. I was completely out of my league when it came to golf ability, plus I didn't have the passion that the rest of my teammates had to be a professional golfer. I wanted to be a sports commentator and storyteller, so while they woke up every day trying to figure out how to get onto the PGA Tour, I was trying to figure out how to work for CBS Sports to call The Masters. To me, that was the event that defined golf, and I wanted to be a voice on that telecast. By my sophomore year, I was getting involved in the Houston media as a volunteer, working at the CBS radio station and the CBS television affiliate. My golf teammates would huddle around in awe while listening to my interviews, not believing that I actually had the press credential and was in the locker room that close to these sports figures. Every so often, I would turn the microphone on my buddies, and we would play-act doing interviews. I always had one role. I was the host of The Masters. Fast forward to 1992, and Fred Couples wins The Masters, and I am in Butler Cabin and am the host of the broadcast. It was the exact scenario we used to pretend when we were in college.

Super Bowl XLI, Indianapolis Colts vs. Chicago Bears, Dolphin Stadium, Miami Gardens, Florida, February 4, 2007

I am a real historian of the sports broadcasting industry and care deeply about my predecessors and the voices of my youth. I've been very fortunate to meet most of them and unfortunately have seen many of them pass on. Jack Whitaker remains one of my all-time favorite people, favorite broadcasters, and favorite influences in my life. I knew Jack had never really gotten the proper credit for being one of the broadcasters for Super Bowl I. He was part of a four-man team that called the game for CBS, with Ray Scott, Frank Gifford, and Pat Summerall; Scott did play-by-play for the first half, while Jack called it in the second half. Before my call of Super Bowl XLI between the Bears and the Colts, I called Mr. Whitaker, who winters in Palm Springs. I told him I was doing a golf tournament in San Diego the week between the AFC Championship Game and the Super Bowl and asked if I could visit with him after the tournament. I went to Palm Springs and sat with him, and one of the pieces of advice he gave me was to be ready for the opening kickoff. When I asked him why, he told me about the start of the second half of Super Bowl I. The kick was returned to around the 40, and all of a sudden, there are arms waving, and the players are getting back into position to do the kick over again. The officials didn't wear microphones back then, so there was no way of knowing exactly what was going on. All he knew was that he had just called a kickoff, and the players were back into kick formation again. It troubled Mr. Whitaker that he had no explanation for his audience as to why there was a re-kick. It wasn't until after the game that he found out that NBC, which was also airing the game, was not back from commercial in time for the kickoff, so the officials gave them a mulligan. He told me that story, which is an amusing one as time marches on, and said just be ready for the opening kick.

Our producer, Lance Barrow, put us on camera out of the commercial right before kickoff. I welcomed everybody back with Phil Simms, mentioned that CBS was the network for Super Bowl I, and named the four announcers that were there to call it. I wanted to channel, somehow if I could, Jack Whitaker, because I was going to get ready for that opening kick he warned me about, so I mentioned him as the ball was being placed on the tee by Adam Vinatieri. Phil makes a comment right before the kickoff, and I turn around and watch the ball land in the arms of Devin Hester at the 8-yard line. Hester returned the ball 92 yards for a touchdown and the only opening kickoff return for a touchdown in Super Bowl history. I'm not into ranking or rating my play-by-play calls, but it is definitely the most satisfying one I've ever had in my career. It felt so sweet to be on top of that play as it unfolded, and I felt as if Jack Whitaker were peering proudly over my shoulder for all 92 yards.

2010 NCAA Men's Basketball Tournament Finals, Butler vs. Duke, Lucas Oil Stadium, Indianapolis, Indiana, April 5, 2010

I had a front-row seat to what nearly became the greatest ending in sports history. I'm not talking about just college basketball, but any sport. Gordon Hayward's midcourt launch at the buzzer very nearly rattled home to give underdog Butler the victory over Duke. It was a great Cinderella story throughout the entire NCAA Tournament that a mid-major was advancing. All roads were leading to Indianapolis, where Butler's campus was just six miles away from Lucas Oil Stadium. Butler won the West bracket, and it was a titanic achievement for them just to get to the Final Four. Then they beat Michigan State in the semifinals to advance to the title game, and the storyline was so irresistible. Here was this Cinderella against one of the iconic programs in any sport, Mike Krzyzewski's Blue Devils. You can't get a storyline much better than that one.

On the day of the game, there is always a little nervous energy for everyone, including the broadcasters. You wait around all day to do a primetime broadcast. I received word that Hayward had actually attended class that day and thought it had to be the first time that had happened in the history of the Final Four. I asked around before the game and found out he had actually attended two classes. Now here we are in the evening, and the ball ends up in his hands off a missed free throw. He takes the shot from the right side of the midcourt stripe. Because the game was being played in a football stadium, the players were actually on a raised stage above us, and their sneakers were at my eye level. Hayward was coming toward us, and when he launched the shot, he was so close to myself and Clark Kellogg that I could have reached out and untied his shoes. That gave me the all-time perfect angle; the only person who had a better view of it was Hayward himself. I could see that it was definitely on the right line, so the only question was whether it was the right distance. It hit off the glass, banged off the front of the rim, tried to come back into the cylinder, and then fell off the front of the rim. If I had to do the math on it, I'd say he was probably an eighth of an inch too high on the backboard. From fifty feet away when he took the shot, that is how close he came to making a shot that would have won the title and gone into the history books as the ultimate finish.

Ross Newhan

Author/Journalist

Recipient of Baseball Hall of Fame's J.G. Taylor Spink Award, 2000

Los Angeles Angels at Baltimore Orioles, Memorial Stadium, Baltimore, Maryland, April 11, 1961

I went to school in Long Beach and had gotten a part-time job at the Long Beach newspaper out of high school. At that time, the *Long Beach Independent Press-Telegram* had an outstanding sports section and covered all of the events the Los Angeles papers did. When the American League expanded and the Angels started playing in 1961, I was next in line for a major beat, and they assigned me to the new expansion team. It was the first baseball expansion, and the hype really built up to the first game on April 11. Everyone was predicting the season would be a disaster for an expansion team, but they won their first game, 7–2. Eli Grba pitched a complete game, Ted Kluszewski hit two home runs, and Bob Cerv hit one. After the game in the clubhouse, you would have thought they just won Game Seven of the World Series. After that game, reality set in, of course, and the season went exactly the way everyone thought it would.

1973 Belmont Stakes, Belmont Park, Elmont, New York, June 9, 1973

The *Los Angeles Times* didn't have a regular race writer at the time, and I was on an Angels trip, so they asked me to cover the Belmont Stakes. I was excited to do it, since my parents were big horse racing fans and I've always been a devotee. I was only at Belmont for one day but got to see one of the most commanding performances in sports history—Secretariat winning by thirty-one lengths. When people often ask me what the one big event is that has stayed with me the most, even though I was a baseball writer for over forty years, this race keeps popping into my mind. I'd never seen a jockey turn around on a horse during a race like Ron Turcotte did to look back for the competition and ultimately, as he was coming down homestretch, checking out the board to see his time. Having the opportunity to write about that really stands out for me.

Los Angeles Dodgers at Atlanta Braves, Atlanta Stadium, Atlanta, Georgia, April 8, 1974

It wasn't only the moment Hank Aaron hit home run number 715. I had covered the end of the 1973 season in Cincinnati, where Aaron, for the first time, really started talking about the types of letters he was getting, the types of encounters he was having on the streets, and the racist atmosphere that was surrounding his pursuit of Babe Ruth. The Braves held him out of one of the games in Cincinnati to give him a better chance of hitting the historic home run in Atlanta at the start of the 1974 season. It was all about the buildup. I remember looking at the clock and trying to record the scene in my mind, but the home run itself wasn't as dramatic as everything that surrounded it. The fact that the commissioner wasn't there played into the story, but it was one of the great moments in baseball history.

1977 World Series, Game Six, Los Angeles Dodgers at New York Yankees, Yankee Stadium, Bronx, New York, October 18, 1977

I've covered many World Series in New York, and a Series there separates itself from any other because of the press coverage, the atmosphere, and the history. Reggie Jackson's performance in this game was so stunning, both in person and in reflection. Hitting three home runs on the first pitch from three different pitchers was simply incredible. At that time, MLB wasn't doing the interview room process, so the clubhouse was just packed and trying to get a quote or two from Reggie afterwards was an act of survival. It was a seminal moment in my World Series coverage.

Reggie Jackson watches the path of his third home run of the game during Game Six of the 1977 World Series. (AP Photo)

2002 World Series, San Francisco Giants vs. Anaheim Angels, Pacific Bell Park, San Francisco, California and Edison Field, Anaheim, California, October 19-27, 2002

Several things stand out to me about the Angels winning the World Series. Down the stretch, to see Anaheim Stadium all in red was something none of us who had covered the club for many years ever thought we'd see in Anaheim. Also, in the previous forty-plus years, the philosophy and continuity was so inconsistent. There were a few homegrown players, but the team never kept them. It was always a win-now philosophy in Anaheim, but the team had only gone to the playoffs three times, with disastrous results in 1982 and 1986. So here was a team in 2002 that had been drafted and came through the system basically as a group. Garret Anderson, Troy Glaus, Darin Erstad, Tim Salmon, John Lackey, Troy Percival, Jarrod Washburn, Francisco Rodriguez . . . these were all products of the organization. To win with that core group of players was basically at odds with their pattern from their first forty years. That kind of thing stuck out, and I felt that winning that Series was going to be a huge building block for the future, and they have been to the playoffs six times in thirteen years since then.

Rob Parker

Broadcaster, WXYZ-TV/Detroit Sports 105.1 FM

1986 World Series, Game Six, Boston Red Sox at New York Mets, Shea Stadium, Flushing, New York, October 25, 1986

I was a young reporter for the *New York Daily News* at the time but grew up a Mets fan and had tickets for the game in the upper deck on the first-base side. Even though I was in the stands, I was torn between being a fan and being a writer, but I chose to be a fan that night. My godfather said to me that if I was able to get tickets to the game, he would go with me, so it was special to spend the moment with him. Even though the Mets were down two runs in the bottom of the 10th, no one had left. When Bob Stanley came in, I turned to my godfather and told him that Stanley was prone to throwing wild pitches. Of course, he then threw an inside pitch off of Rich Gedman's glove, and Kevin Mitchell scored the tying run. Now, Mookie Wilson starts fouling pitches off, and I'm hoping and praying that this team that had steamrolled through the regular season could win the Series that they were supposed to win. Wilson hit the roller toward first base, and I really felt that he was going to beat Bill Buckner to the bag. When it went through Buckner's legs, though, it was total pandemonium. It felt like an out-of-body experience, and you just revel in the moment because you can't believe what you just saw. The oneness of the crowd still gives me goose bumps. To this day, after watching the replay so many times over the years, I still know the call by Vin Scully verbatim. That is how impactful that play was. The last scene I remember was two Red Sox fans who were sitting in my section taking their hats off as they were leaving their seats.

1989 NBA Playoffs Opening Round, Game Five, Chicago Bulls at Cleveland Cavaliers, Richfield Coliseum, Richfield, Ohio, May 7, 1989

The Bulls didn't win the championship this season, but it was the start of Michael Jordan's greatness. When the teams came out on the floor after a timeout with three seconds left, I turned to Clifton Brown of the *New York*

Times, who was sitting next to me courtside, and asked him what Cleveland coach Lenny Wilkens was doing. The Cavs weren't guarding the inbounds pass, but even with the extra defender, they weren't able to keep Jordan from getting free, and he was able to make the game-winning shot over Craig Ehlo in one of the most famous moments of his career. Jordan had been much maligned about his playoff performances to that point. He would score a lot of points, but his teams ultimately didn't win, and people were already saying he would never win the big one. When he made that shot, it was complete silence in the building; all you heard were a couple of Bulls fans in the stands and the celebration of the Bulls players and coaches on the court. The silence was truly deafening. It was one of those shots where you knew the player taking it was special. The entire series hinged on that shot, and if he missed it, they were going home.

1993 NFC Wild Card Playoffs, Green Bay Packers at Detroit Lions, Pontiac Silverdome, Pontiac, Michigan, January 8, 1994

It was the last playoff game ever at the Silverdome, so there is a little history to it. The Lions won the division that year, and Brett Favre was still at the stage of his career where he would make a couple of good plays followed by a couple of bad plays. With about a minute to go, Favre stepped to his left like he was going to run, which didn't make any sense because they needed something downfield, and lets go of a high, arcing ball that looked like a popup. The Lions' defensive back, Kevin Scott, was covering Sterling Sharpe one-on-one but stopped when Favre started scrambling. That left Sharpe all alone in the end zone just to wait for this floater to come down into his arms and win the game. It was another heartbreak for the Lions but was also one of those Brett Favre gunslinging plays that he would become so famous for. This was the first playoff win for Favre and set the tone for so many of the late-game heroics in his career.

2001 World Series, Games Four and Five, Arizona Diamondbacks at New York Yankees, Yankee Stadium, Bronx, New York, October 31 and November 1, 2001

After the events of 9/11, it was a World Series everyone assumed the Yankees were going to win, but they were struggling with the Diamondbacks. In Game Four, when Tino Martinez homered in the bottom of the ninth to tie the game, I can only remember a few other times in my thirty-year career where the stadium shook. You hear it all of the time, but there is nothing like a home run with two outs in the bottom of the ninth. It only tied the game, but it felt like a game- winner. At the very least, it gave the Yankees life. It was an amazing feeling, even as someone who isn't a Yankee fan, just to be there to see what you knew was a special moment that you knew you would remember your whole life. In some ways, Derek Jeter's game-winning home run the next inning paled in comparison to the homer that tied the game.

The next night, for Game Five, a lot of writers were downstairs in an auxiliary press room and working from there so they could get to the locker rooms more easily once the game ended. Everyone was writing the same story they had written the night before, about the Yankees trailing with two outs in the bottom of the ninth, when Scott Brosius comes up and homers to tie the game. All of the writers who were feverishly writing so that they could file as

Derek Jeter celebrates his game-winning home run in the 10th inning of Game Four of the 2001 World Series. (AP Photo/Bill Kostroun)

soon as the game ended stopped writing when Brosius tied the game and looked around at one another with that feeling of déjà vu. It was eerie how everyone did the same thing. Nobody said it, but everyone felt the same thing. They couldn't believe what they just saw. We were underneath the stadium, but once that initial moment passed, we could hear the crowd inside the stadium, and it was shaking again. It was something that I felt privileged to be a part of and be able to see.

2004 NBA Eastern Conference Finals, Game Two, Detroit Pistons at Indiana Pacers, Conseco Fieldhouse, Indianapolis, Indiana, May 24, 2004

The 2004 Pistons team was very special. Once they got Rasheed Wallace, I think that was the greatest team I ever saw. There were no superstars, everyone knew their role, and there was a different hero every night. It was also one of the great defensive teams you'll ever see and had the right coach in Larry Brown. They did everything right. Game Two was in Indiana, but the Pistons couldn't afford to lose and go down two games to none in the series. Late in the game, Reggie Miller looked like he had an easy transition basket off of a Chauncey Billups turnover that would have tied the game, but Tayshaun Prince raced the length of the court to get back and block the shot. To me, Miller made two mistakes on the play. First was slowing down and thinking he had an easy layup. He wasn't known as a dunker, but that is a play where you have to dunk the ball, because if someone is chasing you, the worst-case scenario would be that you get fouled. You also have to know who is on the floor, because Prince was known as a shot blocker. Prince got the ball clean and didn't swat it out of bounds. He hit it just hard enough to direct it to the corner, where Richard Hamilton was able to grab it and seal the victory. It was one of the all-time great plays. I have an original painting in my house of that play, as well as another one in the barbershop that I own. It was a signature play for that team and that franchise.

Gary Parrish

Broadcaster, CBS Sports Network/Columnist, CBSSports.com

Mike Tyson vs. Lennox Lewis, The Pyramid, Memphis, Tennessee, June 8, 2002

The fight was in Memphis, which is where I'm from and live. And it was after the Tyson-Holyfield fights. So Tyson couldn't get licensed in Nevada, and they were looking for a place to do the fight, since they knew it would generate huge pay-per-view and gate numbers. And there was a small boxing promotion company called Prize Fight Boxing based in Tennessee that made a run at it. Next thing you know, the fight's in Memphis, and it ended up being the most lucrative fight in history, at the time.

I was a young reporter at the *Commercial Appeal* newspaper, and I was a boxing fan. I grew up playing *Mike Tyson's Punch-Out!!*, so the idea of being involved in the coverage of the fight was exciting for me. I spent the week leading up to the fight with Tyson's camp, and it all led to this night where every big-name celebrity you can think of was in Memphis. During the preliminary fights, while The Pyramid was still mostly empty, I was sitting in the first row of the stands having a conversation with someone, when Leonardo DiCaprio came over and sat down in the seat next to me, and he was with Tobey Maguire. And though I didn't realize the significance of it at the time, in the ring, fighting while I'm chatting with Leo and Tobey, was Manny Pacquiao, who, of course, went on to be a legend of the sport. I remember the thirty-to-forty minutes leading up to the fight and never experiencing anything else like it. The electricity and star power in the crowd were amazing. That night, though, it became clear to everyone that Mike Tyson wasn't going to be the same Mike Tyson ever again. You could talk yourself into Holyfield being a bad matchup, or that the ear-biting was a crazy episode, but it was still Iron Mike. But when Lennox Lewis knocked him out, he was beaten like he hadn't been beaten since being released from prison. The memories of that night are such a dichotomy—from all of the celebrities being in Memphis to watching a legend from my childhood see his career, for all intents and purposes, end.

2005 Conference USA Championship Game, Louisville vs. Memphis, FedEx Forum, Memphis, Tennessee, March 12, 2005

John Calipari's team that season returned a bunch of players that had played in the NCAA Tournament the year before and added a freshman point guard named Darius Washington. So they were preseason Top 20 and were supposed to be great. It didn't work out that way, however, and they had lots of chemistry problems early in the season. They got better as the season went along, and, while they didn't have much of a chance at an at-large bid because of their early season struggles, they still had a good chance of getting into the NCAA Tournament by winning the Conference USA tournament in Memphis. The Tigers made it to the championship game on their home floor, where they were facing Rick Pitino's Louisville Cardinals, with the conference's automatic bid on the line.

Memphis was down two in the final seconds when Washington took a three-point shot and got fouled with no time left on the clock. The crowd went crazy, because the math was simple—make two of the three shots and the game goes to overtime, make three and the Tigers win and go to the NCAA Tournament. This was a kid whom I had gotten to know during the season. He wasn't too popular among his teammates and wasn't a natural point guard, and he was replacing a senior named Antonio Burks, who was. So Washington was the guy who took a lot of the heat for the problems the team had. Here he is, though, with a chance to erase all of that and be the hero. Because there was no time on the clock, he went to the line by himself, with all of the other players watching from the sideline. He made the first shot, but then missed the second. He was such a good free-throw shooter that no one expected him to miss again, but you could see panic set in on his face after the first miss. The moment was clearly getting to him, to the point where Calipari has said that he wished he had called a timeout just to calm him down, which is contrary to everything a coach usually does. The way he explains it now, if he did that and Washington missed, the blame would not have fallen on the player's shoulders, and Calipari could have taken the heat instead. That was all hindsight, however, and Washington missed and then collapsed right at the free-throw line. He took his jersey and covered his face with it, because, as he later explained to me, his father had always told him that a man doesn't let people see him cry. It was such a vulnerable moment—on his home court and on national television—that his instincts were to cover his face. I've never seen a more gut-wrenching moment that didn't involve a physical injury than that moment on that floor that day.

2006 NCAA Men's Basketball Tournament Regional Semifinals, Gonzaga vs. UCLA, Oakland Arena, Oakland, California, March 23, 2006

It was my last year as the Memphis beat writer, and I was in Oakland covering the team in the Sweet 16. The first half of the doubleheader that day was Gonzaga-UCLA. I got there early enough to go out to the court and see that Gonzaga was up by seventeen points, and then I went back to the press room under the arena. As the game progressed, I started hearing these crazy roars. Felt like the arena was going to collapse on top of us. It was really loud, and the sound was registering to the point where you knew something amazing was going on. Because the game was in Oakland, you see, there were lots of UCLA fans there, so it wasn't a typical neutral-court game, and it was getting loud. So I went out to see what was going on, and Gonzaga was now up just three with 20 seconds left, and UCLA was getting ready to shoot free throws. It was hard to believe they had blown the lead, but they were still ahead. And even if the Bruins made both free throws, Gonzaga would still have the lead and the ball. But after UCLA made both free throws, the Zags committed a turnover that led to an easy basket that would be UCLA's game-winner. The whole place went nuts. The game had turned just like that. It happened so fast. And this ended up being Adam Morrison's final game at Gonzaga. He had become an iconic figure in the sport by that time. After the game, though, what everyone will always remember was him lying on the court, crying. You can cry for lots of different reasons, but what that moment felt like to me was a guy realizing that this was it. He was never going to be Adam Morrison, Rock Star, again. This game was where all of the hype led him, and he was seconds away from being in the Elite Eight and playing for a spot in the Final Four.

Adam Morrison falls to the floor in tears after losing to UCLA in the final seconds of their 2006 NCAA Tournament Regional Semifinal. (AP Photo/Paul Sakuma)

And then it was all ripped away so abruptly. I remember looking at him and thinking he understood what had just happened more than most in his shoes would have. And, sadly, that was the last time he was a meaningful player in a meaningful game.

2008 NCAA Men's Basketball Tournament Finals, Memphis vs. Kansas, Alamodome, San Antonio, Texas, April 7, 2008

There has always been an inherent sense among the people of Memphis that something is going to go wrong, even when things are going well. Every big moment had always been trumped by something else. But when John Calipari came to coach the Tigers, because he is such a good salesman, he had convinced Memphians that the city could be more than it had ever been, and the program could be more than it had ever been, and they loved him because of it. At that time, there was no bigger figure in the city, and he had everyone believing "Why can't it be us?"

In 2008, not only did they have Derrick Rose, but they also had a team that grew up rough, the same way many people from Memphis grow up. They weren't kids from Memphis, but they all could have been, and they had that same attitude that people in the city had. In the championship game, they were up nine with less than two minutes to go, and they were going to win the national championship. You can watch as many basketball games as you want, and you'll rarely see a team blow a lead like that. I remember sitting there and thinking that if someone told me while I was growing up in Memphis that the school would win a national championship in anything, I never would have believed it. And yet it was happening. But then it all fell apart, and, before you knew it, Mario Chalmers hit a three to force overtime, at which point Kansas had momentum and, ultimately, the win.

It is one thing to lose in a national championship game, but this was different. This game was over until it wasn't. And I can still see Chalmers hitting that shot, which was right in front of where I was sitting. I've never seen a title game turn so quickly, and while that shot only sent the game to overtime, if you were in that building, you knew it was over the moment Chalmers's shot went in.

Providence at Creighton, CenturyLink Center Omaha, Omaha, Nebraska, March 8, 2014

I do studio and sideline work for the CBS Sports Network, and we were lucky enough to be in Omaha for Doug McDermott's Senior Day. I was the sideline reporter. And not only was McDermott going to be the National Player of the Year and, statistically, one of the greatest college players of all time, but he was also going for 3,000 points in the game. His father was also the coach of the team. So the game checked so many boxes, and you really hoped the day would go down in a storybook way. In the first half, McDermott went crazy and ultimately ended the game with a career-high 45 points, passing the 3,000-point mark along the way. Then, afterwards, they did the Senior Day ceremony, and he was with his family, and, if you were writing a basketball movie and looking for the final scene, it would be hard to beat this one. It was pretty random that I was there that night, but I remember sitting there thinking how neat it was, especially in an era where most of the best players don't even have a Senior Day.

Jeff Pearlman

Author, *Showtime* **and** *The Bad Guys Won!*

1992 North Atlantic Conference Championship Game, Drexel at Delaware, Delaware Field House, Newark, Delaware, March 9, 1992

This game will always be my greatest observatory sport moment. I was a sophomore at the University of Delaware and was the assistant sports editor at the school newspaper, *The Review*. Delaware had never made it to the NCAA Tournament before. They played in this horrible arena with a rubberized basketball court, a track around it, and bleachers. The Blue Hens were great that season, though. When you go to a school like Duke or North Carolina, you have expectations and assume that you are going to the NCAA Tournament every season. Delaware didn't have those, however, and on this day, 2,000 fans crammed into this hot, crappy gymnasium to see the Blue Hens beat the stuffing out of Drexel. I was sitting at the press table, at the far end of the court, and the building was shaking. It was this innocent joy that doesn't exist at any mid-major school anymore. It was really raw, intense, and celebratory. ESPN would always cover all of the conference championship games, and they sent the late Tom Mees to do the game. Tom was a Delaware graduate, so I made sure to interview him for the paper before the game. Delaware won by twenty-four, and after the game, a guard named Ricky Deadwyler sat on top of the basket and was doing a dance. It was the last game that I enjoyed as both a fan and a member of the media. I was a Delaware student in the process of becoming a member of the media but still had enough student in me to enjoy the euphoria.

1992 NCAA Men's Basketball Tournament First Round, Delaware vs. Cincinnati, University of Dayton Arena, Dayton, Ohio, March 20, 1992

There was a restaurant in the student union at Delaware called The Scrounge, and I was there to cover the selection show when it was announced that Delaware would play Cincinnati in the first round of the NCAA Tournament. The first thought that went through everyone's heads there was that, "Wow, that isn't so bad. This game is winnable." Delaware had a frontcourt that had a lot of size and had only lost three times all season, so it really felt like they could win that matchup. There were some bad signs, though. Early in the season, the Blue Hens lost to Bucknell and Delaware State, so the red flags were there. The student newspaper traveled with the team to the games, and on the trip to Dayton for the game, these guys were convinced they were going to win. What's more, I was convinced they were going to win. I had never covered an NCAA Tournament and was sitting in the press row for the game, so it was a huge deal for me. Delaware won the jump ball and scored to go ahead, 2–0, and that feeling that they could win kept growing. Then, Cincinnati decided to press Delaware, and it makes me laugh thinking about it. It was ridiculous and was the equivalent of Delaware doing that to an intramural team. Cincinnati destroyed Delaware so badly, winning, 85–47. The Bearcats had multiple future NBA players on the team and were athletic and quick. They completely shut down all of Delaware's best players. Despite all of that, though, it was still a joy to be there, and the annihilation after coming into the building with lofty expectations is a better story than if they had lost by five.

Roy Jones Jr. vs. Lou Del Valle, The Theater at Madison Square Garden, New York, New York, July 18, 1998

I used to love boxing when I was a kid, and this was the first fight I ever covered. Sugar Ray Leonard was my favorite boxer while growing up, and Roy Jones Jr. was the closest thing I had seen to Sugar Ray as an adult. Lou Del Valle had a sister who was also a boxer, and whom I had written about for *S.I.* and really liked, so I was acutely aware of this fight and was really into it. I was sitting ringside, and it was the closest I had ever been at a real fight, to the point where I was getting spit on my notebook. Jones had never been knocked down in a fight at this point, so I thought he was totally invincible. Boxing done really well is beautiful, but it usually isn't. Roy Jones Jr., though, was a beautiful boxer. He doesn't appear on many lists of the all-time greats, but he really deserves to be considered one. He could cover up if he didn't want to get hit, and his opponent would become completely inconsequential. Everything he did was with purpose, every muscle had a reason when it was moving. He was the most unique athlete I ever covered.

1999 National League Championship Series, Game Five, Atlanta Braves at New York Mets, Shea Stadium, Flushing, New York, October 17, 1999

I was the number two baseball writer at *Sports Illustrated* at the time, and both the Mets and Yankees were really good, so, generally, Tom Verducci got the Yankees and I got the Mets. The Mets were really fun during that era, and after every game they won, in the clubhouse, they would play "Don't Leave Me This Way" by Thelma Houston. I loved covering that team, but they could never beat the Braves. Obviously, this game was memorable for the way it ended, with the famous Robin Ventura "grand slam single" (Ventura was only credited with a single despite hitting a walk-off grand slam home run because he didn't touch all four bases prior to the on-field celebration). But the other thing that stood out that night was something that happened while we were sitting in the auxiliary press box during the game. At one point, a fan sitting in front of Verducci (who was also covering the game that night) was acting like a jerk. Tom is very quiet, mild-mannered, and dignified, but the guy was hassling him during the game, and all of a sudden, Verducci has him in a headlock and the two of them are fighting. The fan got kicked out, and Verducci went back to looking like a model two seconds later.

Atlanta Braves at New York Mets, Shea Stadium, Flushing New York, September 21, 2001

I was living in New York City and working for *Sports Illustrated*, and 9/11 was a very traumatic event for me. I lived around a mile from the World Trade Center, and you could smell it in the air for weeks. It was a horribly emotional time—everyone wanted to do something, but no one knew what to do. This was the first event I covered for *S.I.* after 9/11, and while the game itself was amazing, the moment when Mike Piazza hit the winning home run off

Steve Karsay was electric. It was as raw and emotional as anything I had ever covered. To me, though, the moment that was truly goose bump-raising and sent chills down your spine was when Liza Minnelli got on the field between innings and sang "New York, New York" and started doing a kick line with the police officers on the field. People just went crazy, and as a New Yorker, it was monumental for me. I'll never forget how amazing that was.

Joe Posnanski

Columnist, NBC Sports

1996 Summer Olympics, Men's 200 Meter Final, Centennial Olympic Stadium, Atlanta, Georgia, August 1, 1996

My first Olympics was 1996 in Atlanta, and I had never really covered track and field outside of some high school stuff, so I'd never been around such a high level of the sport. Michael Johnson was going for the double in the 200 and 400, and when I was in the stadium, it had never occurred to me just how exciting it could be to watch people run. Johnson already had the lead when the race went into the turn, and when he hit the turn, I've never really seen or felt anything quite like it. Everybody in the stadium went crazy at once. It was an eruption. He went flying through the turn, and I'll always like his description of it. He said it was like being in a go-kart going downhill too fast. You're almost on the edge of being out of control, and that is how it felt. It was like his body was going faster than it was capable of going. He just blew everybody away. The race took 19.32 seconds, and in that time, from the beginning of the race to the end, I felt completely different. It is such a shared experience in a way that team sports can't be. Everyone is focused on one person, and even if you were rooting for someone else, you were still sort of pulling for Johnson, because you wanted to say you saw something that you'll never forget.

2000 PGA Championship, Final Round, Valhalla Golf Club, Louisville, Kentucky, August 20, 2000

This was the third of the four majors Tiger Woods won on the way to the "Tiger Slam," and it was far and away the closest of them. I had obviously followed all of his major championships closely, and there was this legend building around him that was so overwhelming at the time that even he couldn't live up to it. It wasn't just that he was winning, it was that he was so dominant while winning. He had just blown away the entire field in both the U.S. Open and the British Open and was the heavy favorite entering the PGA Championship. Tiger was in position to win, but a golfer named Bob May, whom most fans had never heard of, forced a playoff with Woods after both made difficult putts on 18, with May making his first to put a lot of pressure on Woods to make his. It was the first time since he began his dominance that Tiger was being really challenged. This wasn't just about being better than everyone else, but it was the first time as a professional that he had to stand up and show us his heart while being directly challenged. Watching him bring out his best in those final moments was very special.

2000 Summer Olympics, Greco-Roman Wrestling Super Heavyweight Final, Sydney Exhibition Centre, Sydney, Australia, September 27, 2000

This is always going to be my favorite sports moment ever, and I've written at length about it in the past. It was a total fluke that I was even there, because that night, the U.S. baseball team led by Tommy Lasorda was playing for the gold medal. Basically everyone was going to that game, but I had written about that team enough at that point and had enough freedom to cover what I wanted during the Olympics. So I went instead to write about the great Russian wrestler Alexander Karelin, who was the Michael Jordan of the sport. It was a big night for him, as he was trying to win his fourth gold medal and had never given up a point at the Olympics. The place was electric because of this, not electric with Americans, but with Russians and people who were fans of wrestling. I didn't even know the rules of the event but was just watching it to cover Karelin. I don't even think I knew that he was wrestling an American that night and certainly didn't know Rulon Gardner's name. There was a moment during the match where the whole crowd gasped. I didn't know what I was watching but looked up at the scoreboard and saw that Gardner had scored a point. I knew enough that this was a rare thing and also knew enough to know that time was running out for Karelin. Suddenly there was this chance that I was going to see one of the greatest upsets in Olympics history but didn't even know how it happened. Gardner won, and I clearly remember the scene as the final seconds were running out, with the arena going crazy because it was so unexpected, and Karelin holding out his hand to shake Gardner's hand in defeat. You didn't have to know a thing about sports to get the gravity of it. I didn't learn about Gardner's incredible backstory until his press conference. By the end of the night, through a run of luck and bumping into people, I had talked to his mother and his father, and had called his hometown radio station, and each told me an amazing story about him. When I finally sat down to write, my head was going to explode. I literally had too much information. I never could have imagined that I was going to walk into a story as great as this one simply by being in the right place at the right time.

Rulon Gardner holds the arm of Alexander Karelin during the Greco-Roman Super Heavyweight gold medal wrestling match at the 2000 Summer Olympics. (AP Photo/ Katsumi Kasahara)

2001 World Series, Game Four, Arizona Diamondbacks at New York Yankees, Yankee Stadium, Bronx, New York, October 31, 2001

The Diamondbacks were leading the series two games to one and went into the ninth inning with a two-run lead. I was working for the *Kansas City Star* at the time and was writing on a deadline that was very tight, so I basically had to have a column done when the game ended. I had already written my column about the Yankees being dead. They had won the previous three World Series, but a team that no one expected to end their dynasty was about to do exactly that, and it wasn't going to be particularly close. As the ninth inning progressed, the Yankees got a runner on, and Tino Martinez homered to tie the game. Yankee Stadium was going crazy, and all I could think about was that my story was ruined. I now literally had nothing to say and started thinking if I could put the word "not" in various places in the story, as in the Yankees are "not" dead, and if just changing that could make the story work. I ended up tearing up that story and writing again, but now I'm writing based on nothing, because the game was tied. I started writing two columns at the same time, one for each outcome, and just going back and forth between two screens, hardly even watching the game.

When Derek Jeter hit his "Mr. November" homer in the bottom of the 10th, my first thought wasn't even that I had just seen one of the great moments of my life, but that I knew I had to write the column about the Yankees winning. What I ended up sending was gibberish; it was barely English. I sent it in, then had a few minutes to rewrite it for the later editions, and people in the stadium were singing along with Frank Sinatra's "New York, New York." After the song ended, it started again, and people were still singing. No one wanted to leave. Suddenly, this moment was crashing on me. Now I'm seeing it in the light of 9/11, in the light of all of these New Yorkers wanting to capture this moment and in the light of the Yankees dynasty being prolonged by New York's most beloved player. It was overwhelming, and it just kept going. They played the song over and over, and even though I was supposed to be writing, I was caught up in how amazing the moment was. I knew whatever I wrote wasn't going to live up to that moment.

Missouri at Kansas, Allen Fieldhouse, Lawrence, Kansas, February 25, 2012

Having been a columnist in Kansas City for around fifteen years, I came to really understand what Missouri-Kansas basketball meant. It was every bit as big as Duke-North Carolina or Alabama-Auburn in football. It was so intense, and so many people put so much of their daily lives into that rivalry. Missouri had decided to move to the SEC, so this was the last conference game between the teams. Allen Fieldhouse is probably my favorite place in the country to watch a sporting event. It has a little bit of old and a little bit of new, and it is always packed and loud. Missouri ended up building a big lead and looked like they were going to turn the last game into a mockery, but Kansas started coming back, and the arena started getting louder and louder. I often talk with colleagues about the loudest places they've ever been, and I think Allen Fieldhouse that day was the loudest place I've even been. Kansas came all the way back to win, but after it was over, there was this sense that this was never going to happen again. I think it eventually will, but it was pretty clear there was a lot of bitterness over Missouri leaving. Kansas never wanted to play them again, and, going back to the Civil War, there has always been a little antipathy from Missouri about Kansas. You just felt like this was the end of something pretty great, and when things like this end, they usually do in undramatic fashion. This was one of the best games I've ever seen, though, because of the atmosphere and the gravity of the moment.

Ray Ratto

Columnist, CSN Bay Area

1979 NCAA Men's Basketball Tournament Finals, Indiana State vs. Michigan State, Special Events Center, Salt Lake City, Utah, March 26, 1979

This was one of the last Final Fours before the event became a giant trade show, but you knew how important it was and hoped that Michigan State and Indiana State would meet in the championship game. There was a buzz in the arena; it was just crackling. This was the matchup everybody couldn't wait to see, and it was the way the season was defined. You couldn't pick two more different personalities than Magic Johnson and Larry Bird. Johnson was charming even then, while Bird was perpetually uncomfortable in the spotlight. You knew Michigan State had more great players, but the debate didn't boil down to who had the better team or the better coach or anything

Larry Bird helps up Magic Johnson during the 1979 NCAA championship game. (AP Photo)

like that. It was literally about those two guys. The game itself was not a great game, and Bird did not play particularly well. As soon as the game ended, I went right down to the Indiana State bench and watched him sit on the bench with his head in his hands. He was beyond crestfallen, because he knew how important the game was. It turned out to be the seminal moment in the history of the Final Four, which is as big as it is today because of that game. It wasn't the game that did it. It was those two guys. It was one of the few events that lived up to the hype, not that night, but historically, because they ended up defining a decade of the NBA, as well.

Stanford at Cal, Memorial Stadium, Berkeley, California, November 20, 1982

It was John Elway's last game at Stanford, and they needed to win for him to go to the only bowl game he would have played in while there. The Cardinal scored late to take a one-point lead, but then the band thing happens. I was up in the press box, and as the play was unfolding, you see the band coming out onto the field because they were sure the game was over. I saw the play still going on, but my brain couldn't process it. The game was clearly not over, and the band was on the field. But the band wouldn't be on the field if the game wasn't over, right? So the game must be over. The game wasn't over yet, though, so why was the band on the field? I was completely confused and figured the game wasn't going be decided immediately, so I went to the elevator and went down to the field.

By the time I fought through the crowd and made it down there, the officials had decided it was a touchdown and that Cal had won. Paul Wiggin, who was the Stanford coach and as nice a person as possible, was as mad as five people could be. He was beyond angry, because he couldn't imagine a way in which he would be screwed out of the win. The game ended up damaging him so badly that he was always considered a target for firing after that. I followed him as he was trying to find someone to complain to about how his team just got screwed, and he starts following the officials off the field. We all ended up by the door to the officials' locker room, and he was screaming at them the entire time. The officials were trying not to engage him, because they know they can't win that argument. We get right up to the door, and Wiggin gets into the room.

I start following him, because I'm not going to stop until somebody stops me. One of the Pac-10 people put his arm out and held me there, the door closes, and a second later, Wiggin is ushered out, so he never gets an answer. I talked to him, and he still doesn't know why they didn't win. I spent so much time following him that I never got to talk to the trombone player.

1989 World Series, Game Three, Oakland Athletics at San Francisco Giants, Candlestick Park, San Francisco, California, October 17, 1989

I had never been in a place where I saw 70,000 people not die when they probably should have. It was an event in an old, rickety park, which Candlestick Park had always been portrayed as being, so that should have happened, but it was built with Russian concrete, so you couldn't knock it down. It was an unusually hot day for late October, although in the Bay Area, summer runs intermittently, and one of the times where it is usually hottest is late October. I remember people saying it was earthquake weather, which is a classic old wives' tale.

When I went to the park, I was in the press box, and all of a sudden, while we were all sitting there, I hear what sounds like a train running right by the press box. A few seconds later, I knew it was an earthquake, since I've lived in the Bay Area and know what they sound like. This one, though, was bigger and longer. The next thing I noticed was all of the out-of-towners in the press box grabbed their stuff and started fleeing like rabbits, because they aren't experienced with earthquakes and were sure they were going to plummet to their deaths. I followed them out but only grabbed a notebook, because I knew where I needed to be was down on the field. Candlestick was one of those stadiums where you didn't take an elevator down to the field; you had to go down through the stands. As I was heading down to the field, I see people listening to their transistor radios and start hearing the news about the Bay Bridge collapsing and the freeway in Oakland collapsing and the Marina District being on fire. By the time I got down to the field, I was in complete disbelief. It was the end of the world, and I was at a baseball game.

I started talking to players, and all of them were shell-shocked because by the time I got down there, I saw there were no lights on. I knew they have generators and backup generators, so if those were all out, it was really bad. As I was talking to players, I noticed that the Giants were more freaked out than the A's were, and I wasn't sure why until afterwards, when I found out that the A's had more players from the area than the Giants did. After gathering as many quotes as I could, I ran back upstairs and sat down and picked up the phone, but it was dead, so I wasn't going to be able to send my story to the paper. Around five minutes later, the phone kicked in and was one of the only ones working—I'm not really sure why or how, but maybe because we were in San Francisco and I wrote for the *Chronicle*, we were wired differently. I only called in quotes, though, because they weren't really sure how they were going to publish. I went back and forth to the field a couple of times, and every time I did, I'm noticing there are fewer and fewer writers and media people. Many of them left right after the earthquake hit for various reasons. On multiple occasions, while I was on the phone calling in quotes, a police officer would come by and say they needed to clear the area. I didn't want to lose the phone, though, so I would ask the officer if he had called his family yet, and when he said no, I offered to let him use my phone, and in return they let me stay and finish what I needed to do. By the time I finally got kicked out, it was around 8:30 and just about pitch black.

I couldn't get downtown because of gridlock, so I headed home, where I knew the phone worked and I could finish sending in quotes. I lived in the East Bay, though, and the bridge was closed, so I headed south, and every bridge was closed. Between distance and traffic, it took around three hours to finally get home, and by that time, the office was exhausted and told me not to bother anymore. I spent the next ten days covering people in suits telling us why there were no games. It was just surreal, and at the end of the night, with all the pictures we saw, I thought there were thousands of people dead, but because so many people were heading home to watch the game, casualties ended up being a lot lower than they otherwise would have been.

2000 U.S. Open, Pebble Beach Golf Links, Pebble Beach, California, June 15-18, 2000

I'm not a big golf guy, but this was the most comprehensive ass-kicking I've ever seen in any sport, and that includes boxing. Tiger Woods was at the height of his powers, and it was clear that the sport was just him and then a lot of people who played golf. Pebble Beach is a difficult course where you can put the ball in the water on almost every hole, and he just destroyed everybody. You could see on Sunday that nobody had the will to live, and the only question was whether he was going to win by 10, 15, or 20. Was he going to put his foot on everybody's throat and make this a humiliating experience? He did. To this day, it takes people a lot to remember who finished second, and I only remember it because I wrote a sidebar about the two guys who did. I don't speak Spanish, so I'm not really sure what Miguel Angel Jimenez said, but Ernie Els looked like he had seen pterodactyls fly overhead. He played as well as he could, but Tiger Woods ate an entire golf field all weekend. You sat there asking how bad it was going to get for the rest of the field, and it got worse than anybody could have figured.

2001 World Series, New York Yankees vs. Arizona Diamondbacks, Yankee Stadium, Bronx, New York and Bank One Ballpark, Phoenix, Arizona, October 27-November 4, 2001

I don't think it was the best Series I ever saw, except for the fact that everything was backloaded because of 9/11. It turned out to be a great Game Seven, one of the best I ever saw, right up there with the one in 1991. Arizona was basically playing without a closer, but they won a close game in Game Seven. The Yankees were just drained at the end of the Series, especially after going through the nightmare of 9/11. You sort of got the sense that their time had come and gone. They had won four World Series in five years, and you got the feeling that it was the end and things were going to be radically different for them in the future because they were just out of gas. Everything had to go right for Arizona just to get there, even with Randy Johnson and Curt Schilling. They won because Luis Gonzalez hit a ball off the knob of his bat, and it was almost an accident for them to have won. All of those factors really make this World Series stand out. It was a great reminder to me that everything you are sure is going to happen doesn't always happen, so don't sit there and pretend you know the outcome ahead of time. It was one of those rare times where most people were truly surprised at how it ended.

Karl Ravech

Broadcaster, ESPN

1999 Home Run Derby, Fenway Park, Boston, Massachusetts, July 12, 1999

The Home Run Derby in 1999 was part of probably the greatest All-Star celebrations, with Major League baseball parading the greatest players of all time, including Ted Williams, on the field. At that time, steroids were being whispered about, but there was nothing that made people stand up and want to take notice or actually take notice. On a beautiful night in Boston, with Fenway Park lit up and anticipating a magical show, Mark McGwire and Ken Griffey Jr. absolutely beat baseballs over the Green Monster onto the streets. There were so many people chasing baseballs down, and it had a feel-good vibe to it. When you talk about being in the moment in 1999 and the sheer strength and power of these guys, it was like watching Tiger Woods drive golf balls. The pitch would come in and just explode off the bat and not come down. These guys were, as we have since learned, larger than life, to be able to put on a show like they did. Many people are critical of the Home Run Derby, but this one was different, because these players had, in a lot of ways, saved baseball and put it back on the map with their awesome displays of power.

129th Open Championship, Final Round, The Old Course at St. Andrews, Fife, Scotland, July 23, 2000

I was always part of ESPN's coverage of the fall PGA tour, so I was blessed, because I got to go to Hawaii in January for many years. But it also meant I got to cover other PGA events, like the majors. I'm an avid golfer, so it was amazing to see the passion that the people of Scotland have for golf and Tiger Woods at his pinnacle. St. Andrews is famous for the Swilcan Bridge on the 18th hole, and people are lined up on the streets and rooftops around the hole. As Tiger made his way up the fairway, with the tournament never really in doubt, and crossed the bridge to walk to the green, hundreds of people ran through the water in the fairway. I was blown away by the cult-like reverence for Tiger Woods from the belly of golf. It was like a parade celebration for a team that just won the World Series, and he had them walking through water to follow him and chronicle the moment. I was lucky enough to be in the position to do the first interview with him for American television, and he had now won all four majors and completed the career Grand Slam. He was still young, and there was still an innocence about him. The smile was genuine. To be part of history, and witness it where golf was born and it thought of as religion, lets you know that you were part of something special and very unique.

2001 World Series, New York Yankees vs. Arizona Diamondbacks, Yankee Stadium, Bronx, New York, and Bank One Ballpark, Phoenix, Arizona, October 27-November 4, 2001

I was there covering the Series for ESPN, and Chris Berman was also heavily involved with baseball at that time. The morning before the Series started, we were given a tour of Ground Zero, or at least as much as they could show you at the time. We had seen it on TV, but to go there with New York City officials and absorb the massive destruction and tragedy, and see smoke and smell the odor in that area was startling. I was shaking for most of that day. Then marry that to the most exciting World Series that I've been a part of—and I've been at every one since 1995—in a cruel but very real way. It would have made sense for the Yankees to win. In the end, though, the Diamondbacks were able to beat Mariano Rivera. There are TV shows that are trying to mimic reality, but reality is that the story doesn't always follow what most think would be the script. It would be naïve to call it a cruel twist, because we all had witnessed cruelty on a level we had never seen, but the idea that Arizona would come back against Mariano Rivera wasn't in anyone's mind. Curt Schilling tells the story all the time about when he gave up the go-ahead home run to the Alfonso Soriano in the top of the eighth inning, he looked at the Yankees bullpen and saw Rivera warming up and said to himself that he just lost the World Series. That whole combination of events is something I'll never forget and affected me in a way that no other event has ever affected me.

Jay Bell scores on a hit by Luis Gonzalez in the ninth inning to win Game Seven of the 2001 World Series. (AP Photo/Lenny Ignelzi)

2004 World Series, Game Four, Boston Red Sox at St. Louis Cardinals, Busch Stadium, St. Louis, Missouri, October 27, 2004

I grew up in Needham, Massachusetts, so I grew up a Red Sox fan, and all of my friends and family were still licking our wounds from the 1986 World Series. There weren't a lot of good years for Boston sports, and the year before, Aaron Boone (whom I work with now) had destroyed the latest effort to end this curse. In 2004, after the Red Sox were able to rally and come back from the three-games-to-none deficit to the Yankees in the ALCS and get to the World Series, it really felt like there was no competition for them. There was something about beating the Yankees that, as a New Englander but someone objectively covering the series, you knew it was going to happen. I wasn't one of those who ever believed that they were never going to win. There was a level of faith in Theo Epstein to build a team, and he went out and got another New Englander in Curt Schilling in the offseason, and you just knew it was destined to happen. Maybe not in 2004, but in 2005 or 2006, it was going to happen. There was nothing about it in my mind that made me feel otherwise.

The game was on FOX and no one else can get on the field, so all of the other reporters were herded down inside a tunnel leading to the dugout, then once the final out is recorded, you can run out on the field to do your interviews. I have this vivid memory of running onto the field and seeing, for the first time up close, grown men in tears about what they had accomplished. At that point, they weren't just celebrating the World Series. They had become that self-proclaimed group of idiots. They had become the real fabric of what Boston represented. In some ways, they were the Bad News Bears. They were kind of goofy and had adopted the personality of their fan base. Getting on the field, after having watched them while growing up, was a surreal moment for me where I realized not only was I witness to it, but I was also in charge of chronicling it for the preeminent sports network in the world. That was one of those moments where you pinch yourself, because you can't believe you were there for it, and that the team I grew up rooting for had just defeated a curse that was almost nine decades long.

2014 Little League Baseball World Series, Lamade Stadium, Williamsport, Pennsylvania, August 14-24, 2014

This was one of the most mind-blowing, eye-opening events I've ever covered. I was fortunate enough to be in Bristol for the Mid-Atlantic regional championships, and Mo'ne Davis was pitching then. I hadn't heard anything about Mo'ne to this point, and ESPN didn't get involved in the regional championships until the semifinals, but we have all been exposed over the years to girls playing Little League baseball. Many of them were skilled, but none of them were the best player on the team or the person everyone would gravitate to. At first blush, it was all well and good, and we looking forward to seeing her play, and she was going to pitch in the championship game if they could set it up that way. Then we tried to figure out what the quirk was here. Did she throw a knuckleball? What's the twist?

In the championship game, she faced a team from Delaware that had gone pretty far the year before, and if you get to that point, you have to be pretty good. Mo'ne comes out, and there is nothing that would put her in a category with other girls that I had seen play Little League. She threw with a delivery reminiscent of every really, really good Little League player I had ever seen. She was mechanically and fundamentally tremendous, and then you recognize that she isn't giving up any hits and is throwing fastballs by the hitters. It was one of those things that you just knew was different. She pitched a complete game to help the team advance to Williamsport, and I knew then that the story was special. However, I also knew that she was about to face teams from the West Coast, where they play baseball year-round, and that the Mo'ne Davis story was going to end. She was going to come up against boys that were going to hit fastballs and breaking balls.

In her first game, it was no problem at all, and with her team being from Pennsylvania, we were starting to see massive crowds. I told my producer that this was way bigger than baseball, and that this was going to be a cultural story, so let's sit Mo'ne down and make her the ESPN Sunday Conversation. They had played on Sunday, and she agreed to do it. After *SportsCenter* ran it, her notoriety blew up. It was already blowing up, but that interview really pushed it to new heights. She just continued to do things that no one had ever seen, and national news organizations and daytime talk shows were jumping on the story. She was transcendent to the event, and the event had another unique story with an all African-American team from Chicago. There were these two stories, both centered on African-Americans—one a full team, one a girl pitcher. The enormity of it, and the 40,000 people at the games and the millions watching on television, were unprecedented for the Little League World Series. It was, without question, the most dominant Little League story that I had ever seen or even heard of, even bigger than when American teams won the championship. Mo'ne Davis thrust herself into America's conscience, not just in sports. Every girl. Equal opportunity. Inner-city. She checked off every single box, and she did it in a classy, composed, dignified way.

Chris Rose

Broadcaster, MLB Network/NFL Network

1986 AFC Championship Game, Denver Broncos at Cleveland Browns, Municipal Stadium, Cleveland, Ohio, January 11, 1987

This was the first time in my lifetime that the Browns were in the AFC Championship Game and one step away from the Super Bowl. My family were season ticket holders since the Browns came into existence, and we planned vacations around the Browns; from 1979 until the team moved after the 1995 season, I saw or heard every single game either in person, on TV, or on the radio except for one, and that is because I was flying to a funeral.

The Browns had just come off an amazing victory against the Jets the week before, after being down, 20–10, with just under five minutes to go, then forcing overtime and winning in double overtime. The game against the Broncos was tied at 13 in the fourth quarter, when Bernie Kosar hit Brian Brennan for a TD pass. I remember turning to the buddy I was sitting next to, Dave Albright, and saying, "We're fucking going to the Super Bowl!" After the Broncos fumbled the kickoff and recovered it at the 2, it really started to get more apparent that the Browns were headed to the Super Bowl. Ninety-eight yards against that Browns defense just wasn't happening.

And then, someone just started sticking the pins in the Cleveland Browns voodoo doll. If it was third-and-9, they got 10. On a third-and-18, Elway had a big pass to Mark Jackson. Eventually, they scored, of course. Everyone thinks The Drive won the game, but it only tied it. The Browns got the ball first in overtime, and on third-and-2, they gave it to Herman Fontenot, who was a third-down back, and the moment they gave it to him, we all could have walked out of the stadium. We knew the game was over right there. Sure enough, the Broncos stop Fontenot for no gain, get the ball back, and go right down the field for the winning field goal.

If it is possible for 80,000 people all to be silent at one time, except for the sixty-five or so Broncos players and coaches on the field, that was it. I never thought I'd be able to hear what was going on down on a football sideline while I was hundreds of feet away, but I heard it. It was just awful. We took a train to and from the stadium, and that ride home was brutal. It was the first time I'd had the sports carpet pulled out from under me. Unfortunately, it hasn't been the last.

1989 NBA Playoffs Opening Round, Game Five, Chicago Bulls at Cleveland Cavaliers, Richfield Coliseum, Richfield, Ohio, May 7, 1989

I should have known it was going to be a bad day when I was driving to pick up my then-girlfriend and got pulled over for my first speeding ticket while listening to John Fogerty's "Centerfield" (and she was not worth rushing for; I did not end up marrying her). That season, the Cavs dominated the Bulls and didn't lose to them in the regular season, and won Game Four in Chicago to force Game Five back in Cleveland. This was a great up-and-coming team that we thought really had a chance to beat not just the Bulls, but the Pistons and even bring home a championship.

At the end of the game, Craig Ehlo inbounds the ball, gets it back, and drives in for a layup to give the Cavs a one-point lead; I still think he was fouled on the play, but it wasn't called. After the timeout, the Bulls come out, and Brad Sellers, who was a seven-footer who actually grew up in Cleveland, was inbounding the ball and had Larry Nance on him, and was forced to call another timeout. On the next inbound, though, all of a sudden, Nance is not on the ball. He has his back to Sellers, and they are trying to double-team Michael Jordan. I'm screaming from Section 131, Row T, Seat 15, "You cannot do that! Put a man on the ball! Make him throw the ball where you want him to throw it!" So I'm screaming at Lenny Wilkens, and all of the people around me are giving me that look like, "Hey, kid, shut up." When Sellers got the ball to Jordan, it was three seconds that felt like three hours. Jordan went up for the shot, and it was like there were Peter Pan strings attached to his body with people pulling them to keep him floating in the air while Ehlo and Nance fell to the ground. He just levitated, hit the shot, and started celebrating. I remember grabbing my girlfriend and rushing out of there. I just couldn't take it and started running through the concourse chanting, "Here we go Brownies, here we go!"

You sit there and start to realize that Cleveland sports fans are 90 percent scar tissue, and it is because of moments like that. At least we can say we were done in by Elway and Jordan, though.

2000 U.S. Open, Pebble Beach Golf Links, Pebble Beach, California, June 15-18, 2000

This was really the height of Tiger-mania. My wife Michele was pregnant with our first child, so she came to the tournament, which was four spectacular days at Pebble Beach. Tiger just killed the field. I was covering golf for FOX Sports Net at the time and watched him win by 15 shots over Ernie Els and Miguel Angel Jimenez.

The thing I remember the most, though, was watching the other golfers come off the course after their round, look at the scoreboard, and shake their heads. I think they all were questioning whether the score was a mistake. Had they accidentally put a one in front of Tiger's score? Was he really 12-under and not 2-under? He was bringing pro athletes to their knees unlike anything we'd ever seen before. I had a chance to interview him one-on-one, and he was so confident and calm. The thing that stuck with me from it was that he expected it to go like that. He didn't expect it to be close. He was fully aware that he had just beaten the field by 15 strokes, and it wasn't even that close. I love being in the presence of history, because people don't appreciate it. But I had to take a step back and understand that this was unlike anything we had ever seen before, and we are never going to see it again.

2007 Fiesta Bowl, Boise State vs. Oklahoma, University of Phoenix Stadium, Glendale, Arizona, January 1, 2007

Now, Boise State is a household name in college football, but back then, they were the quirky team that played on the Smurf Turf, so everyone wondered how they were going to compete in a bowl game against a powerhouse such as Oklahoma. Well, they came out and punched them in the mouth, and they took it to the Sooners early.

The great thing about a bowl game is that there are fans there who don't have a rooting interest in either of the two teams, so the minute an underdog starts to show some fight, the fans really get into it. Boise State builds a huge lead, but then the Oklahoma athletes start to take over. The Sooners came back to tie it, and you could feel the air go out of the dome in Glendale. It was such a good story for a while, but the team with the pedigree was going to win this thing. I had the chance to watch the fourth quarter of the game from the sideline and was standing right around the 20-yard line. Boise State's quarterback, Jared Zabransky, threw a pick-six to give the Sooners their first lead, and when the Oklahoma player ran past me, I saw the look on Zabranksy's face. He had rolled his eyes up and couldn't believe he had just thrown that pass that probably cost the Broncos the game after all of that hard work. I felt so bad for him that I wanted to give him a hug!

Boise got the ball back, and it was fourth-and-18, when they ran the hook-and-lateral, and the building went nuts. I know you aren't supposed to react to these games, but I didn't give a damn that time. I was jumping up and down on the sidelines, pumping my fists, high-fiving our producers, not believing that we just saw that. And then in overtime, the Broncos get the two-point conversion on the Statue of Liberty play, and the place goes berserk. The game wasn't for the national championship, but we were there for one of the great upsets in history.

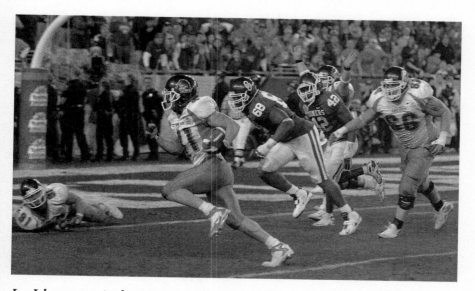

Ian Johnson runs in the game-winning two-point conversion in the 2007 Fiesta Bowl.
(AP Photo/Matt York)

2013 NFL Hall of Fame Announcement, New Orleans Convention Center, New Orleans, Louisiana, February 2, 2013

I had the chance to host the Pro Football Hall of Fame announcement show for NFL Network in 2013. We had no idea before the show who was going in. The media and fans don't know how much the game, and getting the game's greatest honor, really means to these guys. This was the class that included Jonathan Ogden, Larry Allen, and Warren Sapp. These were some of the toughest guys ever, and they were brought to tears by the news. Warren Sapp actually came out and gave me a big kiss on the cheek. I live for moments like that, where people are happy for the right reasons. It was Cris Carter's sixth time as a finalist, and for him to finally get in, after beating the kinds of demons that he did just to stay in the league, let alone be honored as one of the greatest players in the history of the game, was amazing. He couldn't get through a question without tears streaming down his face. What a fantastic moment it was for everybody.

Bob Ryan

Broadcaster, ESPN

Recipient of Basketball Hall of Fame's Curt Gowdy Award, 1997
Elected to National Sports Media Association Hall of Fame, 2011

Minnesota Twins at Boston Red Sox, Fenway Park, Boston, Massachusetts, October 1, 1967

Being in the stands behind home plate for this game will always resonate with me. It was the last day of the season and the culmination of a great pennant race. The Red Sox weren't picked to do much that year and hadn't won the pennant since 1946, and had already started to compile the list of woes about not winning the World Series since 1918. For me, I was a student at Boston College and was spending the summer in Boston for the first time, and rekindled my love of baseball as the Red Sox went through the pennant race. The world was different then, and Fenway Park was not the iconic stadium it is today; it wasn't a cathedral, but an old ballpark that Tom Yawkey was desperate to leave.

The Red Sox needed to win both games over the weekend, and they beat the Twins on Saturday in a dramatic win, with Carl Yastrzemski homering in the seventh inning off Jim Merritt, a lefty brought in specifically to face him. It was Yaz's 44th homer of the season, en route to a partial Triple Crown (he finished tied in home runs with Harmon Killebrew, who ironically hit his 44th in the same game on Saturday). The Sunday matchup was Jim Lonborg against Dean Chance, and with the Red Sox trailing, 2–0, in the bottom of the sixth, Lonborg beat out a bunt to start a five-run uprising, with the key being a two-run single by Yastrzemski. After Rico Petrocelli caught the final out in the ninth inning, everyone still had to wait for the outcome of the Tigers and Angels game, which was the second of two straight doubleheaders to end the season for those teams. If the Tigers won, there would be a playoff game on Monday in Boston, and the only way to follow the game in those days was on the radio. The Red Sox station patched in the game, and while the Red Sox listened in the clubhouse, I was listening on a transistor radio on the trolley going back to my girlfriend's house in Brighton, as the Tigers lost to make the Red Sox American League champions.

1975 World Series, Game Six, Cincinnati Reds at Boston Red Sox, Fenway Park, Boston, Massachusetts, October 21, 1975

I was the beat writer for the Celtics for the *Boston Globe* but helped cover the home games of the World Series for the paper and was assigned to cover the visiting clubhouse. There were so many great moments in this game, starting with the Bernie Carbo homer off of Rawly Eastwick to tie the game in the eighth inning, the Dwight Evans catch off a vicious Joe Morgan line drive, and the double play the Reds turned when they threw Denny Doyle out at home plate. That all led up to the Carlton Fisk home run, which I almost missed. There was a phone call for me from the office, and I was sitting in the left field auxiliary press box. I made it to the phone in the main press box behind home plate just in time and had a great view of the home run from there. Everyone will tell you what an epic game that was.

1976 NBA Finals, Game Five, Phoenix Suns at Boston Celtics, Boston Garden, Boston, Massachusetts, June 4, 1976

The series was supposed to be a walkover for the Celtics, but the team split the first four games to set up Game Five in Boston. In the first part of the game, the Celtics played their best basketball of the entire playoffs, not just the Finals, and were up eighteen points after the first quarter. Phoenix wouldn't go away, though, and just chipped away at the lead and got close, but the Celtics upped the lead back to nine with around three minutes to go. The Suns came back though, and everyone remembers the same play—Paul Westphal's 360-degree left-handed banker—during the comeback. The sequence of events at the end of the first overtime, of course, are unforgettable. John Havlicek made what everyone thought was the game-winner with a shot right from in front of me—a Nolan Ryan fastball-type shot that went so fast, it is hard to figure out how it went in. The fans stormed the court thinking the game was over, but there was still one second on the clock. With the Suns down one, Westphal went over to the scorer's table to find out what would happen if they called a timeout, even though they didn't have one. When he found out they would get called for a technical foul but would get the ball at midcourt, they called the timeout. The Celtics made the free throw, but the Suns inbounded from halfcourt, and Gar Heard tied the game from around eighteen feet. Amid all of the wildness, a fan came out of the stands to attack referee Richie Powers after the first overtime ended. In the third OT, Paul Silas fouled out, and Glenn McDonald came in to score six vital points in just over a minute as the Celtics hung on to win the game.

We did a twenty-fifth anniversary show on the game in 2001, in which Peter May and I dug up every single participant in the game who was still alive, with the two referees being the only ones who had passed away. It was just an epic game filled with some amazing performances, and it still stands up as one of the greatest games in NBA history.

1992 NCAA Men's Basketball Tournament Regional Finals, Kentucky vs. Duke, The Spectrum, Philadelphia, Pennsylvania, March 28, 1992

I believe that even if this game didn't have the storybook ending, with the pass from Grant Hill to Christian Laettner and the ensuing game-winning basket, it still would have been the greatest game I've ever seen. This game was played at the highest level possible, with lots of back and forth, and the final score of Duke 104, Kentucky 103 tells you all you need to know. But the ending was something special. First, Sean Woods makes a play that would have made him a Kentucky legend for the ages. The basket he made, which is almost impossible to describe, was an amazing shot. Duke still had one more shot, and Rick Pitino will have to go to his grave answering to the fact that he didn't guard the inbounds pass. That gave Hill a free look down the court, where he found Laettner, who was so methodical. He thought, put the ball on the floor, spun, and was completely under control and calm and easy. You don't even think about it until you look at the stat sheet, but that shot made him 10-for-10 in the game, and he was also 10-for-10 from the free throw line. That is a pretty good game. That game was utterly spectacular.

Christian Laettner shoots the game-winning basket in overtime to win the 1992 NCAA East Regional Final. (AP Photo/Charles Rex Arbogast)

1999 Ryder Cup, Day Three, The Country Club, Brookline, Massachusetts, September 26, 1999

One of the greatest things about sports is that you just never know when something great is going to happen. Hyped games so seldom live up to it; it is the ones that you don't expect. I cannot exaggerate the dramatic nature and energy that was present on the golf course that day as the United States was launching a counterattack against the Europeans. They were trailing, 10–6, and all of the dialogue was that the Europeans were playing together and the United States didn't like team play and didn't care as much as the Europeans. We all laughed on Saturday when Ben Crenshaw said that he had a good feeling about Sunday. Right away, though, the U.S. takes the lead in the first six matches, and that got everyone's attention. All throughout, there were these individual moments, but you didn't know where to be. One place I was, though, was at the 14th hole, where a lot of the drama took place, including David Duval closing out his match and dancing a jig.

There were two crucial matches back-to-back. First was Justin Leonard against Jose Maria Olazabal, followed by Payne Stewart and Colin Montgomerie. We all thought the second one was going to be the pivotal one. I was in with the first one, which was in the fairway on 17, as the second teed off right behind it, and was about one hundred yards below the green. I saw someone I knew sitting in an NBC golf cart whom I knew a little and watched with him as Leonard sank his famous putt. It was Michael Jordan. I remember writing that it was almost as if golf had become a contact sport. There was something about the atmosphere that made it the most memorable, exciting days that I've had covering an event in forty-six years. I never, ever would have believed that getting out of bed that morning, which is what makes having a job like mine so great.

Sam Ryan

Broadcaster, MLB Network

2007 NFC Championship Game, New York Giants at Green Bay Packers, Green Bay, Wisconsin, January 20, 2008

This was the season that shouldn't have been for the Giants. In November, they were annihilated by the Vikings, and everyone wrote them off at that point . . . including me. I booked a trip to Turks and Caicos for the week after the AFC and NFC championship games, figuring neither New York team was going to be playing at that point. But all of a sudden, the Giants finish strong and make the playoffs. Then they win in Tampa, and then again in Dallas to advance to the NFC Championship Game in Green Bay. As with the other playoff games, no one gave them a shot at winning.

Not only were the Giants the underdog against the Packers, but the temperature was below zero, and the wind chill made it feel like it was thirty below. Just to stand in that cold was ridiculous. I couldn't believe how many

Tom Coughlin looks on in the bitter cold of Green Bay during the 2007 NFC Championship Game. (AP Photo/David Stluka)

layers I was wearing, and it still wasn't enough. Any exposed skin felt like it was burning. The images of Tom Coughlin and his red face are unforgettable, and there were linemen playing with no sleeves. That cold is something I don't think I'll ever experience again, so to play under those conditions, and to stun the Packers and advance to the Super Bowl, was unfathomable. The Giants had become road warriors through the playoffs, and to be there every step of the way through the playoffs was so memorable. No one could have anticipated that it would happen.

Army vs. Navy, Lincoln Financial Field, Philadelphia, Pennsylvania, December 6, 2008

This was the third time I worked as the sideline reporter for CBS Sports at the Army-Navy game, and George W. Bush was going to be at the game and agreed to be interviewed while there, marking the first time a sitting United States president was interviewed live at that game. Vice presidents and former presidents had been interviewed at the game, but this was the first sitting president to be on the pregame show . . . and I was given the assignment of doing the interview. As everyone stressed to me that this was the first time, I became a bundle of nerves. It was a neat experience to be a part of and to see the scale of that operation, and the safety procedures surrounding the president. They brought us to a back room underneath the stadium—it was myself and several military dignitaries who were there for the game. So here I am in this room with all of these people that you have to have the ultimate respect for, given all they do for our country.

When the president came in, there was a receiving line, and he worked his way down the line, one by one. He would shake everyone's hand and have a word or two with each person, and when he got to me, he asked me if I realized just who I was in the room with. The one thing that I remember about President Bush was that he was really funny. When you meet him in person, he really has a lot of personality and is able to make everyone feel a lot more comfortable. My producer was taking pictures, and the press secretary actually came over to tell us not to worry about it, they would take plenty of pictures for us. One month later, they sent me a picture of the interview, and he hand-signed it. That picture is hanging on my wall, and I look like a starstruck little girl.

New York Yankees Ticker Tape Parade, New York, New York, November 6, 2009

This was so neat to be part of. I was working for WCBS in New York, so I got the chance to cover that team on a local basis. I was in the studio for the games hosting pregame and postgame shows, so it was great to get out of the studio and cover the live parade. I didn't know until that morning, though, that I was going to co-anchor the coverage with Chris Wragge. It was cool just watching as the floats went by and talking about all of the different players, and what they had done, and then to be at City Hall for the actual ceremony, and looking out and seeing all of the Yankees fans and their excitement. You just take it in and view it differently, regardless of what team you root for, when you see a city show their love and admiration for one of their teams.

2011 World Series, Game Six, Texas Rangers at St. Louis Cardinals, Busch Stadium, St. Louis, Missouri, October 27, 2011

I was assigned to cover the Cardinals for the Series, while Matt Yallof was on the Rangers. The way we would work the postgame was that one camera crew would come out and do the interview with the winner. So Matt was getting ready to interview the Rangers when they were one strike away from winning the World Series, while I waited in the tunnel, just in case. Well, just in case happened. And for the next two innings, it just went back and forth with the microphone, so that we could both be ready for whatever the outcome was. The David Freese home run was such a great moment for him, after not being an everyday player earlier, and overcoming injuries. He flourished at the most important time of the season. It is baseball. You never know what is going to happen, so for as much to happen in that game as it did, in a game of that magnitude, was simply unbelievable. I'll never forget Bob Costas coming up to me after it was over and telling me that I had just witnessed one of the greatest games in baseball history. And I sat back and really let it sink in and appreciated it.

San Francisco Giants at Cincinnati Reds, Great American Ball Park, Cincinnati, Ohio, July 2, 2013

When you watch a no-hitter on TV, the anticipation of that final out is so much fun. For this one, though, I was sitting in a camera well in the stadium covering it for MLB Network. We got through six innings, then seven innings, and you can start to feel the tension building. The camera well was right next to the Reds' dugout, and Mat Latos kept walking over to where I was sitting, and we were having conversations, keeping me updated on what Homer Bailey was doing between innings and how he wasn't changing his routine. Of course, we all knew this no-hitter was going on, but that it could end at any moment. After it ended and he completed the no-hitter, I was the first person to interview him on the field. What a great moment to be a part of, both as a sports fan and as a baseball broadcaster. I don't think we exhaled until we returned to the production truck after the broadcast ended.

Jeremy Schaap

Broadcaster, ESPN

New York Yankees at Boston Red Sox, Fenway Park, Boston, Massachusetts, October 2, 1978

We all know what happened: Bucky Dent homered to lead the Yankees over the Red Sox in a one-game playoff after trailing by fourteen games in July, earning a profane nickname (at least in the Boston area) in the process. I had just turned nine years old and was a crazy Yankees fan. That was the first season where I really followed the team every day, and it was a special treat to go with my father to Boston for the game. We flew up on the Eastern Airlines shuttle on the day of the game. During the flight, I was sitting next to American League president Lee MacPhail. I was a big baseball fan but didn't know who he was at the time. We spent the flight just talking about baseball, which amused my father. At Fenway, I was too young to sit in the press box, and my father had not secured any tickets. So he was asking the players around the batting cage if anyone had any tickets he could use. One of the players wasn't using his, and that's how I ended up sitting in Bucky Dent's seats when he hit his famous home run.

I had never really experienced being in enemy territory, and from where I was sitting up in left field, I couldn't really tell if the ball was fair or foul. Of course, the Red Sox fans didn't react to the home run, and since I was accustomed to a Yankees homer being greeted by thunderous applause, I thought it was a foul ball. Then I realized what it was and went crazy . . . until I realized that even being nine years old didn't really protect me from the wrath of the home fans. It was a great moment, and I got to spend it with my father in Bucky Dent's seats. Whenever I see Bucky, we still talk about it.

1986 World Series, Game Six, Boston Red Sox at New York Mets, Shea Stadium, Flushing, New York, October 25, 1986

By 1986, I had switched from being a Yankees fan to a Mets fan, which had to do with my father's relationship with George Steinbrenner going south after he wrote an unauthorized biography of the Yankees' owner. My mother's father was a big Mets fan, and he died on September 6 of that year. My grandfather and I were extremely close, which made the next six weeks even more meaningful for me, since I was grieving. We had had the Mets connection and a baseball connection in general. It made the 1986 World Series very emotional for me.

I was at Game Six with my father in the SportsChannel booth, and we started walking out after Keith Hernandez made the second out in the bottom of the 10th. But then Gary Carter singled, and we looked at each other and decided to stick around. So we went back to our seats but were realistic and didn't get our hopes up. But you never forget the sequence: Carter, Mitchell, Knight, Wilson. When the Mets won, it was just a crazy night. That was just a magical moment for me.

Super Bowl XXV, Buffalo Bills vs. New York Giants, Tampa Stadium, Tampa, Florida, January 27, 1991

I was a senior in college and was working for my father at the Super Bowl. I was a huge Giants fan, and even though I was more of a baseball guy, the Giants team that won Super Bowl XXI got me into rooting for that team. I went to school in upstate New York, where there was a big mix of Giants and Bills fans, but for the game, I was able to get a credential and work for my father as a gofer. He spent the game up in the press box, but I was part of the ABC News crew down on the field for the game, helping the cameramen with their gear. Of course, if you want to watch a football game, the worst possible place to do it is on the field, especially at the Super Bowl, where the sidelines are packed with cameramen. When the Bills moved the ball into field-goal range for the game-winning field-goal attempt, I couldn't really tell where the ball was and did the math wrong in my head. Instead of it being a 47-yard attempt, I thought it was 37 yards, so I thought it was a foregone conclusion that Scott Norwood was going to make it. After he missed, there were still a few seconds left on the clock, but all of the media stormed onto the field to get in position, and in that moment, I was so excited, I high-fived Ottis Anderson, which, of course, is professionally frowned upon. I just couldn't help myself, and, in my defense, he was looking for someone to high-five. I'm going to blame him for it. Then, all of a sudden, everyone starts yelling to get off the field, because the Giants still had to take one more snap for the game to end. But that was pretty cool, to be there in that moment, when you think all hope is lost (albeit due almost entirely to my own poor math) and then to see them actually win.

Colorado at Michigan, Michigan Stadium, Ann Arbor, Michigan, September 24, 1994

I grew up in New York, where no one has cared about college football since the Army-Notre Dame rivalry in the 1940s. So college football never really meant much to me, and I had never even been to a Division I-A football game until ESPN assigned me to be a producer for this game at Michigan Stadium. I was working with Steve Cyphers, who did a pregame hit for *College Game Day*. He left to work on another story that night, but I stayed around to cover the game. I was on the field for the game with our crew and was standing around the 3-yard line when Kordell Stewart dropped back and the ball goes up in the air from 65 yards away. I'm sure this is something I've recreated in my memory, but it felt like the place went silent; in my mind, 105,000 people in Michigan Stadium went dead silent while that ball was traveling in the air. If you watch the highlights from the game, you can see me standing right there, and it felt like I could reach out and touch the ball as it was coming down, when a Michigan defender tipped it to Colorado's Michael Westbrook, who caught it for the winning touchdown. From there, it was instant pandemonium. It felt like I was five feet away from Westbrook when he caught it, so I had an incredible perspective on the play. We ran out onto the field to get his reaction and get in the scrum, and all of a sudden, I got hit in the back—and hit *hard*—by something. I turn around to see what was going on, and to this day I'm not completely sure, but I think maybe the ref had thrown a penalty flag and hit me with it. So I picked it up and kept it as a souvenir. This was the first major college football game I had been to in my life, and it ended with one of the most famous plays of the decade.

Mike Tyson vs. Lennox Lewis, The Pyramid, Memphis, Tennessee, June 8, 2002

I had a very good relationship with both Mike Tyson and Lennox Lewis. I thought Lewis was going to win, which he did convincingly. It wasn't

Dempsey-Tunney and it wasn't Ali-Frazier, because both fighters were over the hill, but it was the closest it will come in my career covering boxing. There is nothing like the anticipation before the bell rings for a big fight like this, and there aren't many of them anymore. After Mike got his ass kicked, I was in the locker room interviewing him, and I asked him, "Mike, where do you go from here?" And he said, "I might just fade into Bolivian." It's kind of memorable. During the interview, he was cradling his two-month-old son Miguel in his arms, and he had been totally pummeled. He was beaten up unlike he had ever been beaten up before, and it all just spilled out of him. He kept talking. That was an interview, and a night, I won't forget.

Referee Eddie Cotton restrains Lennox Lewis after he scores a knockdown on Mike Tyson during the fourth round of their championship fight in 2002. (AP Photo/Mark J. Terrill)

Jon Sciambi

Broadcaster, ESPN

1980 NFC Championship Game, Dallas Cowboys at Philadelphia Eagles, Veterans Stadium, Philadelphia, Pennsylvania, January 11, 1981

I grew up a fan of all of the Philadelphia teams, but the Eagles were my team. I think I can still name almost all eleven starters on defense from that season. Of course, as an Eagles fan, I also disliked the Cowboys. Something that really jumps out at me from that game was that the Cowboys had to wear their blue jerseys that day, and they hated wearing them. It was like a jinx when they didn't wear their white jerseys. So even though the Eagles never wore white at home, they did that day to make the Cowboys wear the blue. I know I'll sound like the "Get off my lawn guy" when I say this, but you just don't hear stories of teams doing things like that anymore.

It was freezing that day, and we were bundled up in the stands under blankets. The energy at the Vet was insane. The Cowboys got the ball first, went three-and-out, and on the Eagles' second play, Wilbert Montgomery went 42 yards for a touchdown. I have goose bumps just thinking about it. We were sitting in the corner of the other end zone, so he was running away from us, and we had a great view of the play. The game was over after that, with the Eagles winning, 20–7. As a ten-year-old kid, though, I just loved that team so much.

1997 World Series, Game Seven, Cleveland Indians at Florida Marlins, Pro Player Stadium, Miami Gardens, Florida, October 26, 1997

I was hosting the Marlins' pregame and postgame shows on the radio at the time, so as the game went on, I was basically just a fan watching the game from the back of the broadcast booth. There were 67,000 very tense fans there, and as the game gets late and even tenser, it felt like I was curled up in a ball. It was a one-run game until Florida's Craig Counsell tied it up in the ninth with a sacrifice fly to send it to extra innings.

After Edgar Renteria got the winning hit in the 11th, I went downstairs to do the postgame interviews. The way we got onto the field was through the Marlins dugout, and I remember going up the steps out to the field where the celebration was going on, and the sound of the crowd hit me and stopped me. For that one second, you got to feel what it must have felt like to be playing. The sound of the fans cheering punched you in the face. To me, that game is a great example of why nothing can simulate the drama of postseason baseball, especially a Game Seven that goes into extra innings. The game can end on any given pitch, and the untimed aspect of the game makes it so much different than any of the other sports.

2003 National League Championship Series, Game Six, Florida Marlins at Chicago Cubs, Wrigley Field, Chicago, Illinois, October 14, 2003

People call this the Bartman game, but as a Marlins broadcaster at the time, looking at it from the Marlins' perspective, what really jumps out is that the Cubs were five outs from the World Series and the Marlins were being dominated by Mark Prior. It was 3–0 going into the eighth inning, but the Marlins scored eight runs in the inning. It was just hit after hit after hit. There will always be a dispute over whether Moises Alou actually could have caught the ball that Cubs fan Steve Bartman interfered with, but the Alex Gonzalez error was more crucial.

I was on the call with Dave Van Horne, and the way broadcasts go when there are two play-by-play guys, you alternate doing play-by-play. So that was his inning, and I was doing color commentary. It was remarkable to watch a team rise from the grave the way the Marlins did. We went from trying to figure out how we were going to get out of Wrigley Field during the Cubs' celebration to sitting in a building that was deathly quiet. The turn of events in that inning completely sucked all of the energy out of the fans, but when we were broadcasting the game, it was the error that was our focal point, not the Bartman play. That is really where the game turned.

2004 American League Championship Series, Games Three-Five, New York Yankees at Boston Red Sox, Fenway Park, Boston, Massachusetts, October 16-18, 2004

I had tickets to all three of the games that were played in Boston. The Yankees just pounded the Red Sox in Game Three, to the point where my friends and I left early. We walked back to our hotel and stopped at a few bars along the way, and each time we stopped, the Yankees had scored more runs.

Boston is all about baseball and the Red Sox, and history has changed so much with the team winning three World Series. And it all turned around in Game Four with the David Ortiz home run. We were sitting in the right-field corner, where the homer landed, so in my mind's eye, that moment really stands out. For Game Five, we sat on the Green Monster, and to be up there for the home run that Ortiz hit off the Volvo sign was awesome. After he hit it, I turned to my right and there was a total stranger running at me, and he jumped into my arms. I didn't have a rooting interest in the series, but being there and feeling the emotion of all of the people around me was really cool.

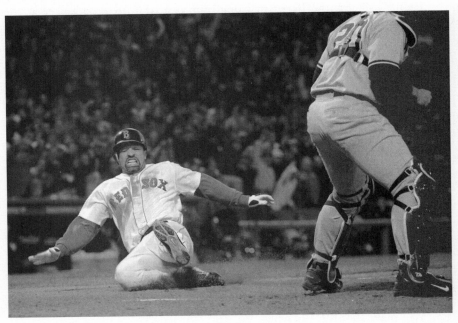

Dave Roberts slides home with the tying run in the ninth inning of Game Four of the 2004 ALCS. (AP Photo/Elise Amendola)

2010 National League Division Series, Game One, Cincinnati Reds at Philadelphia Phillies, Citizens Bank Park, Philadelphia, Pennsylvania, October 6, 2010

I've been at four no-hitters, but this was one of those days where you knew pretty early in the game that you were going to see a no-hitter. Roy Halladay was that good that day. The only guy who hit the ball hard for the Reds was Travis Wood, who is a good-hitting pitcher. It might have been a little extreme to say it after the third inning, when Wood made the best contact of the day. But after the fifth, you could start to say with confidence that he was going to throw a no-hitter that day. The Reds really just had no chance against him.

For me, there wasn't all that much tension to it. I wasn't broadcasting the game wondering if he was going to do it, I was just thinking about how long it would take us to get to the end. It was so neat to see someone so good in a game, and it was fun to tell people just to stick around, because they were going to see a no-hitter if they did.

Charley Steiner

Broadcaster, Los Angeles Dodgers

Larry Holmes vs. Muhammad Ali, Caesars Palace, Las Vegas, Nevada, October 2, 1980

This was the first heavyweight championship fight that I covered, and I was working for the RKO Radio Network. It was the first fight to be held in the Caesars Palace parking lot, where they erected 15,000 bleacher seats. Obviously, it was the tail end of Ali's career and was a wonderful story. I spent a fair amount of time with both fighters at their respective training camps. Ali was larger than life, probably the largest in life of any athlete of the twentieth century, and here was his former sparring partner challenging him for the title. This was in the days of the mega-event in boxing, which don't exist anymore, so folks would show up in Vegas early in the week of the fight, because there was so much stuff going on. In addition, Ali drew a huge crowd from around the world. At that point, I was thirty-one years old and RKO was a relatively new network at the time, so there I go with my Sony over-the-shoulder tape recorder to do interviews. When I got to Caesars Palace, I felt like this rube who had just gotten off some vegetable truck and saw stars and more stars.

During the fight, Ali just got crushed. He looked good going into the ring and was in great physical shape, but he had taken diuretics, so it was an artificially sculpted body. He took an unmerciful beating, and to this day it might have been the saddest event that I've ever covered. To anyone my age, Ali was an idol, so to watch all of that, that particular event tugged at every emotional string. Holmes, who is a lovely fellow, didn't want to beat the shit out of his mentor, but that was his job, and he did.

The 1981 Wimbledon Championships, Gentlemen's Semifinals, John McEnroe vs. Rod Frawley, The All England Lawn Tennis Club, London, England, July 2, 1981

All you really have to do is Google me, Wimbledon, and McEnroe, and you'll get the entire story. It was my first overseas assignment. John McEnroe was at his tempestuous best, and he and Bjorn Borg were in the middle of a short-lived but remarkable rivalry. McEnroe at the time was going out with a young American tennis player named Stacy Margolin, and they were having issues, so every day, the Fleet Street tabloids in London would ask whether they were breaking up. The press room was barely bigger than a phone booth and could comfortably seat around twenty-five people along with some tables. There was a British writer named James Whittaker, and his previous assignment before Wimbledon was whether the then-Lady Diana was a virgin and therefore suitable for Prince Charles. Wimbledon was where sports and gossip all came together as one. McEnroe is a very bright, articulate guy, but the old folks of Great Britain found him to be reprehensible, while the young people loved him. There was never any middle ground. After each match, following the perfunctory tennis questions, Whittaker would always ask, "Is it true, Mr. McEnroe, that you and Miss Margolin are splitsville?" I had never heard the term *splitsville* before, but the Brits were having a great time with it. McEnroe wouldn't answer any of the questions about his personal life, though.

After the semifinal match, Whittaker asked the question yet again "once and for all," and McEnroe went berserk and stormed out, yelling and cursing at the writers as he did it. As the rounds went on during the tournament, this little room would have more and more people in it, and all it needed was one match for the kindling to explode. After McEnroe stormed out, a young British reporter from *Life* magazine and I went over to Whittaker to tell him he was screwing it up for everyone else, and that we just wanted our quotes. At that point, another British reporter named Nigel Clarke inserted himself and started pointing his finger in my face, telling me, "This is none of your business." I said, "Get your fucking finger out of my face," and now it is starting to heat up. All of a sudden, out of nowhere, Nigel steps on a chair and says, "Do you want to settle this outside?" and even before he utters the word "outside," he jumps on me. Now all of a sudden, I'm in a fight. I had been in one fight in my life, during a junior high school football game. There was one camera allowed in that press room, but a freelancer had another camera going, and within hours, this fight is being seen around the world. The police came in and cleared the room, and HBO's Ross Greenburg grabbed me, got me out of the room, and literally hid me in their production truck for two hours while the bobbies were cleaning up the mess.

I went back to the hotel that night not knowing whether I was going to have a job or not. I called into the office, and a young Keith Olbermann answered and told me there was a story on the wire about an American reporter. Before he could even ask, I said it was me. It made the *New York Times* front page the next day. Because it was July 4 weekend, the story was spun that I was defending American honor in the mother country, which sounds a whole lot better than being in a fistfight with a British guy. The next day, I was summoned to the offices of the All England Lawn Tennis Club, where I assumed I was going to have my credential taken away. Instead, I was told that in many ways, they were glad this had happened because they had so many problems with those that shouldn't have credentials. They offered me some tea and sent me on my way. Apparently, a little while later, Clarke was also summoned and was told they were glad he took care of that American. At the post-tournament press conference, Billie Jean King came up to me and said, "That was the best goddamned thing I've ever seen at Wimbledon."

George Foreman vs. Michael Moorer, MGM Grand, Las Vegas, Nevada, November 5, 1994

George Foreman was at the apex of his unbelievable comeback, and I was at just about every one of his fights for ESPN. He had become, not unlike Ali fifteen years earlier, a larger-than-life figure. I spent every day with him, especially the week leading up to the fight. One morning, he was off having breakfast, and I sat down and joined him. He was selling this fight largely based on his craving for cheeseburgers (this was before the Foreman Grill came out), but what was he having for breakfast? Oatmeal, bananas, and prunes. He obviously got caught but asked me not to say anything about it, and we had a great laugh.

Moorer had just beaten Evander Holyfield for the heavyweight title and the question was whether the underdog Foreman could land just one big lucky punch. Round after round, in the center of the ring, Foreman is just getting pummeled. This wonderful, larger-than-life comeback story that captured everybody's attention looked like it was coming to an end. All Moorer had to do was stand ten feet from this guy, even three feet, and he would have won, because he had won every round of the fight until that point. Then he gets nailed. It was the most dramatic reversal of fortune I had ever been around. Out of nowhere . . . BAM, it is over! The forty-five-year-old, now-lovable George Forman had completed the most improbable sports comeback in boxing history with one big punch. I'll never forget meeting him outside of his suite the next morning, before he left to go back to Houston. He left his room, with his garment bag over his shoulder, while a valet had the rest of his bags. While we were walking out and talking, I kept thinking that, for him, it was a business trip. He could have been anyone just leaving a hotel after some time on the road, and he wanted to be home in time for a Sunday church session.

Atlanta Braves at Philadelphia Phillies, Veterans Stadium, Philadelphia, Pennsylvania, September 17, 2001

Baseball had obviously been shut down after 9/11, and I was tasked with doing the first game back in Philadelphia. Nobody quite knew what to think, how to feel, or what reference point to fall back on for the first game after a hideous national tragedy. I was with ESPN at the time, and I didn't know whether I was going to take the train down to Philadelphia from New Haven or drive. It was the day of the game, and I wasn't going to make the decision either to get off I-95 in New Haven for the train or just keep driving until the last minute. I wound up taking the train, and when I boarded, everybody was zombie-like, while I'm going to do a baseball game. I got there in the early afternoon for a 7:00 start, and everybody felt the same way. Was it appropriate for us to be here tonight? Scott Rolen of the Phillies and I will always be friends for the moments we shared before the game. We were just sitting in the stands during the afternoon, and we profoundly didn't know how to react to all of it, so we had this deep conversation about things. At the end of the day, he really didn't want to be there. Around five, I was having a bite to eat with Skip Caray and Harry Kalas, and we are talking to one another about how to do this game. What exactly are we supposed to say and do? I think it was Harry who said, in that big deep voice of his, "Just tell them what we see." It sounds simple, but somebody had to say that to us and for us. When we went on the air, it was a feeling unlike any assignment I've ever had. The first few innings were nondescript, and it was as if everybody were going through the motions just to get some traction emotionally and physically. In the fourth inning, Chipper Jones comes up for the second time, and, God bless the Phillies fans, they boo the hell out of him. I remember saying on the air that this may be our first step back. Fast forward to the end of the game, and the guy who did not want to play, Scott Rolen, hit two home runs and was the star of the game. It was one of those things where nobody knew what to do except go out and do what we all did for a living. That is when it really crystallized for me that our business can really be an elixir to heal the pain or a tourniquet to stop a wound from bleeding.

2003 American League Championship Series, Game Seven, Boston Red Sox at New York Yankees, Yankee Stadium, Bronx, New York, October 16, 2003

In 2003 and 2004, the Yankees and Red Sox played twenty-six times each year, including the postseason. Twenty-six times. These years were the height of the Yankee-Red Sox rivalry. And in 2003, the difference between those two teams was one pitch. I was working Yankees radio at the time with John Sterling, and the way it worked was that after the ninth inning, we would alternate play-by-play each inning, with him doing the 10th, me doing the 11th, and so on. Grady Little stayed with Pedro Martinez longer than most fans think he should have, but going into the game, he knew he had no bullpen, which he told me that afternoon. Little eventually brought in Tim Wakefield to pitch the 10th and kept him in to start the 11th. So we're coming back from the commercial break, which is a little longer in the playoffs than the regular season. WCBS, which carried the games on radio in New York, tacked on a few extra seconds to the break, though, and we were still in commercials as Aaron Boone was walking from the on-deck circle to the batter's box. I was looking down on the field and listening to the commercial, and started thinking that we could have a "Heidi Bowl" moment here. As John took the game out of the break, I knew this wasn't good, because the first pitch was about to be thrown. And Boone ended up hitting the first pitch into the left-field bleachers to win the game and the series. The call ended up being fine, but we were within milliseconds of missing that pitch. Happily, the call has stood up, but it was within inches and seconds of being completely different.

Aaron Boone hits the series-winning home run in the bottom of the 11th inning of Game Seven of the 2003 American League Championship Series. (AP Photo/Dick Druckman)

Dick Stockton

Broadcaster, FOX Sports

Recipient of Basketball Hall of Fame's Curt Gowdy Award, 2001

1954 World Series, Game One, Cleveland Indians at New York Giants, Polo Grounds, New York, New York, September 29, 1954

My father was a great influence for me and is the reason I'm in this business. When I was growing up in Kew Gardens Hills in Queens, he would take me to the Polo Grounds, where we had season tickets for New York baseball Giants games. That was the first sport I was ever attached to. He took me to the first game of the 1954 World Series, when I was still a teenager, and it was the first great moment that I ever witnessed. The Cleveland Indians had won 111 games and snapped the Yankees' string of five straight American League pennants, and were heavy favorites to beat the Giants. Our seats were eight rows behind the visitors' dugout, so our seats faced out toward the right-field line. When Vic Wertz hit the long fly ball to center field, my dad told me to get up and stand on my seat, and when I did, I saw Willie Mays make one of the most famous catches in baseball history. You always thought Mays had a chance to catch every ball hit to center, because he usually did. This ball was hit to the deepest part of the ballpark; centerfield at the Polo Grounds was 483 feet deep. I didn't know that he was going to need to turn around and run like a wide receiver to catch it over his shoulder, though. Dusty Rhodes won the game in the 10th inning with what looked like a popup to the first baseman but actually landed in the overhang in right field for a game-winning, three-run home run. The Giants won the game, 5–2, and ended up sweeping the Indians.

Boston Celtics at Philadelphia 76ers, Convention Hall, Philadelphia, Pennsylvania, 1965 to 1967

I was working at KYW radio in Philadelphia and will never forget the matchups between Bill Russell and Wilt Chamberlain. It was my first job out of college and I was working the overnight shift, so I would go see the 76ers play before work whenever I could. When the Celtics were in town, it was fun to see the two great giants face each other. It was the same thing every time they played—it was the battle of the behemoths. Chamberlain was bigger physically and could do more things offensively, while Russell was a shot blocker and better defensive player.

1975 World Series, Game Six, Cincinnati Reds at Boston Red Sox, Fenway Park, Boston, Massachusetts, October 21, 1975

The thing that was great about this game for me was that it was the first year I had done baseball, and NBC had selected me to be one of the announcers. They used hometown announcers for the games at the time, and it would always be one announcer from the home team paired with Curt Gowdy, Tony Kubek, and Joe Garagiola. It was great fortune that I was assigned to this game. Carlton Fisk's home run capped an incredibly

Carlton Fisk attempts to will the ball fair while following the flight of his 12th-inning game-winning home run in Game Six of the 1975 World Series. (AP Photo/Harry Cabluck)

dramatic game. The Reds were on the brink of winning the World Series before the Red Sox came back to win. Baseball had been on a down cycle the previous three years. Not to criticize the Oakland A's, who won all three, but baseball was in a certain state where it really needed a shot in the arm. I think this Series did that, and this game was the most memorable moment of it, even though the Reds wound up winning in Game Seven. When Fisk hit the home run, I wasn't sure if it was going to be fair or foul, just like everyone else in the stadium, including Fisk. That is one of the more difficult calls to make. It was like Joe Buck's call of Mark McGwire's 61st home run. It wasn't one of those dramatic "Way back, way back, deep to left field, it's gone" home runs. It was a shot down the line and it took a second or two to see if it was going to be fair or foul and whether it was going to clear the wall. I think that was a dramatic call in that you just react to what you see and say what is in your head quickly. You don't have time to think, so all I said was, "And there it goes, if it stays fair . . . home run!" I didn't say anything as Fisk rounded the bases, because the whole scene was electric on television.

1981 NBA Eastern Conference Finals, Boston Celtics vs. Philadelphia 76ers, Boston Garden, Boston, Massachusetts and The Spectrum, Philadelphia, Pennsylvania, April 21-May 3, 1981

For some reason, CBS's number one crew of Gary Bender, Rick Barry, and Bill Russell was assigned the Western Conference Finals between the Houston Rockets and Kansas City Kings, while Kevin Loughery and I were assigned this series. It was the first meaningful playoff series between the teams since the days of Russell and Chamberlain. Of every series I ever covered or witnessed, this was the greatest one of them all. The 76ers led three games to one, but the Celtics came back to win in seven games. There were a couple of fights in the series and a lot of great drama, with five of the seven games decided by two points or less. Game Seven was in Boston Garden, and Larry Bird hit the winning shot to give the Celtics the one-point victory. This was the beginning of the Larry Bird vs Julius Erving rivalry that dominated the '80s in the East.

1983 NCAA Men's Basketball Tournament Finals, North Carolina State vs. Houston, University Arena, Albuquerque, New Mexico, April 4, 1983

I was assigned to the West regional early round games in Corvallis, Oregon, with former Michigan player Steve Grote. No one gave North Carolina State a chance to do anything in the tournament, but they defeated Pepperdine and UNLV to advance to the second weekend. We then did the West final in Ogden, Utah, where they beat Ralph Sampson's Virginia team to get to the Final Four. We all know what happened at that Final Four, of course. Houston was the heavy favorite in the championship game, but there was something about this team of destiny. I was sitting in the stands in Albuquerque and felt that I had a vested interest in N.C. State. I wasn't working the game but had been with them from the beginning of the tournament and saw the way they came from behind again and again, so I felt, "Why not? Why couldn't this huge underdog beat the Phi Slamma Jamma team?" And they did it. When Lorenzo Charles hit the winning basket, I got to see Jim Valvano running around, looking for someone to hug. It is one of those great moments that I carry with me today.

Rob Stone

Broadcaster, FOX Sports

Minnesota Vikings at Tampa Bay Buccaneers, Houlihan's Stadium, Tampa, Florida, October 13, 1996

I worked in the Tampa market at the station that was the home of the Buccaneers games and did their coaches' show. In 1996, the Bucs hired a new coach by the name of Tony Dungy, whom no one knew much about. The Bucs started the season 0–5, and while people liked Dungy, they didn't love him because he hadn't won yet, and it felt like they were still the same old Yuckaneers. He eventually got his first win against the Vikings, and only around 32,000 people were there, but everyone who had covered the Buccaneers felt a different breeze blowing from that point. I remember being on the field during the game and going into the locker room afterwards, and feeling an immense sense of pride, happiness, and satisfaction for Dungy. He had this power over you where you listened to him, you admired his tone, and you wanted him to like and appreciate you because you appreciated him so much. You could really feel that vibe after the game that the players were so happy finally to win for him. Being there for that first win, as he began turning that franchise around, has always stayed with me.

1998 FIFA World Cup Group Stage, United States vs. Iran, Gerland Stadium, Lyon, France, June 21, 1998

It was billed as the mother of all games, because the political tensions between the two countries was off the charts. Most improbably, the countries were paired together in the group stage in Lyon. I was working sidelines and remember hearing all of the stories about the security concerns. There were rumblings that there was going to be a huge protest, banners being unfurled, or people storming the field. I was positioned between the two benches and, during warmups, looked up into the stands and saw military personnel with rifles at the top of the stadium and helicopters buzzing around. I had never experienced this kind of feel around a game. There were questions about whether the teams would shake hands before the game, and the Iran players were told not to budge and to make the United States players come to them. The U.S. had a really poor performance in the match and lost, 2–1, essentially being eliminated from the World Cup. It was the first time I saw sports being bigger than just the game. There was so much more on the line to this one than in a normal game. It impacted lives, politicians, and countries and was way beyond the depth that I was prepared for.

1999 Women's World Cup Final, United States vs. China, Rose Bowl, Pasadena, California, July 10, 1999

I was the sideline reporter for the third-place game, which was played right before the final at the Rose Bowl. We knew this was becoming something bigger than we could ever have imagined and had to think about things like the president coming to the Rose Bowl and how that was going to affect our daily schedule. There was a crazy swarm of energy and anticipation, but I didn't have a place to watch the championship game. All of the passes were being used, so if you didn't have one, you were out of luck, and my duties ended when my interviews after the third-place game were done. Somehow, I was able to finagle my way back into the gates—I went out and found a way back in. After I got inside, I found one of my producers and went from

Brandi Chastain celebrates her game-winning penalty shootout goal in the 1999 Women's World Cup Final. (AP Photo/The San Francisco Examiner, Lacy Atkins)

being on the field for the third-place game to being in the very last row of the Rose Bowl. I was in one of the corners at the other end of the stadium from where the penalty kicks were taking place, but to be in that atmosphere for the greatest moment in American soccer history was absolutely unforgettable. The power of that team still prevails over every girl who plays soccer in the United States to this day.

2009 NCAA Men's Basketball Tournament Finals, North Carolina vs. Michigan State, Ford Field, Detroit, Michigan, April 6, 2009

For a brief time growing up, I lived in Chapel Hill. It was those formative years from preschool through third grade, and all I knew was Carolina Blue, Duke sucks, and UNC hoops is the greatest thing ever. That hasn't left me. As it turned out, my sister got a job in the UNC basketball office, so she had incredible access to the program. The Final Four team that year had Tyler Hansbrough, they were number one in the preseason, and everyone said this was the team to beat. So I said if they made it to the championship game, I was going. After they won on Saturday, I had to figure out how to get to Detroit for Monday's game. I got there, and my sister was able to get tickets for me, her, and our parents, so our whole family that lived in Chapel Hill sat together with great seats. We had better seats than Carolina basketball legends like Antawn Jamison and Phil Ford. The Tar Heels just dismantled Michigan State in the game. When you are a fan of a team, you always get stressed out watching them, particularly in big games, but Carolina jumped out to a 36–13 lead and cruised. So we could sit and relax and enjoy every basket and every second with no stress. We were able to enjoy one of the greatest college basketball teams ever put together and see their crowning achievement in a relaxed setting. I also got to do it with my family, which I cherish.

2010 PBA Tournament of Champions, Red Rock Lanes, Las Vegas, Nevada, January 24, 2010

It was the 45th Tournament of Champions, which is one of the PBA's majors. A woman named Kelly Kulick had made the television broadcast. A woman making the TV part of a bowling tournament had happened once or twice before, but in this case, she was the number one seed, which was crazy, since no woman had ever won on the tour. Not only did she win the whole thing, but she throttled former PBA Player of the Year Chris Barnes in the final, winning by 70 pins. It was over in the ninth frame, and the place was just electric with the appreciation of what was happening. A woman was winning in a male-dominated sport. Not only did a woman win a tournament, but it was one of the biggest of all of them. She was very emotional afterwards, her mom was there to celebrate, and I got emotional calling it. Just watching it again on YouTube gets me teary-eyed. It was a Billie Jean King-type moment for women's athletics, where a woman conquered the men, and did it in dominating fashion. I'm so proud to have been a part of it.

Rick Telander

Columnist, *Chicago Sun-Times*

Super Bowl XX, Chicago Bears vs. New England Patriots, Louisiana Superdome, New Orleans, Louisiana, January 26, 1986

This game was complete and utter dominance, led by the defense. It was a team full of characters, with Mike Ditka, Jim McMahon, Mike Singletary, Dan Hampton, Steve McMichael, and, of course, Walter Payton and the Fridge. I remember the Bears saying they didn't want to knock Patriots quarterback Tony Eason out of the game because they just wanted to abuse him, but they did anyway. The 46–10 outcome was really what everyone expected. That team had a huge following, because they were so charismatic.

1996 NBA Finals, Seattle SuperSonics vs. Chicago Bulls, KeyArena at Seattle Center, Seattle, Washington and United Center, Chicago, Illinois, June 5-16, 1996

This was Michael Jordan's first championship after returning from baseball, but it was also one of the greatest teams of all time, going 72–10 in the regular season. Michael made *Space Jam* in the summer before the season started and had a floor installed at the studio so that he could work out and get ready for the season. Well, when the season started, he just went insane. He punched Steve Kerr and gave him a black eye, and while he was very apologetic about it, Kerr knew that it was just Michael going on one of his lunatic things, and nothing was going to get in his way. He didn't miss a single game in the next three seasons, regular season or playoffs. He was just on a mission, and that season, it was as if none of the other teams in the league had any business even being on the floor with them. When they were rolling, their opponents could barely get the ball up the floor against them. It wasn't just the 72 wins, but it was like the Beatles at their peak. It was a team full of stars—Jordan, Pippen, Harper, Rodman, Kukoc off the bench, Phil Jackson coaching—and when they came to town, they performed. When they won the championship, for Jordan, it was a reaffirmation of his genius and desire.

1998 NBA Finals, Game Six, Chicago Bulls at Utah Jazz, Delta Center, Salt Lake City, Utah, June 14, 1998

The Bulls had never been to a Game Seven in the Finals, but they were trailing late in the game and there was a sense that the Jazz, on their home court with the legendary tandem of Karl Malone and John Stockton, had a shot to get there. But then Jordan stole the ball from Malone and dribbled up court. He could have passed or done a number of other things but instead skidded to a stop, pushed Bryon Russell out of the way, and made one of the most famous shots in history. When he took the shot, it seemed to linger in the air in mid-arc forever, and when it went through, he kept his arm straight out in the air for a moment. He claims he wasn't doing it for a victory salute and that it was just a follow-through, and I kind of understand what he means in that if you keep your arm in the air like that, nothing is going to interfere with the shot. If he could have ended everything like that, and walked away from basketball forever, it would have been the greatest exit ever. Of course, he tarnished it by coming back with the Wizards. But that definitive statement, that stake in the heart of people who had hope, was the essence of Michael Jordan. He was a handsome guy, but just a stone-cold killer who loved to do these things to people.

2000 Summer Olympics, Greco-Roman Wrestling Super Heavyweight Final, Sydney Exhibition Centre, Sydney, Australia, September 27, 2000

Alexander Karelin was a Russian Greco-Roman heavyweight wrestler and was beaten in this match for the first and only time in his career by American Rulon Gardner. It was the most unexpected, stunning thing I've ever seen in sports. Karelin was absolutely terrifying, both to everyone he faced and the audience. He was a monster, like Grendel from Beowulf. People knew that he trained in waist-high snow in Siberia. He had this horrifying body slam where he would lift guys up who weighed 285 pounds with ease, and he faced opponents who would give up rather than be slammed. He just looked fearsome. As it turned out, he was a very good sport, but this monstrous image and vapor around him was terrifying. When it looked like Gardner had a chance to win, I remember people rushing in to the arena, which wasn't very big, to see it. People were there to anoint Karelin as the greatest Greco-Roman wrestler, but it never happened. Gardner was so tough and had such a huge chest, almost circular like a barrel, and he broke Karelin's grip around him, and that was the one point that he used to win that event. I knew nothing about Greco-Roman wrestling but remember these two huge guys going at each other, and it was just amazing.

2004 Summer Olympics, Athens, Greece, August 13-29, 2004

There were two events in Athens that stand out for me. First was the men's marathon, where the leader, Brazil's Vanderlei de Lima, was tackled by a protestor about four miles from the finish line. I was closer to the finish line than where it happened, so I didn't see it, but when de Lima passed by me, he was no longer in first place. When he came running by, no one realized what had happened, but he had this horrified look on his face. He had experienced one of the great breakdowns in civic trust, and it happened at one of the biggest moments of his life. When I found out later what had happened, it was shocking beyond belief.

The other event was the shot put competition, which was held at the ancient Olympia. The athletes came out through the old ruins and threw the shot on the lawn where the ancient Greeks had competed. The sense of history was just overwhelming.

Charissa Thompson

Broadcaster, FOX Sports

Appalachian State at Michigan, Michigan Stadium, Ann Arbor, Michigan, September 1, 2007

It was my first game working as a sideline reporter. Michigan was expected to make a run at the national championship that season but struggled in the first half. I tried to get Lloyd Carr to answer a question on the way to the locker room, but he blew me off, and I couldn't help think that this wasn't going very well for my first game. I knew things weren't going well for the Wolverines but thought that coaches were required to stop to do the interview.

As the game was reaching the sequence at the end, featuring Thom Brennaman's now-iconic call, I knew I was watching something special. It had the chance to be one of the biggest upsets in college football history, with Appalachian State being an FCS school, and I needed to figure out what I was potentially going to ask their coach after this monumental win. Then I had to figure out what to ask Carr this time if they won, as well. When it finally ended, you couldn't believe the silence in the Big House. There was this tiny little section of Appalachian State fans, and that was all you could hear. I remember talking to one of the Mountaineers players before the game, and he told me the whole city of Boone, North Carolina, was

Appalachian State running back Kevin Richardson celebrates the Mountaineers' 2007 win over Michigan in Ann Arbor. (AP Photo/Duane Burleson)

basically shutting down for the game. It was the biggest game they were going to be a part of, and they ended up winning it.

After it was all over, we were in the car back to the hotel. The last game Thom and Charles Davis had called the previous season was the famous Boise State-Oklahoma Fiesta Bowl, and now they had this one. They started talking about where it ranked in the games they had seen, then asked me, and that is when I finally told them that it was my first game.

San Diego Padres at Colorado Rockies, Coors Field, Denver, Colorado, October 1, 2007

I had been the sideline reporter for Rockies games that season but had just left to join *The Best Damn Sports Show Period* in Los Angeles. The Rockies went on this huge run at the end of the season just to get to a one-game playoff to determine the National League wild-card team. I was there as a fan, but there was this emotional attachment for me to this team after covering them all season. It was such a great group of guys, and for them to win so emotionally, with Matt Holliday sliding into home on a really close play to cap a three-run rally in the bottom of the 13th, really meant a lot to me.

2007 NFC Championship Game, New York Giants at Green Bay Packers, Lambeau Field, Green Bay, Wisconsin, January 20, 2008

This one has an asterisk next to it. I was working for *The Best Damn Sports Show Period*, and we were in Green Bay for one of the coldest games ever. During the pregame, we were on the field, and Eli Manning walks out onto the field. Eli is good at playing along with stuff, so I started yelling to him to throw me a pass to start having a catch with him. *Best Damn* was all about having fun, so I was running around on the field doing stupid stuff like that. It was maybe two hours before kickoff, and, if we were lucky, it was five degrees out at the time.

All of a sudden, I look over toward midfield, and Packers coach Mike McCarthy is out there watching me, and I wave at him and keep acting goofy. Around fifteen minutes later, a bunch of security guards come over and ask me to leave the stadium. McCarthy had requested that I be kicked out of the stadium. I had been going back and forth from the field to the FOX pregame set to talk with Terry Bradshaw,

Howie Long, and the guys the whole time I was on the field, so it was obvious I was with FOX, but they insisted I leave. My producer, Joel Santos, told our cameraman to keep rolling, and I'm being escorted out of Lambeau Field, while the security guards are yelling at the cameraman to stop filming (he said he wasn't recording it, but he was). So, while everyone in the stadium froze, we all sat in a hotel bar nearby, watching the game, drinking some wine, where it was nice and warm.

Super Bowl XLII, New York Giants vs. New England Patriots, University of Phoenix Stadium, Glendale, Arizona, February 3, 2008

I was standing in one of the tunnels that lead out to the field, so I couldn't really see the David Tyree catch but watched it, and everything that ensued, on the big screen in the stadium. After Plaxico Burress scored the game-winning touchdown, I remember watching Bill Belichick and other Patriots people start walking off the field. But there was still time remaining on the clock, so they all had to walk back out to the sideline again . . . except for Randy Moss, who just kept walking. That look on their faces, after having lost the game, and their perfect season, the way they just had was unforgettable. I was still new to working in sports at the time and was covering the game for FOXSports.com, but I knew I had seen something special. It was the first Super Bowl I ever attended, and I was able to get my dad tickets for the game, too, so for it to end the way it did really made it extra special for us.

Super Bowl XLIX, Seattle Seahawks vs. New England Patriots, University of Phoenix Stadium, Glendale, Arizona, February 1, 2015

I'm from Seattle and was at the game working for *Extra*, not FOX, so my job all week was to talk to celebrities and work parties and report on the entertainment part of the weekend. So when the game rolled around, it was great finally to be able to talk about sports again. I was on the field before the game with my co-host, A.J. Calloway, and didn't have my FOX hat on (not that I ever really temper my enthusiasm for the Seahawks anyway), and then we went to the different suites during the game to do interviews so I could watch the game.

When Jermaine Kearse made that catch near the goal line on the last drive, I thought, "Here we go. This is it." But then, the feeling turned just like that, in that split second, with the Malcolm Butler interception at the goal line. It went from pure elation to disappointment so quickly, you couldn't believe what had just happened. I'm good friends with Russell Wilson and was talking to him after the game, and he told me he couldn't believe how that game had just ended.

Mike Vaccaro

Columnist, *New York Post*

1999 NBA Eastern Conference Finals, Game Three, Indiana Pacers at New York Knicks, Madison Square Garden, New York, New York, June 5, 1999

A lot of times when you cover a game, what you remember most is the noise. I've never heard sports sound louder than the moment Larry Johnson tied Game Three of this series with the Pacers with a late three-pointer. It was a crazy day in New York sports. Charismatic was going for the Triple Crown at Belmont Park, and the Mets and Yankees were playing a Subway Series game. This was a Knicks playoff run that had fallen out of the sky, but the Pacers were heavily favored in the series and the Knicks had just lost Patrick Ewing to an Achilles injury. If the Pacers had won this game, it basically would have been the end of the string. Then Johnson made the shot. He probably wasn't fouled, and if you look at the video one hundred times, on ninety-nine of them, you won't see any contact, but a foul was called. I've watched this play so many times, and visually, it is so unique because when the ball goes through the basket, you see 19,000 pairs of arms immediately reaching to the sky. Most important, though, I can still remember what it sounded like. I remember turning to Ian O'Connor, who was sitting next to me on press row, and wanting to say something, but knowing he wasn't going to hear it. My words were literally absorbed by the sound around us.

2001 World Series, Game Five, Arizona Diamondbacks at New York Yankees, Yankee Stadium, Bronx, New York, November 1, 2001

Part of what makes this game so special is that what happened this night happened the night before against the same pitcher, so it is remarkable that it happened again. After waiting to file my column until the end of Game Four, resulting in logistical issues getting down to the locker room after the game, I filed this one a little earlier and went downstairs, never thinking that we could possibly see a repeat. We were amassed outside the Yankees' clubhouse and watching on TV, where there was a delay of a few seconds between what happened on the field and what we saw on the monitor. We saw Byung-Hyun Kim getting ready to pitch to Scott Brosius, when all of a sudden there was this implosion of noise and joy. The old Yankee Stadium had a specific sound. You knew when something special was happening, and the sound alone told us Brosius had just hit a home run. Then we actually saw the home run on the TV, and the pictures caught up to the sound. My first reaction was that it was simply incredible. My second reaction, though, was to try and get hold of my office to make sure they didn't run the column I had submitted. It ended up being the first time in my career that I missed my deadline from an event, because what I had sent over was completely worthless. Part of the reason you do this is just for the chance to see something you've never seen before, so to see it on back-to-back nights is just preposterous.

Super Bowl XLII, New York Giants vs. New England Patriots, University of Phoenix Stadium, Glendale, Arizona, February 3, 2008

It is easy to say it now, because it happened, but even though I had picked the Patriots to win in the paper, I wasn't shy about telling people that the Giants could win the game. At the very least, I didn't think the Giants would get humiliated, as a lot of people thought would happen. I thought it would be a good game, and through the first three quarters, you really didn't know how it was going to end. On the final drive, I went to write down the time on the clock when Eli Manning got sacked, only to look up and realize the play was still going on. That is the part of the David Tyree play that stays with me, because of how much it stunned me. Obviously, you don't expect a guy to catch a ball against his helmet, but even beyond that was Manning, who is as stone-footed as you can get, getting away from this frantic pass rush. When you write columns for long enough, you get a feel and rhythm for how things are going to go, and I told the other writers there for the *Post* that I was going to write about that final drive, win or lose. It was either going to be a game-winning drive or end in bitter heartbreak, and either way, it would make a good column. So I focused on as many details on that drive as I could, and that is the one that stood out the most. When Plaxico Burress caught the winning touchdown pass, it was otherworldly, because all of a sudden, this impossible dream was suddenly within reach. Sometimes this job is incredibly easy. This was one of those times. It was all right there in front of you and was everything you could want in a big event.

2012 Atlantic 10 Championship Game, St. Bonaventure vs. Xavier, Boardwalk Hall, Atlantic City, New Jersey, March 11, 2012

When you are as fortunate as I am to get a job in this business in the town where you grew up, you have to suspend a lot of the things you love about sports. You end up rooting for stories as opposed to the teams you grew up being a fan of, because sometimes it involves those teams losing. Because of that, my rooting interests are now confined to St. Bonaventure basketball, which for a very long time was a fruitless task. It is a small school that had a hard time adjusting to modern college basketball and hasn't had a lot of success. When I was there, they had four terrible years. I covered them for two years after graduating, and they were both epically bad seasons. It all came to a head in 2003, when they got caught up in an academic scandal.

Then came 2012, when the Bonnies went on a hot streak late in the season heading into the Atlantic 10 tournament. They won a thrilling game against Saint Joseph's, then, in the semifinals, had a huge lead against UMass. I was on a road trip covering the Knicks and remember watching on my computer in the Milwaukee airport, and as my plane was boarding, UMass started coming back. We pulled away from the gate, and I was trying to figure out a way to keep watching the game while we were moving, and just as we took off, UMass missed a desperation shot, and St. Bonaventure held on to win. After years of frustration, even with a trip to the NCAA tournament in 2000, the feeling of going to the conference tournament final was very emotional. I made a call when I got back to New York and got a credential for the game. I specifically wanted a credential instead of tickets so that I wouldn't root. I couldn't bring myself to be emotional at a game like this, and I ended up actually writing something for my old paper while there. The Bonnies controlled the game from the start, but it was still very nerve-wracking. When people ask me why sports matter, I point to the last 15 seconds of this game. The building was totally silent, because everyone there to root for St. Bonaventure was weeping. There were thousands of men and women bawling like babies. And I'll confess: I was the same way.

Super Bowl XLIX, Seattle Seahawks vs. New England Patriots, University of Phoenix Stadium, Glendale, Arizona, February 1, 2015

When Malcom Butler intercepted Russell Wilson to clinch the win, it was so sudden that there was difficulty processing it. Everyone started to talk about what a terrible play call it was by Pete Carroll, which overshadowed what a great play Butler made. It took everyone in the press box a second or two to figure out what really happened. There was a half-beat of silence followed by the corresponding noises, depending on which team's fans you were hearing. To me, a game isn't great just because you think it is great. It is also because you can't wait to talk about that game with your friends and family. That is what this game was, and you didn't have to have a dog in the fight to feel that way. Days later, people were still talking about it everywhere you went. People just didn't want to let this game go.

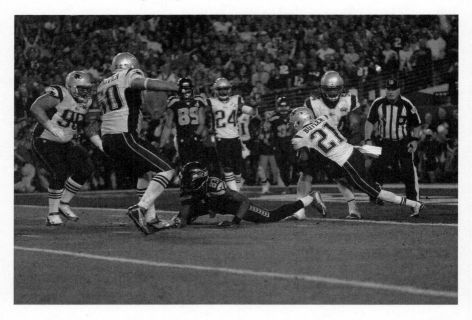

Malcolm Butler intercepts a Russell Wilson pass to seal Super Bowl XLIX. (AP Photo/ Ben Liebenberg)

Adnan Virk

Broadcaster, ESPN

New England Patriots at New York Giants, Giants Stadium, East Rutherford, New Jersey, December 29, 2007

Maybe it was Randy Moss staring me down after I asked a relatively innocuous question and saying, "I'm just happy to shut YOU people up." Maybe it was the perverse joy of sitting through the reliably terse, admirably bland Bill Belichick pre- and postgame pressers. Or maybe it was seeing Tom Terrific in the prime of his career. The Patriots, even with the asterisks of Spygate, Deflategate, et al., are one of the dynastic teams of modern professional sport, and being able to be a part of history and see them run the table in the regular season, culminating in the 38–35 win at Giants Stadium, was memorable.

The 2008 Masters, Augusta National Golf Club, Augusta, Georgia, April 10-13, 2008

I am not a golf guy, and our entire station in Toronto found it uproariously funny that I was selected to cover the Masters in 2008. The event was won by Trevor Immelman, and Tiger Woods was the runner-up, but that's immaterial. What's noteworthy about this experience was getting a taste of why this is ritualistic heaven for golf fans. The luscious greenery, the plentiful azaleas, and even the $1.50 and $2 sandwiches. The entire tournament in Augusta, Georgia, acts as a time capsule for when life may not have been better, but right down to the gentility and civility that abounds, it did seem a lot simpler. Amen to Amen Corner.

Baltimore Orioles at New York Yankees, Yankee Stadium, Bronx, New York, September 21, 2008

If you're a baseball guy, as I am, you can't help but appreciate the nostalgia and appeal of a place like Yankee Stadium. It was the Roman Colossus of its day, and during that Joe Torre-led Yankees run in the late '90s, there was no better place to watch a baseball game. I covered the final weekend there and was lucky enough to chat with superstars from Reggie Jackson to Mariano Rivera to even my favorite broadcaster, Keith Olbermann. They all waxed poetic about what had made this building so indelible and casually reflected on the memories there that would never leave them. Beyond just the stars that I interviewed, I took joy in talking to the hard-working stadium workers behind the scenes who had toiled in obscurity enhancing so many people's experience and receiving so little acclaim for doing so. They all collectively shared in what made the Yankees such a national brand, love them or hate them, and knew how you can never replace your home with some luxurious, money-making facsimile across the street. The real fans can always spot the imposter.

2009 NCAA Men's Basketball Tournament Finals, North Carolina vs. Michigan State, Ford Field, Detroit, Michigan, April 6, 2009

Sports at its best can be an inspiration for the downtrodden and actual escapism for those suffering through tough times. That's what made the 2009 Final Four in Detroit so special and the marvelous run by Tom Izzo and his Michigan State Spartans. Every day as we walked to Ford Field to cover the Final Four, we saw, up close and personal, the decline of one of America's great cities. But what was also undeniable was being swept up in the euphoria of the Spartans' run. I'll never forget sitting courtside as the Spartans roared out of the tunnel for the championship game versus heavily favored North Carolina and the cathartic eruption of noise that burst forth from the crowd of 73,000 at Ford Field. The memory of Izzo, with his raspy voice and regular-guy charm, giving a thumbs-up to the rabid crowd is one that is frozen in my memory. Alas, Tyler Hansbrough and the rest of Roy Williams's Tar Heels were off and running from the beginning, but the state of Michigan seemed to earn a hard-fought victory even if the final scoreboard said otherwise.

2010 NHL Eastern Conference Semifinals, Game Seven, Philadelphia Flyers at Boston Bruins, TD Garden, Boston, Massachusetts, May 14, 2010

There is nothing that can capture the excitement of playoff hockey. The wild swings in momentum, the visceral intensity, the marathon overtimes that can end with one flick of the wrist or one screened shot that tickles the twine.

Through 2013, only three times in 175 tries (a microscopic 1.7 percent) had a team come back from down 3–0 in a playoff series to win. The Toronto Maple Leafs in 1942, 33 years later the New York Islanders, and 35 years after that the Philadelphia Flyers over the Boston Bruins. The Los Angeles Kings also accomplished the feat against the San Jose Sharks in 2014, but I'll never forget being in Boston for the Flyers' miraculous comeback. I had just moved to Connecticut and had started working at ESPN. Once the Flyers rallied to make it a 3–2 series, my wife and I went onto StubHub and procured some tickets. For the low, low price of $150 including tickets, gas, and parking, I can say I was at one of the rarest moments in hockey history. The game itself lived up to the hype; the Flyers were down just as they had been all series but clawed back to win. I also won't forget about filing out of the arena and seeing a Flyers fan who clearly was a little too overzealous in his taunting being jumped and his John LeClair jersey being pulled in every direction possible. Thankfully, we avoided any such violent altercations, with my two-year-old son serving as the likely deterrent!

Lesley Visser

Broadcaster, CBS Sports

Recipient of Football Hall of Fame's Pete Rozelle Award, 2006
Elected to National Sports Media Association Hall of Fame, 2015

1983 NCAA Men's Basketball Tournament Finals, North Carolina State vs. Houston, University Arena, Albuquerque, New Mexico, April 4, 1983

To me, this was the ultimate March Madness. I covered all of North Carolina State's games in the tournament and had known coach Jim Valvano for many years; I've been on the board of "V Foundation" for cancer research for more than twenty years now. It was insanity for him to get to that title. They won seven of nine games after trailing with a minute left that season, and that team had adopted the mindset that it didn't matter if they were trailing

North Carolina State coach Jim Valvano holds the net aloft after his team defeated Houston for the 1983 NCAA Championship. (AP Photo/Leonard Ignelzi)

late in the game, they were going to win anyway. Houston was a dominant team, led by Akeem Olajuwon, who won the tournament's Most Outstanding Player award even though his team lost. I still see a lot of the players from that team today—I worked with Terry Gannon at ABC, while Dereck Whittenburg is also on the "V Foundation" board. To this day, if you ask him, Dereck still calls his play on the winning basket a pass.

1985 NCAA Men's Basketball Tournament Finals, Villanova vs. Georgetown, Rupp Arena, Lexington, Kentucky, April 1, 1985

When people ask me why I do what I do, I say, "Villanova 66, Georgetown 64." I was the lead writer for the *Boston Globe* at the time, and while I was also working for CBS, I was there to cover this one for the *Globe*. I had covered the Big East all season, so, with three teams from the conference in the Final Four that year, I knew most of the players on the floor intimately (with Memphis State being the exception). Villanova coach Rollie Massimino told his team they were going to have to play a perfect game to win the title, and they basically did, missing just one shot in the second half. Georgetown was the defending champion and wanted to join teams like Kentucky, UCLA, Cincinnati, and San Francisco as teams to win consecutive titles. They were so strong and powerful, but Villanova played them all the time in conference games. The Wildcats knew them very well and had no fear of them even though there was a huge disparity in talent. Massimino knew that if he had Ed Pinckney slash to the middle, he could score against the Hoyas from there, which is what he did all game. Georgetown coach John Thompson spread the floor, and it started to become a march to the foul line, just like most Big East games were. It was so powerful after the game when the Wildcats were cutting the net down and put it around the neck of their trainer, Jake Nevin, who was confined to a wheelchair because of Lou Gehrig's Disease.

1992 NCAA Men's Basketball Tournament Regional Finals, Kentucky vs. Duke, The Spectrum, Philadelphia, Pennsylvania, March 28, 1992

There were three of us on the broadcast for CBS—Verne Lundquist, Len Elmore, and myself. This game is considered one of the greatest games of all time, for obvious reasons, even though it wasn't for the championship. I remember Grant Hill saying that people had forgotten that he knew how to play football, so he knew how to make a pass like he made on the final play. I was the sideline reporter, so I got to listen to the huddle before the final play, and all coach Mike Krzyzewski said to them was, "Grant, can you throw it, and Christian, can you catch it?" He didn't ask Laettner if he could make the shot. Kentucky coach Rick Pitino opted not to cover Hill as he inbounded, opting to double-team Laettner instead, which is a move that will always be debated. Pitino has said, though, that it needed to be the perfect pass, the perfect shot, and the perfect guy for the shot for it to work, and it was. As soon as the game was over, before he even did the postgame interview with me, Krzyzewski walked down to shake hands with Kentucky's radio announcer, Cawood Ledford, who had announced he was retiring when the season ended. It has been an honor knowing both of the coaches in this game for many years. In fact, Rick Pitino introduced me to my now-husband, Bob Kanuth, at the Kentucky Derby.

Super Bowl XXXIV, St. Louis Rams vs. Tennessee Titans, Georgia Dome, Atlanta, Georgia, January 30, 2000

I was covering the game for ABC and was on the Rams' sideline inside the 5-yard line for Mike Jones's game-saving tackle, which will always go down as one of the greatest plays in Super Bowl history. The Rams were the "Greatest Show on Turf," and this was billed as a battle between quarterbacks Kurt Warner of St. Louis and the Titans' Steve McNair, so it is ironic that the most important play of the game was by one of the defenses. As that last play started, I was thinking that after all of this, the Rams weren't going to get it done. McNair hit Kevin Dyson on a slant, but Jones stopped him a yard short of scoring to end the game. It was so profound to be standing so close to that play as it happened. The biggest memory for me was Dick Vermeil finally winning a Super Bowl and how emotional he was about it afterwards.

Super Bowl XXXVI, New England Patriots vs. St. Louis Rams, Louisiana Superdome, New Orleans, Louisiana, February 3, 2002

This was the first Super Bowl after 9/11. I remember the first weekend after they resumed playing, the Giants played in Kansas City, and Giants owner

Wellington Mara asked me if I wanted to fly with the team on their charter. I attended a number of funerals for 9/11 victims. The whole season was very powerful for me. In the early to mid-'70s, I was the first woman beat writer for an NFL team, and the team I covered at that time was the Patriots. Putting all of that together, along with their team name being the Patriots, added so many layers for me that day. I was on the field when Adam Vinatieri kicked the game-winning field goal for New England, and when the game ended, it started raining red, white, and blue confetti and streamers in the Superdome. I think that day was one of those that helped pull the whole country back together after the tragedy a few months earlier.

Dan Wetzel

Columnist, Yahoo Sports

2004 American League Championship Series, Game Seven, Boston Red Sox at New York Yankees, Yankee Stadium, Bronx, New York, October 20, 2004

The drama of the Red Sox coming back was unbelievable, and it was the first time you could sense fear in the Yankees. I was staying in midtown Manhattan, and even walking around there during the day, there was this palpable sense among Yankees fans that they thought the team was going to blow this, which the Yankees themselves never felt. It felt like every game in the comeback went to the end, until David Ortiz would do something to win it for Boston. The whole series was getting ridiculous, with Curt Schilling and the bloody sock the night before. Johnny Damon had been horrible in the series, but Terry Francona stuck with him, and he hit a grand slam that was headed right to the overflow press area in right field where I was sitting. When he hit that slam to go up, 6–0, it was obvious the Red Sox weren't going to lose that game. It also sucked all of the air out of Yankee Stadium, as everyone realized the Yankees were going to blow the 3–0 series lead that they had. That series had a lot of great moments, but I'll never forget that one, because that was the moment we all realized this was actually going to happen . . . or was going to lead to the worst choke job in Red Sox history.

2006 Rose Bowl, Texas vs. USC, Rose Bowl, Pasadena, California, January 4, 2006

That game had so many stars—Matt Leinart, Reggie Bush, LenDale White, Pete Carroll for USC, and Vince Young and Mack Brown with Texas. That this game was in the Rose Bowl makes it even better, since that is the best venue there is for college football. I was standing near the end zone where Texas scored on the final drive. USC just couldn't stop Young on that drive. He was so much better than anyone on the USC defense, and on the last play, he came charging right into the corner where I was standing. The roar of the crowd and the screams of horror from the USC side as he scored were pretty awesome. And it was coming right at me. Everything happens so quick down on the field, and you don't realize how big and fast these guys really are until you watch from down there.

2008 U.S. Open Playoff, Torrey Pines Golf Course, La Jolla, California, June 16, 2008

I followed Tiger Woods around every day during the tournament. At times, he was playing outrageously well. On Saturday, he chipped one in on 17, and after he hit it, he just stopped and smiled, because he knew it was ridiculous. He hurt his knee during the tournament, but on Monday during the playoff, he had everything going. You had this journeyman golfer named Rocco (Mediate), and then you had Tiger, the most dominant guy on the tour.

Tiger Woods kisses the championship trophy after winning the 2008 U.S. Open in a sudden-death playoff against Rocco Mediate. (AP Photo/Chris Carlson)

It was just the two guys playing on Monday, and every hole was just jammed with people watching the ultimate match play. Tiger was playing on the bad wheel, and you didn't know whether he would be able to make it through, how much it was affecting him, or whether there was a little gamesmanship by Tiger and if he was just playing it up. His first Masters might have been his greatest triumph, but this Open win is a very close second. It was also the last glimpse at the old-school Tiger Woods—so dominant and charismatic, and capable of such great theater, but he's never recaptured it.

2012 Summer Olympics, Men's 100 Meter, Olympic Stadium, London, England, August 5, 2012

I was at the 100 meter in both Beijing and London, and will never forget the overwhelming sense of excitement in the stadium. And even though everyone in the stadium has different interests, because there are multiple events going on in any given session, Bolt was so unbelievable and was such a charismatic presence that the whole place just stopped to watch him. It didn't matter who you were or where you were from, you wanted to watch Usain Bolt run. The 100 is such a primal sport, and so basic, like two people saying, "I'll race you to that tree." But here's Bolt, with his ability after 30 or 40 meters to hit full speed when he gets upright and takes off, who's just utterly unbelievable. The whole place ends up gasping in awe. In London, the race featured the most accomplished field of runners ever. They were all great athletes and had spent four years practicing just to beat Bolt, and he just destroyed them all. A number of runners had their personal-best times in the race, but it didn't matter. These guys had run faster than anyone had ever run, and they still got smoked by Bolt. It was the ultimate domination, with the whole stadium cheering for him, because everyone knew they had just seen something unbelievable.

2014 Winter Olympics, Men's Hockey Preliminary Round, United States vs. Russia, Bolshoy Ice Dome, Sochi, Russia, February 15, 2014

What will always stand out to me from this game was the shootout. It was a hugely hyped game, and the Russians were obviously hugely popular with the game being held in their home country. As the shootout went into extra rounds, the U.S. kept putting T.J. Oshie out to shoot, and every time he got the puck, he started doing his sweeping, round, peculiar approach toward the net. The Russians were screaming every time, like they were watching a car accident about to happen. He would just come in and score almost every time. I also noticed that all of the concession workers in the arena had left their stands and were watching the play. If you wanted to steal a hot dog, you could. Every arena worker had flooded the stairways and open areas because they were not going to miss this. And every time Oshie went back out for another shot, they all had that "Not him again" look on their faces. It was just a great, dramatic ending, and the Olympics at its best.

Trey Wingo

Broadcaster, ESPN

Los Angeles Dodgers at St. Louis Cardinals, Busch Stadium, St. Louis, Missouri, May 26, 1992

I worked in St. Louis for six years before coming to ESPN and was covering the Cardinals when Ozzie Smith got his 2,000th hit. It was on an inside-out swing where the ball fell into play down the right-field line, and he ended up on third base with a triple. The relief on his face when he got there resonated with me. Ozzie came up as a defensive wizard who couldn't hit his weight, and he weighed about 140. The idea that he could get 2,000 hits, to him, I think was very significant, because it proved in his mind that he was a legitimate hitter. He worked really hard throughout his career on his hitting. The defense came easy for him, but he worked hard at becoming a professional hitter. After the game, we did all of our normal interviews but still hadn't gone on air yet. I asked him if he would come on to do a live shot at the top of the show. It was basically just the two of us left at the stadium, and he was beaming. We talked about how great the night was and then did the live shot. I remember leaving to go back to the station thinking that was pretty cool. He stuck around afterward to hang out with me and shared the moment with me in a very private way. Some days at work are better, and that was a really good day.

Super Bowl XXVII, Dallas Cowboys vs. Buffalo Bills, Rose Bowl, Pasadena, California, January 31, 1993

I grew up a Dallas Cowboys fan. Both my parents and all of my family are from Texas, even though I grew up in Connecticut. The Cowboys were great when I was a kid, then they were a disaster for a while after that, but I was always a fan. When they made the Super Bowl, I said that if I was able to get tickets, I was taking my dad. He isn't a huge sports fan, but he likes the Cowboys. There was a time when I was a kid that my dad was so busy with his job that we didn't talk much, but we could always talk about football, and we could always find time to talk about the Cowboys. So when I got the tickets, I invited him. We had better seats than Jack

Nicholson. We were on the 50-yard line at the Rose Bowl, and he was walking up and sat down five rows behind us. I turned to my dad and said, "We have better seats than The Joker." Then to see the Cowboys go out and destroy the Bills, it was just great to be there with him when that happened. I'll always remember that. We wound up going the next year, and then again a couple of years later, so my dad and I went to all three of the Super Bowls the Cowboys won. They were all great, but they say you never forget the first one, and to be there with him was awesome.

1996 NHL Western Conference Semifinals, Game Seven, St. Louis Blues at Detroit Red Wings, Joe Louis Arena, Detroit, Michigan, May 16, 1996

Jon Casey was in goal for the Blues because Grant Fuhr had injured his knee earlier in the playoffs, but he blanked the Red Wings in regulation and the game went to overtime tied, 0–0. Early in the second overtime, Steve Yzerman let a shot rip that went just over Casey's shoulder and just under the crossbar for the only goal of the game. That shot was a rocket, and I had never in my life been anywhere where I felt a stadium shake like Joe Louis Arena did at that moment. This was when the Red Wings were at the peak of their power and was also the last game in Wayne Gretzky's short tenure with the Blues. The Blues had put so much emphasis on that season because Gretzky was going to be a free agent, but when Yzerman rifled that shot, the Joe erupted, and it just sank the Blues.

2003 NBA All-Star Game, Philips Arena, Atlanta, Georgia, February 9, 2003

The whole weekend was really an homage to Michael Jordan, who was in his final go-round, so it was neat to be there. I sat next to Bill Walton during the game, which is an experience by itself. The game itself was nuts and went back and forth before the West final won in double overtime, 155–145. Kevin Garnett won the MVP, and I did the postgame interview with him. I asked him if he felt bad about stealing Michael's moment, and he told me that they were out there to win a game, and he did what he could.

Earlier that week, I was at the Ritz and started talking to Stuart Scott but didn't notice whom he was sitting with at the bar. It turned out to be Tiger Woods, and the two of them were holding court, but I didn't even realize that is who Stuart was with. We said hi to each other kind of awkwardly, so that was a little weird. On my way back to my room after that, I was texting my dad to tell him what had just happened, and my head was down as the elevator door opened, so when I walked in, I ran right into somebody who says, "Hey, Wingo, watch where you're going." It was Michael Jordan. I was so flummoxed about the first situation that I walked right into Michael.

Super Bowl XLII, New York Giants vs. New England Patriots, University of Phoenix Stadium, Glendale, Arizona, February 3, 2008

At the Super Bowl, after the game they shepherd you down from the press areas to a waiting area in the bowels of the stadium so that you are ready to go out on the field as soon as the game ends. Halfway through the fourth quarter, hundreds of media members start heading downstairs, but none of us are near a TV monitor, so we can't see the game. I called Mark Schlereth, who was at home, and told him that since I wasn't near a TV, I needed him to tell me what was going on in the game so we knew what to do when the game ended. As he gave me details, I was telling everyone else around me what was happening. So he is giving me details, but starts talking in football language, like, "It looks like a fire drill two-man zone." I told him to stop telling me what the offensive line was doing and just focus on where the ball goes and what happens. He does that, and says, "Eli drops back, scrambles around, made the pass, first down." By this point, we were in a spot where we could see a monitor, so I told him I was good and thanked him for the help, then watched the Giants score the winning touchdown on the catch by Plaxico Burress. After the game ended and they let us on the field, I make a beeline for Burress, and I'm the only one talking to him. I get this great interview with him, the guy that caught the game-winning pass in the Super Bowl to end the Patriots' unbeaten season. After we are done, I see an enormous mob around David Tyree and ask myself, "Why are they talking to that scrub?" As it turns out, the play that Schlereth described to me was the famous Tyree catch, in which he basically pinned the ball against his helmet while being tackled. That was all the information my good friend Schlereth was able to give me. Not that Eli was almost sacked or that Tyree caught the ball against his helmet. Just completion and first down is what my friend Mark told me. I love him and think he is one of the best analysts I've ever worked with, but he will never be a play-by-play guy.

Tracy Wolfson

Broadcaster, CBS Sports

1998 Winter Olympics, Women's Figure Skating, White Ring, Nagano, Japan, February 20, 1998

This was my first big job at CBS, and I was a tape librarian for the figure skating events. Michelle Kwan was everyone's favorite and you really wanted to see her win the gold, but Tara Lipinski came in that night and stole the gold away from her, which was shocking. I wasn't a reporter yet, so I didn't have to be unbiased during the event. I'll never forget how emotional it was in the building that night, and feeling really bad for Kwan. I'm not going to lie; I definitely shed a tear. To this day, I can still feel that disappointment for her. I have had the chance to talk to Kwan about that night and told her I cried about it, and she said, "You and me both!" When people ask me what events I would like to cover in my career, the Olympics is definitely one of them, and my experience in Nagano before my on-air career started is one of the reasons why.

2005 U.S. Open, Men's Quarterfinals, James Blake vs. Andre Agassi, Arthur Ashe Stadium, Flushing, New York, September 7, 2005

I grew up a big tennis fan and went to the U.S. Open many times, so it was cool being able to cover it early in my career. The match went well past midnight, ending at 1:15 in the morning, but the building was still almost full when Agassi closed out the five-set victory. The emotion of the crowd cheering for two Americans on America's biggest tennis stage made it even cooler, and, at age thirty-five, it would end up being Agassi's last U.S. Open run (he would lose to Roger Federer in the final). There is something special with the New York crowd when an American fan favorite makes a long run late in his career, and this night brought that out of everyone in attendance.

Super Bowl XLVII, San Francisco 49ers vs. Baltimore Ravens, Mercedes-Benz Superdome, New Orleans, Louisiana, February 3, 2013

The game itself wasn't anything special but was made memorable when the lights went out in the Superdome. I never expected to be on the Super Bowl broadcast and was told I wasn't getting on unless the lights went out. Sure enough, that is exactly what happened, and there I am trying to figure out the story. The 49ers' second-half comeback after the lights came back on was fun to be around, as well, even though it fell short. That was the biggest event I've ever been a part of on the air, even if I wasn't supposed to be.

2013 NCAA Men's Basketball Tournament Final Four, Georgia Dome, Atlanta, Georgia, April 6-8, 2013

Being a Michigan grad, it was a nice surprise when Michigan made it to the national championship game and having the chance to cover it for CBS. It was a big challenge to try and stay unbiased, but, at the same time, root for them under the table where no one could see. There is always that fine line I have to be careful not to cross whenever I cover the Wolverines. I had my family with me in Atlanta for the Final Four for the first time, and everyone I knew from college was there, too. It turned out to be a tremendous game and a great Final Four.

Alabama at Auburn, Jordan-Hare Stadium, Auburn, Alabama, November 30, 2013

This game stands out not just because of the enormity of the game, but for how it ended. I was on the sideline for so many big games that season, but to witness the ending of this game—in which Auburn's Chris Davis returned a missed field goal 109 yards with no time remaining to win the game—was something else. I had already gotten my interviews ready in my head. I knew I was going to talk to Nick Saban and AJ McCarron after the game ended, but as the winning play unfolded, you just couldn't believe it was really going to happen. That was followed by that reaction of "What do I do now?" and the immediacy of having to switch ends and trying to find the Auburn people I needed to talk to. As a sideline reporter, that is the biggest challenge. You never want to let that interview get away, so being able to report on it from the center of the mayhem after the game, trying to tackle Davis to talk to him, and interviewing Auburn head coach Gus Malzahn, this was one of the biggest moments I've been a part of. I was always a college football fan growing up and went to Michigan, but never knew just how passionate SEC fans were. A game like this one shows just how important college football is to people in that part of the country.

Chris Davis returns a missed field-goal attempt 109 yards to score the game-winning touchdown in the 2013 Iron Bowl. (AP Photo/Dave Martin)

Matt Yallof

Broadcaster, MLB Network

1999 AFC Wild Card Playoffs, Buffalo Bills at Tennessee Titans, Adelphia Coliseum, Nashville, Tennessee, January 8, 2000

I was covering the Bills for WKBW in Buffalo and was assigned to do pregame and postgame reports. To be perfectly frank, the details of the game are vague, aside from the final minute of play. I was standing with my cameraman behind the goalpost when Steve Christie kicked the field goal to give the Bills the lead. I remember this because we were walking, getting our postgame story ready, and talking to each other about going to the game in the next round. We were talking about whom the Bills may be playing next and where we might be going—all those things you get excited about when you are covering a team that is advancing in the playoffs.

So, I wasn't even watching the kickoff, but we could hear, as we were walking from the end zone to the sideline, the crowd start to swell. And it is getting louder and louder and louder, to a point where it was nearly deafening. I turned around to see what was going on, just in time to see Kevin Dyson coming into the end zone. He ran out of the end zone toward the sideline,

Kevin Dyson scores to complete the "Music City Miracle" in a 1999 AFC Wild Card playoff game. (AP Photo / Al Messerschmidt)

right past where we were standing. This was, for my money, the loudest football stadium I've ever been in. A lot of people where I was standing didn't know what was going on. I know I didn't know what was going on, because I didn't see the start of the play. We just assumed the game was over.

After the celebration on the field died down, we went into the Bills' locker room, and you could hear a pin drop. It was completely quiet, except, all of a sudden, you heard this wailing and screaming behind a closed door, and it was Bills head coach Wade Phillips having a complete meltdown in the visiting coach's office.

2000 National League Championship Series, Game Five, St. Louis Cardinals at New York Mets, Shea Stadium, Flushing, New York, October 16, 2000

The pandemonium started when Todd Zeile cleared the bases in the fourth inning with a double. I was sitting in the overflow media section in the mezzanine of Shea, and that hit put the game out of reach. The Mets hadn't been to a World Series since 1986, so there was an entire legion of fans that hadn't seen the Mets play in the Series. The rest had waited fourteen years for them to get back. Personally, I grew up a Mets fan but had never witnessed them clinch anything in person. I remembered 1986 and watching on TV, so it was pretty cool to be a part of that. What I remember most was after Zeile's hit, looking up, and seeing the upper deck of Shea Stadium literally moving. The concrete was moving like a wave. It is what I imagine it would look like if a minor earthquake hit New York, where the stadium was built to have a little give. And it was giving. As everyone was celebrating, I kept thinking about whether the stadium was going to fall. It really had the feeling that the upper deck was going to fall on the mezzanine.

After the game, it was like a frat party in the clubhouse. When the Mets win, they do it right. When the Yankees win, it is more businesslike. So in the room were all the Mets, and a few celebrities, as well. Two of the people I saw as soon as I walked in the room were Susan Sarandon and Tim Robbins, who were standing on the side, drinking champagne. Mets manager Bobby Valentine was break dancing in the middle of a circle of players. There was probably a half inch of champagne on the floor, so everyone's feet were soaked. The clubhouse was just destroyed. It was right around the time the song "Who Let The Dogs Out" was popular, and I asked Lenny Harris for an interview. All he wanted to do, though, was look in the camera and yell, "I let the (bleeping) dogs out!"

2002 NFC Championship Game, Tampa Bay Buccaneers at Philadelphia Eagles, Veterans Stadium, Philadelphia, Pennsylvania, January 19, 2003

I have almost no memory of the game, but it was the most raucous crowd I'd ever seen. The Eagles fans were angry, because the team had lost the previous year in the NFC Championship Game, and this was supposed to be their year, in the last year of Veterans Stadium. The Eagles were supposed to win this game and make it to the Super Bowl. Mid-game, it was clear they weren't going to win, and the fans started to act up. There were people in the bathrooms trying to rip urinals off the wall. I saw guys trying to pull seats out of concrete. But it wasn't just about trying to get a souvenir. These fans were mad.

It was the combination of a lot of bad things. It was a cold winter day, there was a lot of alcohol flowing, the Eagles were losing a game they were expected to win, it was the last game in a stadium that wasn't the most popular to begin with, and it was that fan base (which I love, after working in Philadelphia for six years). After the game was over, we were outside, getting ready to do our live shot for Comcast SportsNet postgame coverage, and it was the only time in my twenty-five-year TV career where I was truly scared. Someone actually threatened my life—me, a 5-foot-9 guy from Long Island who had nothing to do with the outcome of this game. That was just one disaster of a day for Philadelphia.

2011 World Series, Game Six, Texas Rangers at St. Louis Cardinals, Busch Stadium, St. Louis, Missouri, October 27, 2011

I was assigned by MLB Network to cover the Rangers for the entire World Series. As the reporter for the winning team, you can't wait for the end, because all of your work has a happy ending. We were positioned in the tunnel that leads into the dugout, so that we could get all of our postgame interviews on the field as soon as the game ended. Obviously, our stay in that little area was delayed and delayed, because the game kept going and going.

I remember talking to my producer while we were waiting, and we were both saying that the Rangers outfielders couldn't allow any hits to go over their heads. Unfortunately for them, that is exactly what happened, starting the incredible sequence of events at the end of the game. The triple by David Freese tied the game in the bottom of the ninth, but Josh Hamilton came back in the very next inning and hit a huge home run to put the Rangers back ahead.

Every World Series has a signature moment, and we all assumed the Hamilton homer was going to be it. What a story it would have been, with everything that Hamilton had gone through to get to the majors. That didn't happen, of course, as Freese came through once again. The fans in St. Louis are different. There wasn't any anger between the moments of excitement. There wasn't any panic. They were just watching, as if they were sitting in the audience at a play. It was just a very nice atmosphere. There wasn't any visceral anger after they blew the lead. There wasn't any panic when they were down to their final strike twice. It was just exciting, and it was something that struck me.

There were two images that stuck with me. One was a baby who was sleeping on his father's shoulder as this was all unfolding, and thinking to myself that this kid was going to grow up being told he was at this game, yet slept through it. The other image was after the Rangers blew it twice. I saw Nolan Ryan in the Rangers' tunnel. At the time, he was the team's president, and he was ashen white. He looked like he had just seen a ghost. We knew there was a Game Seven coming, but I don't think anyone at that point believed the Rangers could come back from what they just went through.

2014 World Series, Game Seven, San Francisco Giants at Kansas City Royals, Kauffman Stadium, Kansas City, Missouri, October 29, 2014

About an hour before the game, I was lucky enough to get Madison Bumgarner to do an interview with me for MLB Network. The big question leading into the game was whether he was going to pitch out of the bullpen and how much he would pitch if the team decided to use him. When I asked him to talk for a few minutes, he was as affable and as easygoing as he would be in the middle of February. I asked him if he was going to start the game sitting in the bullpen or sitting in the dugout, and he said he didn't know, and that he hadn't talked to Giants manager Bruce Bochy about it yet. All I could think to myself was, "What do you mean you didn't talk to him about it yet?"

We all know what unfolded next. Inning after inning, we were all just amazed by what this guy was doing. He wasn't just pitching, he was dominating. The game ends, and everyone is putting his performance into historical context, as far as numbers are concerned. That part is instantaneous now, with researchers and social media. We head out onto the field, where the Giants are celebrating, and he was the third guy I was able to interview on the field, before moving into the locker room, and his pacing and his cadence in the interview was exactly the same as it was in our interview before the game. I looked at him and asked him if he understood what he had done, and how historic it was, and all he could say was, "Thanks for saying that. All I was trying to do was make my pitches." It was the calm in the face of what he accomplished, not just the performance, that was so memorable for me.

INDEX

Grambling vs. Morgan State, Yankee Stadium, Bronx, New York, September 20, 1969: Freddie Coleman

1970 NBA Finals, Game Five, Los Angeles Lakers at New York Knicks, Madison Square Garden, New York, New York, May 4, 1970: Harvey Araton

1970 NBA Finals, Game Seven, Los Angeles Lakers at New York Knicks, Madison Square Garden, New York, New York, May 8, 1970: Marv Albert, Jerry Izenberg

Muhammad Ali vs. Joe Frazier, Madison Square Garden, New York, New York, March 8, 1971: Dave Kindred

Philadelphia Phillies at Cincinnati Reds, Riverfront Stadium, Cincinnati, Ohio, June 23, 1971: Hal McCoy

1973 Belmont Stakes, Belmont Park, Elmont, New York, June 9, 1973: Jerry Izenberg, Dave Kindred, Ross Newhan

1973 National League Championship Series, Game Five, Cincinnati Reds at New York Mets, Shea Stadium, Flushing, New York, October 10, 1973: Freddie Coleman

1973 South African Open, Ellis Park Tennis Stadium, Johannesburg, South Africa, November 14-27, 1973: Frank Deford

Los Angeles Dodgers at Atlanta Braves, Atlanta Stadium, Atlanta, Georgia, April 8, 1974: Ross Newhan

Muhammad Ali vs. Joe Frazier, Araneta Coliseum, Quezon City, Philippines, October 1, 1975: Jerry Izenberg

1975 World Series, Game Six, Cincinnati Reds at Boston Red Sox, Fenway Park, Boston, Massachusetts, October 21, 1975: Hal McCoy, Bob Ryan, Dick Stockton

1975 World Series, Game Seven, Cincinnati Reds at Boston Red Sox, Fenway Park, Boston, Massachusetts, October 22, 1975: Hal McCoy

Georgia Tech at Notre Dame, Notre Dame Stadium, South Bend, Indiana, November 8, 1975: Terry Gannon

1976 Daytona 500, Daytona International Speedway, Daytona Beach, Florida, February 15, 1976: Dave Kindred

1976 NBA Finals, Game Five, Phoenix Suns at Boston Celtics, Boston Garden, Boston, Massachusetts, June 4, 1976: Bob Ryan

1977 World Series, Game Six, Los Angeles Dodgers at New York Yankees, Yankee Stadium, Bronx, New York, October 18, 1977: E.J. Hradek, Ross Newhan

New York Yankees at Boston Red Sox, Fenway Park, Boston, Massachusetts, October 2, 1978: Jeremy Schaap

1979 NCAA Men's Basketball Tournament Finals, Indiana State vs. Michigan State, Special Events Center, Salt Lake City, Utah, March 26, 1979: Ray Ratto

Colorado Rockies at Atlanta Flames, The Omni, Atlanta, Georgia, March 1, 1980: Jiggs McDonald

1980 Stanley Cup Finals, Game Six, Philadelphia Flyers at New York Islanders, Nassau Coliseum, Uniondale, New York, May 24, 1980: E.J. Hradek

The 1980 Wimbledon Championships, Gentlemen's Final, Bjorn Borg vs. John McEnroe, The All England Lawn Tennis Club, London, England, July 5, 1980: Frank Deford

Larry Holmes vs. Muhammad Ali, Caesars Palace, Las Vegas, Nevada, October 2, 1980: Charley Steiner

1980 NFC Championship Game, Dallas Cowboys at Philadelphia Eagles, Veterans Stadium, Philadelphia, Pennsylvania, January 11, 1981: Andrea Kremer, Jon Sciambi

1981 NBA Eastern Conference Finals, Boston Celtics vs. Philadelphia 76ers, Boston Garden, Boston, Massachusetts, and The Spectrum, Philadelphia, Pennsylvania, April 21-May 3, 1981: Dick Stockton

The 1981 Wimbledon Championships, Gentlemen's Semifinals, John McEnroe vs. Rod Frawley, The All England Lawn Tennis Club, London, England, July 2, 1981: Charley Steiner

1981 AFC Wild Card Playoffs, Buffalo Bills at New York Jets, Shea Stadium, Flushing, New York, December 27, 1981: Steve Levy

1982 Smythe Division Semifinals, Game Three, Edmonton Oilers at Los Angeles Kings, The Forum, Inglewood, California, April 10, 1982: Bob Miller

1982 World Series, Game Seven, Milwaukee Brewers at St. Louis Cardinals, Busch Stadium, St. Louis, Missouri, October 20, 1982: Joe Buck

Stanford at Cal, Memorial Stadium, Berkeley, California, November 20, 1982: Ray Ratto

1983 Big East Conference Championship Game, Boston College vs. St. John's, Madison Square Garden, New York, New York, March 12, 1983: Freddie Coleman

1983 NCAA Men's Basketball Tournament Finals, North Carolina State vs. Houston, University Arena, Albuquerque, New Mexico, April 4, 1983: Dick Stockton, Lesley Visser

1983 Stanley Cup Finals, Game Four, Edmonton Oilers at New York Islanders, Nassau Coliseum, Uniondale, New York, May 17, 1983: Jiggs McDonald

1984 Summer Olympics, Los Angeles, California, July 28-August 12, 1984: Freddie Coleman

1984 Summer Olympics, Greco-Roman Super Heavyweight Final, Anaheim Convention Center, Anaheim, California, August 2, 1984: Jerry Izenberg

1985 NCAA Men's Basketball Tournament Finals, Villanova vs. Georgetown, Rupp Arena, Lexington, Kentucky, April 1, 1985: Bob Ley, Lesley Visser

San Diego Padres at Cincinnati Reds, Riverfront Stadium, Cincinnati, Ohio, September 11, 1985: Hal McCoy

Super Bowl XX, Chicago Bears vs. New England Patriots, Louisiana Superdome, New Orleans, Louisiana, January 26, 1986: Rick Telander

The 1986 Masters, Final Round, Augusta National Golf Club, Augusta, Georgia, April 13, 1986: Jim Nantz

1986 World Series, Game Six, Boston Red Sox at New York Mets, Shea Stadium, Flushing, New York, October 25, 1986: Mike Breen, Bob Costas, Steve Levy, Rob Parker, Jeremy Schaap

1986 AFC Championship Game, Denver Broncos at Cleveland Browns, Municipal Stadium, Cleveland, Ohio, January 11, 1987: Chris Rose

1987 NCAA Men's Basketball Final Four, Louisiana Superdome, New Orleans, Louisiana, March 28-30, 1987: Jim Nantz

1987 NCAA Men's Basketball Tournament Finals, Indiana vs. Syracuse, Louisiana Superdome, New Orleans, Louisiana, March 30, 1987: Scott Ferrall

1987 Patrick Division Semifinals, Game Seven, New York Islanders at Washington Capitals, Capital Centre, Landover, Maryland, April 18, 1987: Jiggs McDonald

Indiana at Northwestern, Welsh-Ryan Arena, Evanston, Illinois, January 11, 1988: Mike Greenberg

Los Angeles Dodgers at Cincinnati Reds, Riverfront Stadium, Cincinnati, Ohio, September 16, 1988: Hal McCoy

1988 World Series, Game One, Oakland Athletics at Los Angeles Dodgers, Dodger Stadium, Los Angeles, California, October 15, 1988: Marv Albert, Bob Costas

1988 World Series, Game Two, Oakland Athletics at Los Angeles Dodgers, Dodger Stadium, Los Angeles, California, October 16, 1988: Doug Gottlieb

1989 NBA Playoffs Opening Round, Game Five, Chicago Bulls at Cleveland Cavaliers, Richfield Coliseum, Richfield, Ohio, May 7, 1989: Rob Parker, Chris Rose

Los Angeles Kings at Edmonton Oilers, Northlands Coliseum, Edmonton, Canada, October 15, 1989: Jiggs McDonald, Bob Miller

1989 World Series, Game Three, Oakland Athletics at San Francisco Giants, Candlestick Park, San Francisco, California, October 17, 1989: Bob Ley, Chris Myers, Ray Ratto

Florida at Auburn, Jordan-Hare Stadium, Auburn, Alabama, November 4, 1989: Gregg Doyel

1989 AFC Wild Card Playoffs, Pittsburgh Steelers at Houston Oilers, Houston Astrodome, Houston, Texas, December 31, 1989: Scott Ferrall

1990 West Coast Conference Semifinals, Portland at Loyola Marymount, Gersten Pavilion, Los Angeles, California, March 4, 1990: Chris Myers

1990 NCAA Men's Basketball Tournament First Round, Loyola Marymount vs. New Mexico State, Long Beach Arena, Long Beach, California, March 16, 1990: Doug Gottlieb

Super Bowl XXV, Buffalo Bills vs. New York Giants, Tampa Stadium, Tampa, Florida, January 27, 1991: Mark Feinsand, Jeremy Schaap

1991 NCAA Men's Basketball Tournament Semifinals, UNLV vs. Duke, Hoosier Dome, Indianapolis, Indiana, March 30, 1991: Colin Cowherd

1991 U.S. Open, Fourth Round, Jimmy Connors vs. Aaron Krickstein, National Tennis Center, Flushing, New York, September 2, 1991: Ian Eagle

1991 World Series, Game Seven, Atlanta Braves at Minnesota Twins, Hubert H. Humphrey Metrodome, Minneapolis, Minnesota, October 27, 1991: Dave Kindred

1992 North Atlantic Conference Championship Game, Drexel at Delaware, Delaware Field House, Newark, Delaware, March 9, 1992: Jeff Pearlman

1992 NCAA Men's Basketball Tournament First Round, Delaware vs. Cincinnati, University of Dayton Arena, Dayton, Ohio, March 20, 1992: Jeff Pearlman

1992 NCAA Men's Basketball Tournament Regional Finals, Kentucky vs. Duke, The Spectrum, Philadelphia, Pennsylvania, March 28, 1992: Bob Ryan, Lesley Visser

Dinner at Steve Spurrier's House, Gainesville, Florida, March 28, 1992: Gregg Doyel

The 1992 Masters, Final Round, Augusta National Golf Club, Augusta, Georgia, April 12, 1992: Jim Nantz

Los Angeles Dodgers at St. Louis Cardinals, Busch Stadium, St. Louis, Missouri, May 26, 1992: Trey Wingo

1992 NBA Finals, Game One, Portland Trail Blazers at Chicago Bulls, Chicago Stadium, Chicago, Illinois, June 3, 1992: Andrea Kremer

1992 Summer Olympics, Men's Basketball, Palau Municipal d'Esports de Badalona, Badalona, Spain, July 26–August 8, 1992: Kenny Albert, Marv Albert

1992 Summer Olympics, Men's 4x100 Meter Relay Final, Estadi Olimpic de Montjuic, Barcelona, Spain, August 8, 1992: Frank Deford

1992 Summer Olympics, Men's Basketball Final, Palau Municipal d'Esports de Badalona, Badalona, Spain, August 8, 1992: Harvey Araton

Army vs. Navy, Veterans Stadium, Philadelphia, Pennsylvania, December 5, 1992: Freddie Coleman

Super Bowl XXVII, Dallas Cowboys vs. Buffalo Bills, Rose Bowl, Pasadena, California, January 31, 1993: Mike Greenberg, Trey Wingo

1993 NCAA Men's Basketball Tournament Finals, North Carolina vs. Michigan, Louisiana Superdome, New Orleans, Louisiana, April 5, 1993: Jeffri Chadiha

1993 Patrick Division Semifinals, Game Six, Washington Capitals at New York Islanders, Nassau Coliseum, Uniondale, New York, April 28, 1993: Jiggs McDonald

1993 Patrick Division Finals, Game Seven, New York Islanders at Pittsburgh Penguins, Civic Arena, Pittsburgh, Pennsylvania, May 14, 1993: Jiggs McDonald

1993 Campbell Conference Finals, Game Seven, Los Angeles Kings at Toronto Maple Leafs, Maple Leaf Gardens, Toronto, Canada, May 29, 1993: Bob Miller

1993 NBA Finals, Game Three, Phoenix Suns at Chicago Bulls, Chicago Stadium, Chicago, Illinois, June 13, 1993: Ric Bucher

Cleveland Indians at New York Yankees, Yankee Stadium, Bronx, New York, September 4, 1993: Keith Law

Philadelphia Eagles at New York Jets, Giants Stadium, East Rutherford, New Jersey, October 3, 1993: Kevin Burkhardt

Riddick Bowe vs. Evander Holyfield, Caesars Palace, Las Vegas, Nevada, November 6, 1993: Colin Cowherd

Miami Dolphins at Philadelphia Eagles, Veterans Stadium, Philadelphia, Pennsylvania, November 14, 1993: Andrea Kremer

Phoenix Suns at Golden State Warriors, Oakland-Alameda County Coliseum Arena, Oakland, California, November 16, 1993: Ric Bucher

1993 NFC Wild Card Playoffs, Green Bay Packers at Detroit Lions, Pontiac Silverdome, Pontiac, Michigan, January 8, 1994: Rob Parker

1994 Winter Olympics, Men's 1000 Meter Speed Skating Final, Vikingskipet Olympic Arena, Hamar, Norway, February 18, 1994: Harvey Araton

Minnesota Twins vs. Chicago White Sox, Ed Smith Stadium, Sarasota, Florida, March 14, 1994: Mike Greenberg

Vancouver Canucks at Los Angeles Kings, The Forum, Los Angeles, California, March 23, 1994: Bob Miller

1994 Stanley Cup Finals, Game Seven, Vancouver Canucks at New York Rangers, Madison Square Garden, New York, New York, June 14, 1994: Kenny Albert, Marv Albert, Ian Eagle, Steve Levy

1994 NBA Finals, Game Five, Houston Rockets at New York Knicks, Madison Square Garden, New York, New York, June 17, 1994: Mike Breen

Chicago Cubs at Cincinnati Reds, Riverfront Stadium, Cincinnati, Ohio, July 16, 1994: Thom Brennaman

Colorado at Michigan, Michigan Stadium, Ann Arbor, Michigan, September 24, 1994: Jeffri Chadiha, Jeremy Schaap

George Foreman vs. Michael Moorer, MGM Grand, Las Vegas, Nevada, November 5, 1994: Charley Steiner

Morgan State at Georgetown, Capital Centre, Landover, Maryland, November 30, 1994: Chris McKendry

Chicago Bulls at New York Knicks, Madison Square Garden, New York, New York, March 28, 1995: Mike Greenberg

California Angels at Baltimore Orioles, Camden Yards, Baltimore, Maryland, September 6, 1995: Kenny Albert

1996 Fiesta Bowl, Nebraska vs. Florida, Sun Devil Stadium, Tempe, Arizona, January 2, 1996: Colin Cowherd

1996 NHL Eastern Conference Quarterfinals, Game Four, Pittsburgh Penguins at Washington Capitals, USAir Arena, Landover, Maryland, April 24, 1996: Steve Levy

1996 NHL Western Conference Semifinals, Game Seven, St. Louis Blues at Detroit Red Wings, Joe Louis Arena, Detroit, Michigan, May 16, 1996: Trey Wingo

1996 NBA Finals, Seattle SuperSonics vs. Chicago Bulls, KeyArena at Seattle Center, Seattle, Washington and United Center, Chicago, Illinois, June 5-16, 1996: Rick Telander

ABCD Camp, Fairleigh Dickinson University, Teaneck, New Jersey, July 8-11, 1996: Bruce Feldman

1996 Tour de France, Stage 17, Pamplona, Spain, July 17, 1996: Terry Gannon

1996 Summer Olympics, Opening Ceremonies, Centennial Olympic Stadium, Atlanta, Georgia, July 19, 1996: Bob Costas

1996 Summer Olympics, Centennial Olympic Park, Atlanta, Georgia, July 27, 1996: Scott Ferrall, Chris Myers

1996 Summer Olympics, Men's 200 Meter Final, Centennial Olympic Stadium, Atlanta, Georgia, August 1, 1996: Joe Posnanski

1996 Summer Olympics, Women's Basketball Finals, Georgia Dome, Atlanta, Georgia, August 3, 1996: Mike Breen

1996 American League Championship Series, Game One, Baltimore Orioles at New York, Yankees, Yankee Stadium, Bronx, New York, October 9, 1996: Mark Feinsand

Minnesota Vikings at Tampa Bay Buccaneers, Houlihan's Stadium, Tampa, Florida, October 13, 1996: Rob Stone

Waco Wizards at Austin Ice Bats, Luedecke Arena, Austin, Texas, October 19, 1996: Michelle Beadle

USC at UCLA, Rose Bowl, Pasadena, California, November 23, 1996: Peter Schrager

1996 NFC Championship Game, Carolina Panthers at Green Bay Packers, Lambeau Field, Green Bay, Wisconsin, January 12, 1997: E.J. Hradek

1997 NHL Eastern Conference Quarterfinals, Game Four, Philadelphia Flyers at Pittsburgh Penguins, Civic Arena, Pittsburgh, Pennsylvania, April 23, 1997: Scott Ferrall

1997 NBA Finals, Game Five, Chicago Bulls at Utah Jazz, Delta Center, Salt Lake City, Utah, June 11, 1997: Marv Albert

1997 World Series, Game Seven, Cleveland Indians at Florida Marlins, Pro Player Stadium, Miami Gardens, Florida, October 26, 1997: Gregg Doyel, Jon Sciambi

Villanova at Duke, Cameron Indoor Stadium, Durham, North Carolina, December 10, 1997: Gregg Doyel

Chicago Bulls Home Game, United Center, Chicago, Illinois, 1997-98 season: Michelle Beadle

1998 U.S. Women's Figure Skating Championships, CoreStates Center, Philadelphia, Pennsylvania, January 11, 1998: Terry Gannon

1998 Winter Olympics, Women's Figure Skating, White Ring, Nagano, Japan, February 20, 1998: Tracy Wolfson

1998 NBA Finals, Game Six, Chicago Bulls at Utah Jazz, Delta Center, Salt Lake City, Utah, June 14, 1998: Harvey Araton, Ric Bucher, Bob Costas, Ian Eagle, Rick Telander

1998 FIFA World Cup Group Stage, United States vs. Iran, Gerland Stadium, Lyon, France, June 21, 1998: Rob Stone

1998 FIFA World Cup Final, Brazil vs. France, Stade de France, Saint-Denis, France, July 12, 1998: Bob Ley

Roy Jones Jr. vs. Lou Del Valle, The Theater at Madison Square Garden, New York, New York, July 18, 1998: Jeff Pearlman

Arizona Diamondbacks at Pittsburgh Pirates, Three Rivers Stadium, Pittsburgh, Pennsylvania, September 3, 1998: Keith Law

1999 NBA Eastern Conference Finals, Game Three, Indiana Pacers at New York Knicks, Madison Square Garden, New York, New York, June 5, 1999: Mike Vaccaro

1999 Women's World Cup Final, United States vs. China, Rose Bowl, Pasadena, California, July 10, 1999: Chris McKendry, Rob Stone

1999 Home Run Derby, Fenway Park, Boston, Massachusetts, July 12, 1999: Karl Ravech

1999 Ryder Cup, Day Three, The Country Club, Brookline, Massachusetts, September 26, 1999: Bob Ryan

1999 National League Championship Series, Game Five, Atlanta Braves at New York Mets, Shea Stadium, Flushing, New York, October 17, 1999: Jeff Pearlman

1999 AFC Wild Card Playoffs, Buffalo Bills at Tennessee Titans, Adelphia Coliseum, Nashville, Tennessee, January 8, 2000: Mike Hill, Matt Yallof

Super Bowl XXXIV, St. Louis Rams vs. Tennessee Titans, Georgia Dome, Atlanta, Georgia, January 30, 2000: Mike Hill, Lesley Visser

2000 NHL Eastern Conference Semifinals, Game Four, Philadelphia Flyers at Pittsburgh Penguins, Mellon Arena, Pittsburgh, Pennsylvania, May 4, 2000: Steve Levy

2000 NBA Western Conference Finals, Game Seven, Portland Trail Blazers at Los Angeles Lakers, Staples Center, Los Angeles, California, June 4, 2000: Colin Cowherd

2000 U.S. Open, Pebble Beach Golf Links, Pebble Beach, California, June 15-18, 2000: Ray Ratto, Chris Rose

129th Open Championship, Final Round, The Old Course at St. Andrews, Fife, Scotland, July 23, 2000: Karl Ravech

2000 PGA Championship, Final Round, Valhalla Golf Club, Louisville, Kentucky, August 20, 2000: Joe Posnanski

2000 Summer Olympics, Greco-Roman Wrestling Super Heavyweight Final, Sydney Exhibition Centre, Sydney, Australia, September 27, 2000: Joe Posnanski, Rick Telander

2000 National League Championship Series, Game Five, St. Louis Cardinals at New York Mets, Shea Stadium, Flushing, New York, October 16, 2000: Matt Yallof

2000 World Series, New York Mets vs. New York Yankees, Shea Stadium, Flushing, New York, and Yankee Stadium, Bronx, New York, October 21-26, 2000: Mike Hill

2001 Daytona 500, Daytona International Speedway, Daytona, Florida, February 18, 2001: Chris Myers

Seattle SuperSonics at New York Knicks, Madison Square Garden, New York, New York, February 27, 2001: Mike Hill

2001 NCAA Division III Men's Basketball First Round, Hampden-Sydney at William Paterson, William Paterson Recreation Center, Wayne, New Jersey, March 3, 2001: Kevin Burkhardt

Atlanta Braves at Philadelphia Phillies, Veterans Stadium, Philadelphia, Pennsylvania, September 17, 2001: Charley Steiner

Atlanta Braves at New York Mets, Shea Stadium, Flushing, New York, September 21, 2001: Jeff Pearlman

Bernard Hopkins vs. Felix Trinidad, Madison Square Garden, New York, New York, September 29, 2001: Mike Hill

2001 American League Division Series, Game Three, New York Yankees at Oakland Athletics, Network Associates Coliseum, Oakland, California, October 13, 2001: Mark Feinsand

2001 World Series, New York Yankees vs. Arizona Diamondbacks, Yankee Stadium, Bronx, New York, and Bank One Ballpark, Phoenix, Arizona, October 27-November 4, 2001: Thom Brennaman, Ray Ratto, Karl Ravech

2001 World Series, Game Three, Arizona Diamondbacks at New York Yankees, Yankee Stadium, Bronx, New York, October 30, 2001: Joe Buck

2001 World Series, Game Four, Arizona Diamondbacks at New York Yankees, Yankee Stadium, Bronx, New York, October 31, 2001: Joe Posnanski

2001 World Series, Games Four and Five, Arizona Diamondbacks at New York Yankees, Yankee Stadium, Bronx, New York, October 31 and November 1, 2001: E.J. Hradek, Rob Parker

2001 World Series, Game Five, Arizona Diamondbacks at New York Yankees, Yankee Stadium, Bronx, New York, November 1, 2001: Mike Vaccaro

2001 World Series, Game Seven, New York Yankees at Arizona Diamondbacks, Bank One Ballpark, Phoenix, Arizona, November 4, 2001: Mark Feinsand, Jerry Izenberg

2001 GMAC Bowl, Marshall vs. East Carolina, Ladd-Peebles Stadium, Mobile, Alabama, December 19, 2001: Steve Levy

Super Bowl XXXVI, New England Patriots vs. St. Louis Rams, Louisiana Superdome, New Orleans, Louisiana, February 3, 2002: Jeffri Chadiha, Lesley Visser

2002 Winter Olympics, Men's Ice Hockey Finals, United States vs. Canada, E Center, Salt Lake City, Utah, February 24, 2002: E.J. Hradek

Yao Ming's Final Home Game with Shanghai Sharks, Pudong Yuanshen Gymnasium, Shanghai, China, March, 2002: Ric Bucher

2002 NBA Playoffs Opening Round, Game Five, Indiana Pacers at New Jersey Nets, Continental Airlines Arena, East Rutherford, New Jersey, May 2, 2002: Ian Eagle

2002 NHL Western Conference Finals, Game Seven, Colorado Avalanche at Detroit Red Wings, Joe Louis Arena, Detroit, Michigan, May 31, 2002: Jon Morosi

Mike Tyson vs. Lennox Lewis, The Pyramid, Memphis, Tennessee, June 8, 2002: Gary Parrish, Jeremy Schaap

2002 FIBA World Championships Finals, Yugoslavia vs. Argentina, Conseco Fieldhouse, Indianapolis, Indiana, September 8, 2002: Mike Breen

2002 World Series, San Francisco Giants vs. Anaheim Angels, Pacific Bell Park, San Francisco, California, and Edison Field, Anaheim, California, October 19-27, 2002: Ross Newhan

2003 Fiesta Bowl, Ohio State vs. Miami, Sun Devil Stadium, Tempe, Arizona, January 3, 2003: Stewart Mandel

2002 NFC Championship Game, Tampa Bay Buccaneers at Philadelphia Eagles, Veterans Stadium, Philadelphia, Pennsylvania, January 19, 2003: Matt Yallof

2003 NBA All-Star Game, Philips Arena, Atlanta, Georgia, February 9, 2003: Trey Wingo

2003 NBA Western Conference Finals, Game Six, San Antonio Spurs at Dallas Mavericks, American Airlines Center, Dallas, Texas, May 29, 2003: Doug Gottlieb

USC Football Practice, Howard Jones Field, Los Angeles, California, August 6, 2003: Bruce Feldman

Detroit Tigers at Toronto Blue Jays, SkyDome, Toronto, Canada, September 6, 2003: Keith Law

Tampa Bay Devil Rays at Toronto Blue Jays, SkyDome, Toronto, Canada, September 25, 2003: Keith Law

2003 National League Championship Series, Game Six, Florida Marlins at Chicago Cubs, Wrigley Field, Chicago, Illinois, October 14, 2003: Thom Brennaman, Jon Sciambi

2003 American League Championship Series, Game Seven, Boston Red Sox at New York Yankees, Yankee Stadium, Bronx, New York, October 16, 2003: Kenny Albert, Mark Feinsand, Charley Steiner

2003 NFC Divisional Playoffs, Green Bay Packers at Philadelphia Eagles, Lincoln Financial Field, Philadelphia, Pennsylvania, January 11, 2004: Kevin Burkhardt, Mike Garafolo

2004 Aaron's 499, Talladega Superspeedway, Talladega, Alabama, April 25, 2004: Scott Ferrall

Massachusetts at Syracuse, Carrier Dome, Syracuse, New York, May 1, 2004: Liam McHugh

2004 NBA Western Conference Semifinals, Game Five, Los Angeles Lakers at San Antonio Spurs, SBC Center, San Antonio, Texas, May 13, 2004: Ric Bucher

2004 NBA Eastern Conference Finals, Game Two, Detroit Pistons at Indiana Pacers, Conseco Fieldhouse, Indianapolis, Indiana, May 24, 2004: Rob Parker

2004 Belmont Stakes, Belmont Park, Elmont, New York, June 5, 2004: Liam McHugh

2004 Summer Olympics, Athens, Greece, August 13-29, 2004: Rick Telander

2004 Eastern League Championship, Game Three, Altoona Curve at New Hampshire Fisher Cats, Gill Stadium, Manchester, New Hampshire, September 18, 2004: Keith Law

2004 American League Championship Series, New York Yankees vs. Boston Red Sox, Yankee Stadium, Bronx, New York, and Fenway Park, Boston, Massachusetts, October 12-20, 2004: Joe Buck

2004 American League Championship Series, Games Three-Five, New York Yankees at Boston Red Sox, Fenway Park, Boston, Massachusetts, October 16-18, 2004: Jon Sciambi

2004 American League Championship Series, Game Four, New York Yankees at Boston Red Sox, Fenway Park, Boston, Massachusetts, October 17, 2004: Chris Myers

2004 American League Championship Series, Game Seven, Boston Red Sox at New York Yankees, Yankee Stadium, Bronx, New York, October 20, 2004: Kenny Albert, Dan Wetzel

2004 World Series, Game Four, Boston Red Sox at St. Louis Cardinals, Busch Stadium, St. Louis, Missouri, October 27, 2004: Karl Ravech

2005 Conference USA Championship Game, Louisville vs. Memphis, FedEx Forum, Memphis, Tennessee, March 12, 2005: Gary Parrish

134th Open Championship, Second Round, The Old Course at St. Andrews, Fife, Scotland, July 15, 2005: Terry Gannon

2005 U.S. Open, Men's Quarterfinals, James Blake vs. Andre Agassi, Arthur Ashe Stadium, Flushing, New York, September 7, 2005: Tracy Wolfson

USC at Notre Dame, Notre Dame Stadium, South Bend, Indiana, October 15, 2005: Stewart Mandel

2006 Rose Bowl, Texas vs. USC, Rose Bowl, Pasadena, California, January 4, 2006: Michelle Beadle, Colin Cowherd, Bruce Feldman, Stewart Mandel, Dan Wetzel

2006 NCAA Men's Basketball Tournament Regional Semifinals, Gonzaga vs. UCLA, Oakland Arena, Oakland, California, March 23, 2006: Gary Parrish

2006 NCAA Men's Basketball Tournament Regional Finals, George Mason vs. Connecticut, Verizon Center, Washington, DC, March 26, 2006: Stewart Mandel

Atlanta Falcons at New Orleans Saints, Louisiana Superdome, New Orleans, Louisiana, September 25, 2006: Mike Greenberg

2007 Fiesta Bowl, Boise State vs. Oklahoma, University of Phoenix Stadium, Glendale, Arizona, January 1, 2007: Thom Brennaman, Chris Rose

Super Bowl XLI, Indianapolis Colts vs. Chicago Bears, Dolphin Stadium, Miami Gardens, Florida, February 4, 2007: Jim Nantz

UFC 68, Nationwide Arena, Columbus, Ohio, March 3, 2007: Gregg Doyel

Milwaukee Brewers at Detroit Tigers, Comerica Park, Detroit, Michigan, June 12, 2007: Jon Morosi

2007 Women's British Open, The Old Course at St. Andrews, Fife, Scotland, August 2-5, 2007: Terry Gannon

Appalachian State at Michigan, Michigan Stadium, Ann Arbor, Michigan, September 1, 2007: Thom Brennaman, Charissa Thompson

Texas Tech at Oklahoma State, Boone Pickens Stadium, Stillwater, Oklahoma, September 22, 2007: Liam McHugh

San Diego Padres at Colorado Rockies, Coors Field, Denver, Colorado, October 1, 2007: Charissa Thompson

New England Patriots at New York Giants, Giants Stadium, East Rutherford, New Jersey, December 29, 2007: Adnan Virk

2007 NFC Championship Game, New York Giants at Green Bay Packers, Lambeau Field, Green Bay, Wisconsin, January 20, 2008: Sam Ryan, Charissa Thompson

Super Bowl XLII, New York Giants vs. New England Patriots, University of Phoenix Stadium, Glendale, Arizona, February 3, 2008: Joe Buck, Jeffri Chadiha, Mike Garafolo, Charissa Thompson, Mike Vaccaro, Trey Wingo

2008 NCAA Men's Basketball Tournament Finals, Memphis vs. Kansas, Alamodome, San Antonio, Texas, April 7, 2008: Doug Gottlieb, Gary Parrish

The 2008 Masters, Augusta National Golf Club, Augusta, Georgia, April 10-13, 2008: Adnan Virk

2008 U.S. Open Playoff, Torrey Pines Golf Course, La Jolla, California, June 16, 2008: Dan Wetzel

2008 Summer Olympics, Men's 4x100 Meter Medley Finals, Beijing National Aquatics Center, Beijing, China, August 17, 2008: Andrea Kremer

Baltimore Orioles at New York Yankees, Yankee Stadium, Bronx, New York, September 21, 2008: Adnan Virk

Army vs. Navy, Lincoln Financial Field, Philadelphia, Pennsylvania, December 6, 2008: Sam Ryan

Super Bowl XLIII, Pittsburgh Steelers vs. Arizona Cardinals, Raymond James Stadium, Tampa, Florida, February 1, 2009: Mike Garafolo, Andrea Kremer

2009 NCAA Men's Basketball Tournament Finals, North Carolina vs. Michigan State, Ford Field, Detroit, Michigan, April 6, 2009: Rob Stone, Adnan Virk

The 2009 Wimbledon Championships, Gentlemen's Final, Andy Roddick vs. Roger Federer, The All England Lawn Tennis Club, London, England, July 5, 2009: Harvey Araton

New York Yankees Ticker Tape Parade, New York, New York, November 6, 2009: Sam Ryan

2010 PBA Tournament of Champions, Red Rock Lanes, Las Vegas, Nevada, January 24, 2010: Rob Stone

2010 Winter Olympics, Men's Hockey Final, United States vs. Canada, Canada Hockey Place, Vancouver, Canada, February 28, 2010: Kenny Albert

2010 NCAA Men's Basketball Tournament Finals, Duke vs. Butler, Lucas Oil Stadium, Indianapolis, Indiana, April 5, 2010: Ian Eagle, Jim Nantz

2010 NHL Eastern Conference Semifinals, Game Seven, Philadelphia Flyers at Boston Bruins, TD Garden, Boston, Massachusetts, May 14, 2010: Adnan Virk

Cleveland Indians at Detroit Tigers, Comerica Park, Detroit, Michigan, June 2, 2010: Jon Morosi

2010 Stanley Cup Final, Game Six, Chicago Blackhawks at Philadelphia Flyers, Wachovia Center, Philadelphia, Pennsylvania, June 9, 2010: Mike Garafolo

2010 National League Division Series, Game One, Cincinnati Reds at Philadelphia Phillies, Citizens Bank Park, Philadelphia, Pennsylvania, October 6, 2010: Jon Sciambi

Auburn at Alabama, Bryant-Denny Stadium, Tuscaloosa, Alabama, November 26, 2010: Bruce Feldman

2011 NCAA Wrestling Championships, Wells Fargo Center, Philadelphia, Pennsylvania, March 17-19, 2011: Jason Gay

2011 World Series, Game Six, Texas Rangers at St. Louis Cardinals, Busch Stadium, St. Louis, Missouri, October 27, 2011: Joe Buck, Jon Morosi, Sam Ryan, Matt Yallof

WWE Survivor Series, Madison Square Garden, New York, New York, November 20, 2011: Michelle Beadle

2012 Australian Open, Men's Finals, Rafael Nadal vs. Novak Djokovic, Rod Laver Arena, Melbourne, Australia, January 29, 2012: Chris McKendry

Missouri at Kansas, Allen Fieldhouse, Lawrence, Kansas, February 25, 2012: Joe Posnanski

2012 Atlantic 10 Championship Game, St. Bonaventure vs. Xavier, Boardwalk Hall, Atlantic City, New Jersey, March 11, 2012: Mike Vaccaro

St. Louis Cardinals at New York Mets, Citi Field, Flushing, New York, June 1, 2012: Kevin Burkhardt

2012 Stanley Cup Final, Game Six, New Jersey Devils at Los Angeles Kings, Staples Center, Los Angeles, California, June 11, 2012: Bob Miller

2012 Summer Olympics, Men's Tennis Semifinals, The All England Lawn Tennis Club, London, England, August 3, 2012: Jason Gay

2012 Summer Olympics, Men's 100 Meter, Olympic Stadium, London, England, August 5, 2012: Dan Wetzel

2012 Summer Olympics, Men's Keirin, London Velopark, London, England, August 7, 2012: Jason Gay

2013 NFL Hall of Fame Announcement, New Orleans Convention Center, New Orleans, Louisiana, February 2, 2013: Chris Rose

Super Bowl XLVII, San Francisco 49ers vs. Baltimore Ravens, Mercedes-Benz Superdome, New Orleans, Louisiana, February 3, 2013: Tracy Wolfson

2014 FIFA World Cup Qualifier, United States at Mexico, Estadio Azteca, Mexico City, Mexico, March 26, 2013: Bob Ley

2013 NCAA Men's Basketball Tournament Final Four, Georgia Dome, Atlanta, Georgia, April 6-8, 2013: Tracy Wolfson

2013 NBA Finals, Game Six, San Antonio Spurs at Miami Heat, AmericanAirlines Arena, Miami, Florida, June 18, 2013: Mike Breen

San Francisco Giants at Cincinnati Reds, Great American Ball Park, Cincinnati, Ohio, July 2, 2013: Sam Ryan

Alabama at Texas A&M, Kyle Field, College Station, Texas, September 14, 2013: Bruce Feldman

2013 World Series, Game Six, St. Louis Cardinals at Boston Red Sox, Fenway Park, Boston, Massachusetts, October 30, 2013: Jason Gay

Alabama at Auburn, Jordan-Hare Stadium, Auburn, Alabama, November 30, 2013: Tracy Wolfson

Toronto Maple Leafs at Detroit Red Wings, Michigan Stadium, Ann Arbor, Michigan, January 1, 2014: Liam McHugh

2014 BCS Championship Game, Florida State vs. Auburn, Rose Bowl, Pasadena, Coliseum, January 6, 2014: Stewart Mandel

2014 Winter Olympics, Men's Hockey Preliminary Round, United States vs. Russia, Bolshoy Ice Dome, Sochi, Russia, February 15, 2014: Liam McHugh, Dan Wetzel

Providence at Creighton, CenturyLink Center Omaha, Omaha, Nebraska, March 8, 2014: Gary Parrish

2014 Stanley Cup Final, Game Five, New York Rangers at Los Angeles Kings, Staples Center, Los Angeles, California, June 13, 2014: Bob Miller

2014 NBA Finals, Game Five, Miami Heat at San Antonio Spurs, AT&T Center, San Antonio, Texas, June 15, 2014: Michelle Beadle

2014 Little League Baseball World Series, Lamade Stadium, Williamsport, Pennsylvania, August 14-24, 2014: Chris McKendry, Karl Ravech

2014 U.S. Open, Women's Final, Caroline Wozniacki vs. Serena Williams, Arthur Ashe Stadium, Flushing, New York, September 7, 2014: Chris McKendry

2014 National League Division Series, Game Two, San Francisco Giants at Washington Nationals, Nationals Park, Washington, DC, October 14, 2014: Jon Morosi

2014 World Series, Game Seven, San Francisco Giants at Kansas City Royals, Kauffman Stadium, Kansas City, Missouri, October 29, 2014: Kevin Burkhardt, Jeffri Chadiha, Matt Yallof

Super Bowl XLIX, Seattle Seahawks vs. New England Patriots, University of Phoenix Stadium, Glendale, Arizona, February 1, 2015: Bob Costas, Mike Garafolo, Charissa Thompson, Mike Vaccaro